DISABILITY ETHICS

A FRAMEWORK FOR PRACTITIONERS, PROFESSIONALS AND POLICY MAKERS

PAUL JEWELL

DISABILITY ETHICS

A FRAMEWORK FOR PRACTITIONERS, PROFESSIONALS AND POLICY MAKERS

PAUL JEWELL

Common Ground

First published in Australia in 2010
by Common Ground Publishing Pty Ltd
at On Diversity
a series imprint of The University Press

Copyright © Paul Jewell 2010

All rights reserved. Apart from fair dealing for the purposes of study, research, criticism or review as permitted under the Copyright Act, no part of this book may be reproduced by any process without written permission from the publisher.

The National Library of Australia Cataloguing-in-Publication data:

Disability Ethics: a framework for practitioners, professionals and policy makers
Jewell, P. D. (Paul Damian), 1947-

Includes bibliographical references.
978 1 86335 754 8 (pbk.)
978 1 86335 755 5 (pdf)

1. Applied ethics.
2. Disabilities.

174.2

Table of Contents

Chapter 1: The Ethical Challenge 1
    The Challenge 1
    Practitioners and professionals 2
    Providers and policy makers 2
    Consumers, clients and advocates 2
    Citizens 2
    The best terms to use 3
    Some brief definitions 3
    Theory, practice and actual cases 4
    Morals, ethics and professional ethics 4
    Three reasons for professional ethics 6
    Some typical ethical dilemmas concerning provision for people with
        disabilities 7
    A survey of ethical theories 10
    Distractions to be avoided 15
    Conclusion 15
    Constructing and applying a framework for professional ethics 16

Chapter 2: A Community-Based Approach to Professional Ethics. ... 19
    A community-based approach in a nutshell 19
    People as members of communities 20
    The Client as first priority 22
    Models of professional-client relationships 23
    Choosing the appropriate professional-client model 25
    Boundaries to professional relationships 26
    Relations with employers 27
    Relations with families 28
    Relations with the wider community 29
    Relations with the profession 29
    Obligations of the profession 30
    Justice – a community-based approach 31
    Some illustrations in practice 32
    Features of a community-based approach to ethics 37
    Some limitations of community-based approach to ethics 38
    Conclusion 40

Chapter 3: A Consequences-Approach to Professional Ethics 43
A consequences-approach in a nutshell 43
Adding consequences and principles to a community- based approach to ethics 43
The obvious appeal of consequences 45
Some dilemmas concerning consequences 46
Concerns about the consequences approach, and responses to concerns 48
Features of a consequences-approach to ethics 58
Some limitations of a consequences-approach to ethics 59
Conclusion 61

Chapter 4: A Principles-Based Approach to Professional Ethics 63
A principles-based approach in a nutshell 63
Respect for persons 63
Applying the concepts 66
The principle of respect for human rights 66
Formal agreements, codes and conventions 67
The capabilities approach 70
Five advantages of a principles approach in ethics 72
Combining the principles approach with the community approach ... 73
Difficulties with the principles approach 74
Some dilemmas involving a principles approach 77
Features of a principles approach to ethics 81
Conclusion 83

Chapter 5: A Code of Ethics 85
A Code of Ethics and Practice for Disability and Rehabilitation Professionals 85
Preamble 85
Vision statement of Disability and Rehabilitation Professionals' Association 86
Mission statement of Disability and Rehabilitation Professionals' Association 86
Beliefs of Disability and Rehabilitation Professionals 86
General Principles: Overview 87
Ethical and Professional Statements 89
Assessment and Evaluation 92
Advertising and Presentations 93
Professional Relationships 93
Privacy and Confidentiality 94

Programming, intervention / therapy and support 96
Supervision of students 97
Research and Publication 97
Resolving ethical issues 98
Appendix A - Commonwealth Legislation - Guidelines 99
Appendix B - State Legislation - Guidelines 99
Appendix C - International Statements, Treaties & Alliances - Guidelines 99

Chapter 6: Making Ethical Decisions 101
A methodical approach to an ethical issue 102
A strategy for making ethical decisions 103
A strategy for making ethical decisions – expanded 103

Chapter 7: Confidentiality 117
The default position – all information is confidential 119
Exceptions to confidentiality 123
The Tarasoff case 125
Implications of the Tarasoff case for disability professionals 127
Legally required disclosure 128
Insurance and welfare 128
Confidentiality and its limits 129
Two ethical dilemmas concerning confidentiality 131
Confidentiality issues in a database 133
Conclusion 140

Chapter 8: Ethics in Public Policy 143
Ethical dimensions of public policy 144
The sterilisation controversy 146
Ethical analysis 152
Conclusion 158

Chapter 9: The Ethics of Identity 161
'Disabled people' or 'people with disabilities' 161
The medical model 163
The social model 164
Impairment 166
Prioritising the person 168
Positive badging 169
A perspective from Philosophy 172
Resolving the contradiction 175

    Summarizing the debate about terminology 176
    Exclusion through theories of human nature 176
    Expanding the concept of human nature 179
    Theories of ethics and human nature 182
    The threshold 182
    Conclusion 183

Chapter 10: Justice **185**
    Justice in professional ethics 186
    Social justice 187
    Defining justice with a focus on needs 188
    Defining justice as individual liberty 189
    A theory of justice 190
    Criticisms of Rawls' theory of justice 192
    Rethinking Rawls' theory 195
    Retributive justice 196
    Conclusion 198

Chapter 11: An Ethical Society **201**

References and Notes **205**

Bibliography **219**

Chapter 1
The Ethical Challenge

The Challenge

The social arrangements with which we are familiar work well for most of us most of the time. We work, we earn, we pay taxes. We engage professionals when we need their advice. We expect that there will be doctors whose expertise can be relied upon if we are ill and other health professionals who will assist us on our way to recovery. We expect that there will be schools staffed with knowledgeable teachers, hospitals staffed with caring nurses and courts presided over by fair judges. We vote for politicians who offer policies we favour. We require government to provide us with security, protect our freedoms, and restrain people who are a threat to social order. We look to government to help out those of us who cannot help themselves in desperate situations or times of emergency.

These social arrangements rest on some shared assumptions and values. They assume that people are, by and large, free, self-determining persons. They assume that we respect each other's rights and independence, and, at the same time, that we choose to co-operate rationally and productively with each other. Most of the time this is a reasonable assumption.

Our social arrangements are challenged when this assumption does not hold. What policies should government have in place for people who are not independent, or not rational, or not co-operative, or not productive? If, by some catastrophe, through accident, disability or mental illness, you became such a person, how should you be dealt with by professionals and government services? If, on the other hand, you are a professional, how should you go about making decisions for clients who are not well-placed to make decisions for themselves? Are there standards of professional ethics that can deal with this situation? Are there ethical standards that can be applied by managers of service organizations, or by policy writers, or by government officials? Are there ethical standards that concerned citizens should demand of government, of service organizations and of professionals who provide for people made vulnerable by disabilities?

To answer these questions, I will explore a range of ethical theories and examine how they meet this challenge. I will examine their strengths and weaknesses and test their application to actual ethical dilemmas drawn from the life stories of people with disabilities.

As I do so, I will develop a framework that will serve as a guide for making ethical decisions. I intend this framework to be useful to the following groups of people.

Practitioners and professionals

Practitioners whose primary role is to provide services to people with disabilities.

Professionals whose clients include people with disabilities. This includes social services such as Health, Education, Welfare, and Aged Care.

Students in these fields.

Providers and policy makers

Managers of organizations that provide services to clients with disabilities.

People engaged in writing or implementing policies concerning the provision of disability services.

People engaged in writing or implementing policies that have an impact on the lives of people with disabilities: for example in local government, transport, or building codes.

Students in these fields.

Consumers, clients and advocates

People engaged in influencing, or advocating for, policies that impact on people with disabilities.

And, of course, people with disabilities, their families, friends and supporters.

Citizens

People who are interested in social justice.

People who are interested in public policy, the role of government and government responsibilities.

Students in these fields.

The best terms to use

There is a debate about the best language to use. Referring to somebody as a 'disabled person' looks like a commonplace and acceptable expression, but does it draw attention to the disability, by putting that word first, rather than putting the person first? Saying 'people with disabilities' or 'a person with impairments' is rather clumsy. It does shift the focus somewhat, but still connects the disability to the person, rather than to the social barriers which are really the disabling factors. The debate is complicated, so I will take it up in more detail in chapter nine 'The Ethics of Identity'. Meanwhile, I will use the terms interchangeably.

Sometimes I will refer to *clients*, sometimes to *disabled people* and sometimes to *people with disabilities*.

Some brief definitions

For the purposes of this discussion, I offer the following definitions that I will later expand.

***Ethics**: the study of how people should treat each other.*

This includes the notions of right and wrong, values, relationships, justice, fairness, consequences, autonomy, rights and respect.

***Professionals**: people with high levels of expertise and responsibilities in the provision of services.*

For the sake of brevity and convenience, I will use the term *professionals* to mean practitioners, professionals, providers, managers, policy makers and government officials.

***Clients**: the recipients of professionals' services.*

Some people prefer other terms such as consumers, customers and recipients. While there is debate about the relative merit of these terms, I will use the word *clients*. In particular, I refer to people whose ability to function as independent self-determining persons has been compromised by developmental disability, by illness or by accident. Some have a diminished ability for rational decision making. Others, by contrast, have a physical disability that leaves them dependent and vulnerable to being treated *as if* they had diminished decision-making capacity.

***Professionals ethics**: the standards that should guide professionals' interactions with clients within their professional roles and responsibilities.*

For the purposes of this discussion, professional ethics includes ethical standards that should guide practitioners, professionals, providers, managers, policy makers and government officials. I will use the term 'professional' to apply to all those occupations.

Theory, practice and actual cases

I will examine several theories of ethics to see how they apply to the provision of services to people with disabilities. I will cite many actual cases, which will illustrate how policies, professional practices and ethical guidelines impact on these people. Most discussions of the role of government, of social policy and of professional ethics are primarily concerned with the rights of autonomous citizens and clients. My discussion moves beyond this by examining the challenges inherent in providing for people whose autonomy is compromised.

Morals, ethics and professional ethics

An official who takes bribes is unethical. If that same person is a cruel and neglectful parent, a cheating spouse and a malicious gossip, then we would rightly judge such behaviour as immoral. A useful definition of ethics is *the study of how people should treat each other*. Some concepts of ethics and morals go further and encompass other considerations such as animals, the environment, personal satisfaction or religious prescriptions. We do not, however, have a consensus on these matters. We do agree that stealing from people is unacceptable, that lying to them is wrong, that cruelty is repugnant. It would not be useful here to make a distinction between the terms 'moral' and 'ethical', either in their current usage or in their etymological origins, except to note that the convention is to say 'professional ethics' rather than 'professional morals'[1].

Professional ethics is the analysis and practice of the special obligations that result from the professional's role and responsibilities. We might pay little attention to gossip amongst neighbours, but if a doctor gossips about the conditions of patients, that would be a serious breach of medical ethics. We might accept a gift for doing a friend a favour, but a teacher should certainly not accept a gift in exchange for raising a student's grade. If ethics is about how people should treat each other, then professional ethics is about the special obligations, constraints and boundaries that determine how professionals should treat clients. *Professionals* includes practitioners, managers and policy makers. Not all professionals deal directly with clients. Some manage organizations, some write policy and some advise government. Professional ethics is relevant to them too, because policies and government services impact profoundly on how people are treated.

Ethics is not a matter of individual opinion, nor of personal conscience. It cannot be, if it is about how we should treat each other. Presumably, we all want to live in an ethical community, that is one where people treat each other with respect and care about each other's welfare. Perhaps, then, the prime ethical challenge is to persuade people to be nice to each other. It is sometimes thought that if only we could achieve that, all our problems would be solved. It is true that good will is essential, but it is not enough [2]. To act ethically ourselves, and furthermore, to construct well-functioning communities, requires skill and the application of practical reasoning [3]. As members of a community, we have to work out the practical details concerning the best ways to respect each other and care for each other's welfare. How should we balance being honest with being polite? Should young offenders be treated leniently or sternly? Should we care for everybody equally, or should we be particularly concerned for members of our own families? Attachment to one's immediate family seems intuitively right, but to what extent is the care of a person with a disability a family responsibility or the responsibility of the rest of the community through government agencies? The resolution of these issues requires debate and negotiation. There are no clear-cut absolute answers to these questions, but neither are they matters of mere personal opinion. Some ways of treating people are better than others. Some social arrangements have better outcomes than others. Skilled, practical, ethical reasoning will produce better results than good will alone.

Theories of ethics provide advice about how we should treat each other. They have been proposed, developed and debated by philosophers, and over time they become part of the culture. Some influential philosophers, such as David Hume and Immanuel Kant, are historic figures. Others, such as Martha Nussbaum and Ronald Dworkin, are working today, and currently influencing us. From our culture, we absorb our everyday ideas about right and wrong, about how we should treat other people and how we expect to be treated [4].

Some ethical theories focus on freedom, rights, respect, impartiality and consistency [5]. Some start with the fact that people live in communities. They talk about caring for each other, human relationships, roles and agreements [6]. Other theories concentrate on the fact that we have interests that we wish to satisfy. They focus on people's welfare and happiness [7]. Much of the time, the variety of ethical theories complement each other, but sometimes they conflict.

Culture is not fixed. Our ideas concerning how we should treat each other and how we expect to be treated is subject to debate, negotiation and adjustment to changing circumstances and contemporary ideas. We attempt to provide each other with reasons to behave in one way or another [8]. Our discussions are characterised by such words as *good, bad, right, wrong, interests, welfare, rights* and our conclusions are of the kind "I recommend we undertake this action" or "That institution has an obligation towards those people". Human nature being what it is, and the fact that people are typically more acutely aware of their own needs and desires than those of others, the discussion may be sparked by claims of the kind "The community should act to satisfy my needs" or "Society should refrain from impinging on my freedoms" [9].

The challenge in all this is to hammer out *mutual* agreements. Ethics is a discussion of how people should treat *each other*. It is easy for me to assert my rights, or demand my wishes be satisfied, or even complain that someone else is doing the wrong thing. The real ethical challenge involves forging agreements with each other about what is the right thing to do.

Three reasons for professional ethics

One reason is that a professional has a special responsibility when dealing with clients. For example, any of us might be sympathetic when someone is ill, but a nurse has a particular responsibility for patient care.

The second is that a professional has a degree of knowledge, power and authority that the client lacks. All clients are vulnerable to some extent. For example, many of us engage accountants because we need advice in managing money and meeting taxation requirements. We lack the specific skills and resources, and need assistance to complete the necessary tasks. Some clients are particularly vulnerable because of age, illness or disability. Professionals have the ability to do a great deal of harm or a great deal of good, and so need to take special care to fulfil their professional obligations.

The third reason is that professions are recognised and regulated by the State. Some of this regulation is entrusted to the profession itself through peer review and licensing boards, some by legislation, and some by community expectation and convention. A professional has a relationship not only with the client, but also with other professionals and with the wider community. For example, a lawyer may not defend a client by any means possible, such as deceiving the court, but must work within rules that are designed to promote justice.

Which occupations count as professions and which do not is a matter of some debate [10]. Various lists of characteristics have been compiled [11]. Essential features include:
- A high level of expertise in the provision of services and advice to clients and/or the wider community. This expertise is typically gained through higher education.
- Formal recognition of the profession through membership of a professional body. These bodies demand standards of qualifications and behaviour with peer review of professional conduct and conditions for registration.
- Professional ethics, typically stated in a Code of Ethics [12].

These three features are essential because of the work professionals do. Professional work differs from many occupations that are more routine, or that deal with objects rather than persons. In many occupations, a worker is accountable only to the immediate supervisor. Professionals have wider and more challenging accountability, to clients, to the wider community, and to their peers through a professional body or registration board. In contrast to following routines, professionals are called upon to make decisions, solve problems, offer recommendations and, importantly, care about the impact of their decisions on the welfare of their clients.

Clearly, the provision of services to people with disabilities is a professional task, with challenges to be met, decisions to be taken and with clients whose welfare is at stake. The tasks may involve individual support, or managing an organization, or formulating policy, or making representations and recommendations to government. Each of these requires great expertise, accountability and commitment to client welfare. As with other professions, there is a need for professional ethics specific to the challenges inherent in disability provision.

If ethics is the study of how people should treat each other, then professional ethics is concerned with how professionals should act when dealing with their clients.

Some typical ethical dilemmas concerning provision for people with disabilities

The consideration of ethical dilemmas is a useful exercise when developing and evaluating professional ethics. Dilemmas are best seen as extreme examples of ethical challenges. Ethical challenges are part of the ordinary business of disability service provision. Respect for people and an awareness of their needs is an everyday requirement, whether in writing policies, managing organizations or providing professional services.

It is best to circumvent dilemmas before they result in crisis and conflict. Ethics is more about positive and effective practice than it is about the identification of wrong-doing or the resolution of conflict. Nonetheless, even the most skilled and well-intentioned practitioners will find themselves confronted with ethical dilemmas.

The word 'dilemma' means more than 'problem'. When we confront a dilemma, we are faced with two competing choices of action, and it is not clear which is preferable. Typically there are reasons both for and against each action, and neither represents a perfect solution. Fortunately, they are uncommon, but when they do occur, they place severe demands on ethical expertise, hence their usefulness for this book. The dilemmas described in this and subsequent chapters are drawn from the experiences and observations of practitioners. Some, such as court cases, are in the public domain. Otherwise, the characters in the stories are fictional out of respect for the privacy of real individuals, but the dilemmas are authentic.

Some of the dilemmas concern the practicalities of every day living. Others are matters of life and death.

Jim at the community group

Jim is 42 years old and has a moderate intellectual disability. He lives in supported accommodation and works full-time as a supported employee in a large factory. He enjoys socializing and particularly looks forward to 'Friends in Peace', which is an inclusive religious service held every Wednesday evening in a community church. Many local people come to these meetings, as well as about 20 people with an intellectual disability. Jim is an enthusiastic and regular attendee.

Jim has swallowing difficulties, and an assessment by a speech pathologist has resulted in a modified diet of 'soft foods only'. At 'Friends in Peace', a variety of foods are served for supper. They are home-made by church volunteers and include biscuits, cakes, pies, fruit, and yoghurt. Despite the soft food diet recommendation, Jim often chooses to eat hard food on these occasions. If recreation staff attempt to intervene, he becomes aggressive.

Developmental Educators have told Jim about his dietary needs and he is aware of them. A list of suitable items which Jim likes has been compiled and some of these are made available at 'Friends in Peace'. Nonetheless, Jim seizes hard foods when Recreation Assistants are busy with other clients and attempts to eat them quickly, which worsens his difficulties and causes him to cough and choke.

Jim benefits a great deal from attending 'Friends in Peace'. Apart from the confrontations over food, he is calm and relaxed, enjoying the opportunity to see his friends, to socialize, and to participate in the community. There are no other community programs that offer the same benefits. It is not feasible to remove the hard foods from the community supper.

Jim's position raises a number of practical and theoretical questions.

Does Jim have the right to eat whatever he chooses?

Do the risks in doing so over-ride his rights?

What are the ethical obligations of the Recreation Staff?

Are their roles and responsibilities different from that of the speech pathologist or the church community?

Given these circumstances, should Jim be prevented from attending 'Friends in Peace'?

Martin at school

Martin is a nine-year-old boy with Autism. He frequently spits in class and is sent home from school. This can happen up to four times a week.

Martin is in a 'special class' with seven other children at the local primary school. He learned the spitting behaviour from another student in the class. Efforts to discourage him, such as 'time out in the quiet room' have been ineffective. Although he has Autism, he has a good understanding of language and of consequences. He has learned that spitting results in his being able to go home, which is what he prefers. Health concerns have been raised by support staff, with one member becoming sick, allegedly from inhaling Martin's saliva when he spat at her.

As well as the health issues, leaving Martin in school is disruptive to his fellow students' education. Sending him home encourages spitting behaviour, and disrupts both his own education and his parents' work lives.

Should Martin be sent home when he spits?

Angela at the shops

Angela is a mature-aged woman with Down Syndrome who lives in a residential setting with five other adults who have intellectual disability. Angela has a habit of stealing, which is getting worse. She visits the local shopping centre a couple of times a week and invariably steals small items from the supermarket.

Angela steals items she does not need, in particular packets of pencils. It has been suggested by a psychologist that she has Impulse Control Disorder. If she is caught stealing she denies it and any recollection of the event. On the other hand, she appears to know that stealing is wrong and she will get into trouble if caught.

If steps are taken to curtail Angela's visits to the shops, it is predicted that other residents will be the target of her thefts. To date, she has not been charged but it is likely this will eventually happen.

Should Angela be blamed for her behaviour?
Should she be protected from being charged?
Should she be prevented from going to the shops?
Do her carers have any obligations to the shopkeepers?

Baby Charlotte in hospital

Charlotte was born prematurely with severe and multiple disabilities. She has not left the hospital where she was born, and never will. She has respiratory problems which will probably result in a fatal infection within a year. She has kidney problems and brain damage. She is blind and deaf. She is incapable of voluntary movement or response. She evidently experiences pain, but not pleasure.

The damage to her respiratory function, her kidneys and her brain cannot be repaired or reversed. It is expected that she will soon need artificial ventilation to stay alive. Her parents believe that she should therefore receive a tracheostomy. The doctors involved do not think this is in Charlotte's best interests. Even if they do everything possible, the chances of her surviving the next twelve months are low, with estimates from doctors ranging from 25% to 5%.

The dispute between the parents and the doctors has become a matter for a decision by a Family Law Court.

Should a judge be the person to make decisions concerning Charlotte's life, welfare and medical treatment?
Should medical decisions be made by doctors alone?
Should decisions about Charlotte's best interests be made by her parents?
If a judge is to make the decision, should it be to prolong Charlotte's life?[13]

A survey of ethical theories

Clearly, the resolution of these dilemmas is not easy, and calls for expertise. Ideally, that expertise would include the application of theory to practice. A number of ethical theories have been developed over time, proposed by philosophers and refined by debate. They have fashioned social customs and beliefs, and been absorbed into the social fabric. They guide people's values, decisions and actions, although the people using them may not be aware of the theories' origins or histories. The theories differ from each other significantly, and how any one of us resolves the dilemmas will depend upon which theory we favour.

What follows is a brief survey of the most common and influential ethical theories. From them, I will select those that appear to have the most useful application to disability ethics. In the remainder of this book, those selected will be examined in more detail. I will examine their strengths and weaknesses, particularly those regarding the challenges of disability provision. I will suggest some modifications, and develop a framework for resolving issues, constructing policy and making decisions that are ethically justified.

An ethical issue is one where there is discussion about how best to proceed [14]. It is an *issue* because what constitutes the best course of action is not immediately obvious and a decision is called for. There are choices to be made. The issue is *ethical* in nature because the course of action has an impact on the wishes and welfare of the people involved [9]. Some of the theories described briefly below will be more useful then others in making decisions about disability issues. The first three theories are the most dominant in contemporary society, so, in subsequent chapters, I will focus on them, albeit with acknowledgement of the others.

As mentioned earlier, when I use the term 'professional ethics' in this discussion, I include frontline practitioners, related professionals, management and government policy, and I use the term *client* to include consumers and recipients of services and policies.

Three dominant ethical theories

1. Communitarianism

This approach starts from the idea that it is human nature for people to care about each other, form relations with each other and come to agreements about how to treat each other. If the prime ethical question is 'How should people treat each other?' the Communitarian answer is 'However they agree to treat each other'.

Communities can and do evolve shared values and develop agreements about how to put these values into practice. A version of the communitarian approach is the theory of social contract. This proposes that people are obligated to each other because they are party to social agreements. The contract may be formal or tacit. It may be actual or hypothetical. A number of important philosophers have contributed to the development of the communitarian approach. David Hume proposed that people are capable of sympathising with each other's plights, and communities are based on shared understandings and agreements. Thomas Hobbes and John Locke said it was rational for people to co-operate with each other rather than conflict, and John Rawls proposed that a just society exhibited social arrangements that fair-minded people would agree to [15].

This group of theories about community, agreements and social contracts looks very promising for professional ethics in disability provision. It should help us discuss commitment to care, the role of the professional, relationships with clients and other stakeholders, and the role of government. We could envisage a Code of Ethics as a social contract, along with organisational policies and mission statements. Membership of a professional body, registration and peer review could also fall under communitarianism. So could discussions concerning justice, legislation and social policy.

The justification of the democratic form of government relies upon the notion of social contract, so the legal and ethical obligations of professionals, providers and policy makers are underpinned by a community-based approach to ethics.

2. Deontology

Deontology focuses on the idea that people should respect each other as autonomous beings and that we should treat each other accordingly.

The term *deontology* is not very informative, unlike *Communitarianism* which has the word *community* in it. *Deontology* comes from the Greek word *deon* meaning duty, or something you are obliged to do, but that does not inform us what our duty is, or what we might be obliged to do. It might be more helpful to refer to Deontology as a *principles-based* approach, because it argues that some actions are right and some are wrong *in principle*, simply because of the sort of actions they are. It is associated with the philosopher Immanuel Kant and it is very influential [16]. Kant proposed two important principles. One was that we should treat people as ends in themselves and avoid manipulating them for our own purposes. The other was that we have a duty to adhere to universal rules, rather than be swayed by emotion, desires, expediency or circumstances.

These two principles are useful in discussing rights, justice and equal treatment. A respect for people and their autonomy can be expressed as a respect for their rights. From a duty to adhere to universal principles we can derive a justification for acting rationally, consistently and impartially.

Notions of autonomy, rights, impartiality and consistency will clearly need to be important considerations in the development of ethics in disability provision. They can also inform Communitarianism approaches, such as the members of the United Nations agreeing on a Convention on the Rights of Persons with Disabilities. This Convention echoes the United Nations' Universal Declaration of Human Rights[17]. The notion that ethics consists of committing to universal principles will clearly be useful in developing an ethical framework that is applicable to disability issues.

3. Consequentialism

According to Consequentialism, it is the results that matter. The main consequentialist theory is known as Utilitarianism, which recommends we consider whether our decisions and actions are useful in producing good outcomes. Do our decisions increase the welfare, happiness and interests of the people affected? If so, we are being ethical. Utilitarianism was initially proposed by the philosophers Jeremy Bentham and John Mill, who asserted that increasing happiness was really the only goal of ethics and the only measure of right and wrong. Agreements and principles should merely be ways of achieving good results [18].

Increasing the welfare of clients is clearly a prime goal in disability provision. Decisions, recommendations and conduct that result in harm are reprehensible. Policies and organisational arrangements that ignore their actual impacts on people are lacking in justification. Utilitarianism appears so straightforward as to be obviously correct, but it is predictable that there will be complications. Dilemmas may arise when people's interests are incompatible, where a decision has good results for one person but poor outcomes for another. Alternatively, principles and consequences may conflict, whereby respecting the rights of a client may entail a risk to the client's welfare. Nonetheless, a consideration of clients' welfare is the very reason for the existence of professions and policies. A consequences-based approach is essential to ethics in disability provision.

Some other ethical theories

4. Virtue Ethics

The idea of Virtue Ethics takes a somewhat different approach from the theories I have so far surveyed. According to Virtue theory, the right thing to do is what a good person would do. To become a good person, one should develop habits of behaviour which then constitute the character of a virtuous person. An honest character is someone who consistently and reliably tells the truth. An early proponent of this theory was the philosopher Aristotle, who recommended that people should acquire technical competence in their occupations along with moral dispositions such as courage and honesty [19].

One difficulty with Virtue theory is that, as a community, we do not have an agreed list of virtues. Aristotle's original scheme included courage but not compassion; in a modern society we might consider the latter more important than the former. Religions have also proposed varying lists of virtues (and contrasted them with vices), which makes their application to professional ethics contentious [20]. Aristotle's starting point, though, is useful. He pointed out that a 'good' quality is tied to function. A good knife is one that is sharp and cuts well. A good builder is someone who has the skills and knowledge that produce excellent buildings. Using this idea, it should be possible for us to formulate a list of qualities that would allow a disability carer to be an excellent carer, an organization's chief to be a good manager, or a policy-writer to produce effective policies. There is a danger, though, that Virtue theory concentrates on the nature of the professional rather than on the needs of the client.

5. Emotivism

Emotion is an important influence in our ethical judgements, but philosophers are divided about its proper place. As mentioned above in section 2 on principles, Kant thought that ethical judgement should be entirely rational and not be swayed by emotion [16]. Hume, in contrast, thought that the emotion of sympathy was the foundation of all ethics [6]. Other philosophers treat ethical statements as nothing more than an expression of a feeling. This doctrine, known as Emotivism, says that ethical statements tell us something about the speaker, typically whether they approve or disapprove of something, but nothing about the actions or state of affairs being praised or condemned [21].

A combination of rational thought and emotional judgement is probably the basis of ethical decisions for most people. Certainly in the provision of disability services, caring about clients' welfare and wanting the best outcomes are important emotions. Anger at injustice and a desire to make the world a better place are essential drivers of social change. It is true, though, that emotions cannot be exchanged between people in the same way that reasons can, so the construction of policies and professional ethics need more than emotions. Similarly, accountability for decisions and justification of policies need a rationale, rather than just "I felt like it was the right thing to do at the time".

6. Intuitionism

We all have intuitions: that is, we know something to be true even though we cannot explain how we know. We can often tell when someone is distressed, even if they deny it and put on a brave face. Ethical Intuitionism is the idea that some actions are simply right and some are wrong, and that people can tell the difference, without necessarily being able to explain it. Being cruel to children might be an example of behaviour which we intuitively know is wrong.

The difficulty is that one person's intuition may conflict with another's, and if intuitions cannot be explained, there is no way of settling the matter, coming to a judgement or making a decision. Worse still, there is no way of distinguishing intuition from prejudice. There are good reasons why we should not be cruel to children. We can explain those reasons with reference to Communitarianism, Principles and Consequentialism, rather than merely shrug our shoulders and fall back on intuition. A sound intuition probably can be explained, and, in the context of professional ethics, explanations are required[22].

7. Relativism

Cultural relativism is the view that what constitutes ethical or unethical behaviour depends on what community one is in, and what that community's customs are. Alcohol is acceptable in some parts of the world, but not in others, for example. Individual relativism takes the notion further, basing ethics on individual persons' values and commitments, which clearly differ from person to person[23]. Relativism is a persuasive idea. Ethics is a matter of human judgement, and there is no universally agreed criterion we can turn to in order to resolve confusion or disagreements. Considering the theories surveyed so far, Communitarianism sees ethics as a result of groups of people developing agreed ways of interacting. Relativism, then, appears to be compatible with Communitarianism. In contrast, Deontology appeals to universal principles. Despite this, it has respect for the individual at its core. Consequentialism counts the results for actual people, which appears to be an objective process. Clearly, though, what one person counts as a good outcome differs from another's wishes. Relativism encourages respect for individuals, tolerance of difference and participation in shared, consultative decision-making. Relativism therefore has much to recommend it.

However, Relativism has a serious drawback. Taken to its logical conclusion, Relativism asserts that right and wrong are merely matters of opinion and that anyone's opinion is as good as anyone else's. Community standards of behaviour are merely arbitrary conventions, comparable to etiquette, like holding a dinner fork in the right or left hand. This view is at best unhelpful and at worst dangerous. Surely cruelty to children cannot be a matter of personal taste or social custom. An individual who practises it is depraved, and a society that tolerates it is in dire need of reform. Extreme Relativism makes all ethical discussion pointless.

In real life. people need to ascertain how to get along with each other, and how to construct fruitful social arrangements, including professional ethics and public policy. Relativism might make a contribution to the tolerance of individual differences, but not to standards of professional ethics and public policy.

Summary

It is apparent from this survey that when it comes to making decisions and policies in disability provision, some ethical theories will be more useful than others. Whilst acknowledging the Relativist view, and recognising the contributions of emotion and intuition, in this book I will concentrate on the first three theories. I will examine the application of:
- the notions of communities, agreements and professional roles

- principles derived from deontology
- the calculations of consequences.

Distractions to be avoided

The nature and needs of the client should always be at the heart of deliberations about professional ethics. After all, professional services exist because there are clients who need the services. There are two distractions from a client-centred approach that should therefore be resisted.

One distraction is a focus on the nature and needs of the provider of the services. Organizational policies, the rules of professional bodies, and relations with other professionals should all be instrumental in serving the needs of the client. It is one of those unfortunate facts of human nature that organizations tend to arrange their procedures in ways that are convenient for the organization, rather than the clients it serves. Professional ethics is not primarily about maintaining the reputation of the profession, nor about loyalty to employers, nor about setting fees for professional services. It is primarily about the client.

The second distraction is to concentrate on the ethical theories, rather than on their application to actual people. This is a danger with theories in general. With regard to the three dominant theories above:
- Communitarianism - Respect for the norms, customs and expectations of communities should not overwhelm the realisation that communities are made up of individuals.
- Principles - There is a danger that universal principles can be too abstract, instead of being reflections of people grappling with life choices[20].
- Consequences - The calculation of consequences can be taken to mean 'the greatest good for the greatest number' or, even worse 'what is good for the economy'. The economy has no needs, only people do. The best results for a number of people should be an aggregation of the satisfaction of individuals[14]. Furthermore, professionals have special obligations to their clients, who merit priority.

Conclusion

For the purposes of this discussion, I have defined Ethics as the study of how people should treat each other.

I have defined Professional Ethics as the study of how people should behave when carrying out their professional duties and, in particular, how they should treat their clients.

Discussion of ethics in the context of disability provision should have a focus on the nature, needs and circumstances of people with disabilities,

particularly as recipients of professional services. The scope of the discussion includes:
- Community obligations, public provision of services, and legislation
- Rights, entitlements and welfare of people with disabilities
- Organisational policies and procedures
- Obligations of practitioners and professionals towards clients who have disabilities.

In a survey of ethical theories that influence people's judgments, there are three dominant theories. They are
- Communitarianism
- Deontology
- Consequentialism

Constructing and applying a framework for professional ethics

In the next chapter, I will examine how a community-based approach to ethics can be applied to disability issues. I will discuss professional roles and responsibilities and the place of professional codes of ethics. I will provide several instances of ethical dilemmas that challenge disability professionals. I will note the strengths and weaknesses of the community-based approach and suggest the need for standards derived from a consideration of consequences and principles. I will take up these considerations in subsequent chapters.

In chapter three, I will examine a consequences approach to professional ethics. I will examine its obvious appeal and also its serious difficulty, which is how to balance good and bad consequences. I will provide some instances of ethical dilemmas relevant to the calculation of consequences and examine the relative responsibilities of the professional and the client.

In chapter four, I will examine principle-based approaches to ethics. These approaches include deontology, a capabilities approach and a rights-based approach. I will discuss how principle based approaches differ from a consequence-based approach and how dilemmas can result from those differences.

Chapter five comprises a code of ethics for disability professionals.

In chapter six, I will develop a framework for making ethical decisions and show how it can be applied to an everyday ethical challenge. I will provide a methodical strategy for making ethical decisions that includes identifying the issue and the stakeholders, applying the approaches discussed in previous chapters, and coming to a resolution and recommendation.

A pervasive challenge to professionals, particularly professionals whose clients are vulnerable, is managing the responsibilities associated with confidential information. I will examine that issue in chapter seven. I will discuss an important legal case, and present some typical dilemmas. I will also examine the challenges faced by government policy-makers in setting up a national data base.

I will continue to apply ethical theories to government policy-making in chapter eight, using as an example the issue of sterilising girls who have intellectual disabilities. I will examine the role of the law and the Family Court and the impact they have on people with disabilities and their families.

As my discussion moves from particular cases illustrated in early chapters to challenges at the level of policy and society, I will provide a philosophical perspective in chapters nine and ten. In chapter nine, I will discuss the issue of identity, the challenges this issue presents to disabled people, and the debate concerning whether the term 'people with disabilities' is preferable. I will discuss the relative merits and flaws of the medical model and the social model in the perception of disability.

In chapter ten, I will discuss justice. I will distinguish between distributive justice and retributive justice. I will note the impact of the criminal justice system on people with disabilities. I will discuss the contribution of the philosopher John Rawls to the theory of justice, and apply his theory to justice in disability issues.

In chapter eleven, I will recapitulate the previous chapters. I will point out how various ethical theories struggle with disability issues and show what modifications they need in order to be effective for disability professionals.

Chapter 2
A Community-Based Approach to Professional Ethics.

In this chapter, I will examine a community-based approach to ethics. First, I will look at how a community-based approach can be used as a basis for ethics generally. Then I will apply it to disability ethics more specifically. I will identify the strengths and flaws of this approach in the construction of professional ethics. I will also note any additions that need to be made to the theory so that it can be applied to disability issues.

A community-based approach in a nutshell

This approach starts from the idea that it is human nature for people to care about each other, form relations with each other and come to agreements about how to treat each other.

From this it follows that professionals have obligations to be sympathetic to clients, should fulfil their responsibilities and the expectations that arise from their professional roles, and should work within the terms of the relevant agreements, contracts, policies and laws.

People as members of communities

People are fundamentally social beings. We live, work and play in groups. We relate to friends, families, employers, colleagues and fellow citizens. We are also individuals, with our own needs, interests, desires, tastes, values and ideologies. Sometimes these individual differences conflict, and sometimes they are in harmony. It is for this reason that people face the challenge of figuring out how they should treat each other. Forming satisfactory and fruitful social arrangements is both a human drive and a practical necessity.

Co-operating with each other is a practical necessity if we are to have our individual needs met. Our entire lives, from the buildings we occupy to the coffee we drink, require the co-operation of thousands of people. We have constructed a vast web of agreements with each other. Some of these agreements are formal, such as contracts to supply goods and services. Some are informal, such as which member of a household usually buys the coffee. A community is a group of people who have some shared goals, circumstances and understanding. A co-operative relationship, a set of agreements, roles and expectations arises as a result.

Some social arrangements are, of course, imposed by the powerful for selfish reasons. Some of these may even be touted as 'good for the community' to disguise their proponents' intentions. Discussion of this can be found in Sociology and Politics [1]. I will not discuss that issue here for two reasons. One is that the project of this book is *prescriptive*, rather than *descriptive*. It does not describe what other people *do*, but sets out to develop guidelines to prescribe what we *should* do. This relates to the second reason, which is that this book's perspective is drawn from Philosophy, rather than Politics or Sociology. It is best to leave discussion of power relations to the social sciences rather than be diverted from the specific task of developing professional ethics in disability provision.

Making agreements

If we use a community-based approach, we can think about ethics as the process of forming and negotiating agreements, roles and expected behaviour. According to this approach, the right thing to do is to act in a manner which is appropriate to one's role, and is respectful of the norms, values, agreements, policies, conventions and rules of the community.

Members of a community also have an obligation to contribute to the formation of conventions and rules that promote the shared understandings and goals of the community [2]. Rules should not be an arbitrary and external imposition, but should be the expression of shared values and communally-held intentions [3].

It is clearly rational for people to come to agreements about how to treat each other, rather than to be in constant conflict [4]. People then have an obligation to respect these agreements. This argument is known as the 'social contract' theory and is the foundation for the ideals of democracy [5].

It is true that getting on with other people can be tiresome, and that the demands of communal living are relentless [6]. Sometimes the idea of living peacefully alone in the wilderness seems idyllic in comparison [7]. Nevertheless, the practicalities of ordinary life dictate that we need to participate in a well-ordered society in order to meet our needs.

So one argument for a community-based approach to ethics is that we are both rational and self-interested individuals who are smart enough to see that we need to live in communities in order to satisfy our needs, and we therefore need to co-operate with each other and conform to the community's rules.

Caring for each other

There is also another quite different justification for a community-based approach which says that, as well as being rational individuals, people are emotional and they are social. This is important, because, as the philosopher David Hume pointed out, it is emotions that drive our actions, not reasoning [8]. It is the emotional side of our nature that makes us want to do things. Our rational side just advises us on how best to get things done. Hume famously said that our reasoning side is the slave of our emotional side, and that is the way it should be.

Amongst the emotions, there is one that is important for ethical theory: the feeling of sympathy that we have for others. Ethics is a result of intertwined features of human nature. We are rational and emotional. We are social and sympathetic. We care about what happens to ourselves and we care about what happens to others, too. What drives our actions is emotion, and what drives our ethical actions is the emotion of sympathy [9].

Friends and family, workplace and world

The conventions of a community are an expression of these features of human nature. They may be traditions that have evolved over time, or they may be explicit responses to community needs. They may be unspoken expectations arising amongst close-knit people in small groups, or formal contracts and legislation binding large numbers of people.

From a community-based approach to ethics, we can develop the following ideas:
- When we are acting as members of a family, or household, or with close friends, there are informal expectations that grow out of these close-knit relationships and these expectations should guide our ethical decisions.
- In our work relationships, there may be mission statements, or policies, a code of ethics or defined obligations to guide our ethical behaviour.
- As citizens, we have obligations to each other, some of which are laid down in legislation.
- As human beings, we are in a sense, citizens of the world, and capable of sympathising with any and all other human beings, recognizing an ethical bond with them.

Clearly, the community-based approach to ethics is particularly applicable to professional ethics in disability provision. Any profession is a social arrangement, and therefore a result of a community convention. The provision of disability services can be seen as the community's formal expression of people in the community recognising other's needs. The actual work of a professional in the field is in a web of relationships – with clients, with their families, with employers and with society at large.

The Client as first priority

Using a community-based approach, we can understand how people in a community would recognise needs, and identify some of these needs as requiring the skills of dedicated experts. To achieve this, the community sets up and employs professions of people who have the necessary expertise and dedication.

The sole reason for the existence of a profession is the existence of clients with needs. If there were no people with disabilities who needed provision for their needs, there would be no professionals in disability services. It follows that professional ethics should be founded on the needs of the client.

Using a community-based approach, it can be argued that:
- Ethics is about how people should treat each other.
- Recognising that people with disabilities have needs, the community has established professions to provide for those needs.
- Responding to clients' needs is therefore the prime obligation of disability services professionals.
- Professional ethics is about how professionals should treat clients.
- Professionals have relations with parties other than clients. They probably work for an employing organization. They often work with other professionals and with clients' families. From time to time, these relationships will conflict and dilemmas will arise. In such situations, the needs of the client, that is, the person with the disability, should be the first priority.

In disability services, negotiating relationships with clients and other parties is more complex than in some other professions. When the owner of a business engages an accountant for financial and tax advice, the relationship is uncomplicated. The business owner is the person who engages the accountant, the person who describes the needs and gives instructions, and the person who pays the fees. There are only two parties involved in the agreement. The relationship involves only the professional and the client. The wider community has already provided a precise legislative framework within which the transactions take place.

In disability services, some contracts are similar. The client can identify the needs, engage the appropriate professional and pay for the relevant services. In many instances, the arrangement is more complicated. There may be many parties involved. In the case of a child with a disability, the professional might be contracted by an organization, and the fees come from the government. The responsibility for the child's welfare rests with the parents, who also have responsibility for any other children in the family. The disability professional may need to work with the staff of the child's school, who have responsibility for all the students' welfare. The school principal's obligations, the siblings' needs, the parents' views and the organization's budget may all place demands on the professional's decisions. Maintaining the priority of the child's needs may be difficult in such circumstances, but should remain the prime ethical consideration.

Models of professional-client relationships

If a community-based approach to ethics is about relationships, what sort of relationship should a professional have with a client? The ethicist Michael Bayles discusses five models of the professional-client relationship [10]. They are agency, contract, friendship, paternalism and fiduciary.

The most appropriate model depends on the characteristics of the profession and the characteristics of the client.

1. Agency

When a professional is an agent of the client, the client has the authority and the responsibility, and the agent carries out the client's instructions. We can envisage the legal profession as operating most readily in this model, the medical profession less so, and schoolteachers, perhaps, not at all [11]. There are two difficulties with this model. One is that it assumes the professional is accountable to the client and to no other parties. The wider society, the client's family and associates, as well as the professional's employer, might all constrain or influence the professional's decision. The agency model allows the professional to shrug off responsibility for decisions and outcomes. The second difficulty is the assumption that the power and responsibility lies mostly with the client. Even with the most autonomous of clients, the professional has knowledge and expertise the client lacks. That is why the client needs the professional in the first place.

Nonetheless, in some circumstances, agency has much to recommend it. It is too easy for a professional to assume the power and responsibility that should rest with the client. The client's autonomy should be respected and the capacity for self-determination recognised and facilitated. Many clients' practical autonomy is severely compromised, and for them, agency is not feasible. On the other hand, many people with disabilities quite properly resent being treated as second-class citizens and being relieved of decisions that are properly theirs [12]. An agent may be just what some clients need.

2. Contract

Some client-professional relationships are, in fact, legally contracts. The idea of a contract is part of community-based ethics. The contract model is attractive in that it assumes an equal distribution of authority and responsibility between professional and client. A good contract is also clear about what those responsibilities are, thus facilitating both self-determination and good outcomes. The contract model, though, makes an assumption similar to that of the agency model about the practical autonomy of the client. The assumption is that a contract is taken to be an arrangement between free and equal parties. In all likelihood, neither the freedom nor the equality is real. A client with a disability is more dependent on the service provider than the provider is on the client. In most professional relationships, the client chooses the professional. In contrast, it is frequently the case that a client with a disability does not get to choose who the provider will be. It may also be that the nature of the disability unavoidably dictates the client's needs and that the professional has a commitment to provision of care, with neither having the freedom to withdraw from the relationship. Matters may be further complicated by the contract being between the professional and an organization, or perhaps between an organization and the government, rather than the client with the disability being the contracting party.

Nonetheless, the contract model does have advantages. It can provide clarity, transparency and respect for the parties involved.

3. Friendship

Contracts are usually impersonal, such as the agreement for the provision of a telephone service. The provision of disability services, by contrast, is characterised by shared goals and a commitment to another's welfare, and is thus more akin to friendship than contract. Friends also prioritise their friends' interests over other acquaintances and strangers, which is akin to a professional prioritising a client's interests. Ties of affection may also develop between disability support workers and their clients. However, the friendship model of professional-client relationship is fraught with difficulties. As with contract, friendship is assumed to be between equals and mutual. In practice, disability care is one way, or at least unbalanced. The nature of the relationship is such that the professional is expected to apply expertise in the promotion of the client's interest, but the client is not required to so care for the professional's interests. Of course, the two parties may well have a mutual regard and respect for each other, but that is not a requirement of the relationship.

There is debate in disability ethics, with some arguments proposed that there should be a policy of discouraging professional-client friendships in favour of distant impartiality, whilst other arguments point to the positive power of emotional ties and the all too frequent lack of friendship opportunities in clients' lives.

4. Paternalism

Parents care about their offspring and have knowledge and expertise that their children lack. Paternalism is decision-making by experts on behalf of, and about, people who do not have the skills, knowledge or maturity to make decisions for themselves. If we admit the fact that the relationship between the professional and client is not between equals, then perhaps paternalism is an acceptable model. Admittedly, paternalism is frowned upon by many ethicists, particularly Deontologists. It overrides autonomy and informed consent whilst allowing manipulation and the disguise of dominance [13]. Because disability services necessarily entail an imbalance of power, there is fertile ground for paternalism and its drawbacks.

In many circumstances, paternalism is unavoidable, and indeed a commendable approach. Caution should be exercised though, so that it is not applied at the expense of clients' autonomy where they have the capacity for self-determination.

5. Fiduciary

A balance may be struck between the extremes of agency and paternalism in the fiduciary model, which, as the word implies, is based on trust. The difference in power between client and professional is acknowledged, and the vulnerable client places trust in the more powerful professional. This is not, however, blind trust. The client consents to the recommendations of the professional and the professional accepts the responsibility of considering alternatives and conveying all relevant information to the client.

The fiduciary model appears to be an attempt to achieve the best approach by combining the acceptable features of the other models. It thereby runs the risk of being regarded as a motherhood statement lacking in practical application.

Choosing the appropriate professional-client model

Organizations should consider carefully the nature, circumstances and needs of clients when formulating their policies and procedures. Similarly, their staff should select the appropriate model. Professionals may have personal preferences for one or other of these models. Some may have the patience, wisdom and personality suitable to being a benign authority practising paternalism. Others may be outgoing and affectionate and friendly. If we put the client at the heart of our considerations, it becomes apparent that each of these models depends upon some notion or other of the client's practical autonomy, that is the capacity for self-determination. It is inescapable that self-determination will be compromised by disability. Indeed, compromised self-determination could be the definition of disability. An estimation of the client's capacities and needs should be the deciding factor in choosing the appropriate model, rather than have it determined by the nature or personal preferences of the professional.

Which of these models is best will depend upon the client's needs, circumstances and capabilities. Problems can arise if there is a disagreement about which model is appropriate. A client who needs an agent should not be treated with paternalism, for example. In a community-based approach to ethics, the obligations of the professional are derived from the professional's agreed role and a *shared* understanding of the appropriate relationship model.

Boundaries to professional relationships

A contract or agreement between two parties typically says what they are expected to do and what they are expected not to do. There is an amusing but serious sign used by some shopkeepers which says, "We have an arrangement with the bank. We do not give credit and they do not sell groceries". The phone company supplies a phone service only, and a phone company technician may enter property for installation or repair purposes, but not for other reasons. Contracts set boundaries to behaviour, and there are similarly boundaries expected in professional relationships. Some of these boundaries may be unspoken expectations, some may be in a Code of Ethics, and some may be in a contract. (See chapter five for a code of ethics.) If we think about the relationship between a professional and a client with disabilities, a number of boundaries seem appropriate. There are practical limits to the amount of time and expertise available. On a different plane, judgements need to be made about the boundaries between the personal and professional spheres.

There are important ethical questions that a professional needs to be clear about. What is the nature of my job? What is my role? What is my relationship with the client? What are the community's expectations about how I should behave? What can I be reasonably expected to do? What falls outside my professional obligations?

Boundaries of expertise

By definition, a professional has special expertise. A professional is not obliged to meet all the needs of a client, only those related to the profession. A distinction may need to be drawn between client needs that are disability related and other needs. Furthermore, a professional should not offer or provide services which are beyond the professional's expertise and qualifications. The relationship between client and professional should operate within appropriate boundaries.

It follows then, that the professional has an ethical obligation to be clear about those boundaries and explain them to the relevant parties.

Boundaries of time

Since the professional relationship is a response to the client's needs, it should cease when the services are no longer being provided or if they are no longer benefiting the client. The provision of services may also be limited to particular times (and places). Suitable information and notice of these constraints should be provided to parties affected by them. Where required, alternatives should be proposed and discussed.

Personal boundaries, opinions and judgements

In any relationship, the people involved will share some opinions and differ in others. Some opinions, perhaps about sex, politics or religion, may be strongly held and potentially disruptive. Relativism, as discussed in chapter one, is a useful approach here. At any rate, personal opinions and differences should not compromise professional decisions [14]. A distinction should be made and a boundary drawn. If this is not possible, as a last resort the professional may have an obligation to withdraw and arrange for an alternative [15].

Friendship boundaries

There is an unresolved debate about the proper intersection of friendship and professional relationships. A community approach to ethics is founded on the notion that people are social beings who empathise with each other's views and circumstances – in short, form friendships. It is natural for friendships to form amongst people who associate with each other, and it would be wrong to prevent it. Furthermore, it should be recognised that people with disabilities may have fewer opportunities to associate with others and thereby form friendships. A personal-friendship relationship added to a professional-client relationship may be valuable to both parties. Since friends care about each other's welfare, and a professional cares about a client's welfare, the two sorts of relationships can complement each other to the benefit of both. This was discussed earlier in the section on models of professional-client relationships.

Against this view is the argument that friendship is between equals and is reciprocal. Clients are not expected to care for the professional's welfare, and the client-professional relationship is not one between equals. The terms of contract may dictate the end of the professional relationship, with distressing effects on the friendship. The subjective ties may compromise the professional's objective judgement. For these, and other reasons, some organizations' policies prohibit friendships with clients.

In professional ethics, boundaries may need to be drawn between the personal and professional domains, and be clear to both parties, with particular regard to the potentially vulnerable position of clients with disabilities.

Relations with employers

In some other professions, it is common for the client to approach the professional, seek advice and pay for the service. In provision for disability, the arrangement is usually more complex. Typically, professionals are accountable to an employer. The situation of 'serving two masters' – the client and the employer – has the potential to generate a conflict of obligations and consequent ethical dilemmas. These will hopefully be rare, because the employing organization has the same goal as the professional, which is to provide for the needs of the client. In that sense, the manager of the organization is also a professional with ethical obligations. It is usual, in fact, for managers to be members of the same profession as the employees.

Employment contracts and organization policies can be seen as agreements and therefore an expression of communitarian ethics. As such, they should be clear about their intentions and the various obligations of the parties involved. Clients, professionals, employers and other affected parties should be able to operate ethically and productively within the stated boundaries. Ideally, such documents would be open to review and renegotiation. Employment and policy statements that are not clear, or are not respectful of the parties involved, are not useful as ethical guidelines.

Even though they share the same ultimate goal, differences may arise between professionals and employers because, where the professional is concerned with the particular needs of the individual client, the organization has to consider wider picture issues such as budget restraints, what services it may and may not offer, and the eligibility criteria for potential clients.

These challenges represent an essential difficulty in a community-based approach to ethics – how can we best co-operate in groups whilst maintaining and valuing our individual natures? [16]

Relations with families

Relations between disability providers and the families of people with disabilities can be difficult. Often the family is both a recipient of the services and a provider of care at the same time, which complicates the relationship [17]. Because the family receives services, it is at a disadvantage when it comes to sharing decision-making and responsibility. In practice, the professional is relatively powerful.

The family and the disability professional are likely to have the same agenda, but quite different perspectives. They both provide care but, for the professional, this provision is to a client, rather than to a loved one. A professional has boundaries and has reason to be impartial and dispassionate. Family members are exactly the opposite.

Professional expertise is also different from family understandings. Professionals gain their knowledge through comparisons with many clients. The family members know one case, but very intimately. Ideally, these two levels of expertise will be combined, but negotiating a relationship that allows this relies upon the professional's willingness to do so, and the family's inclination to trust the advice of the professional.

Some professionals adopt the 'expert model'. They are in charge, their expertise directs the care and the family members are expected to be passive recipients of the services [18].

Other professionals prefer the 'transplant model'. They aim to teach the parents how to care for their child and thereby transplant their expertise into the family.

Alternatively, there is the 'negotiating model', which is more compatible with a community-based approach to ethics. A negotiating model ideally respects the rights and responsibilities of the parents and other family members, recognises their expertise, and negotiates a fruitful partnership based on agreed shared goals.

Relations with the wider community

Communitarian ethics proposes that people have obligations to each other because they are social beings who form relationships with each other. Professionals have the same obligations that all members of a community do, such as treating other people with honesty, respect and compassion, and, in addition, professionals have obligations which are specific to their professional roles.

The democratic system of government can be seen as community ethics in practice, and legislation can be seen as an expression of community values. There is legislation concerning families, legislation that prohibits discrimination, and laws regulating finance, for example. Some general legislation will be pertinent to disability issues, such as regulations concerning the aged, children, and welfare provisions. There is also legislation specific to disability issues, governing matters that range from building codes to guardianship. While ethics and law are not the same thing, ideally legislation is a result of ethical concerns. Professionals should be aware of both the intention and the letter of the law, and use that knowledge in their ethical decision-making.

The United Nations' Convention on the Rights of Persons with Disabilities is also a formal expression of community values [19]. Other relevant United Nations' documents include the Universal Declaration of Human Rights and the Convention on the Rights of the Child [20].

Relations with the profession

Trust is an essential feature of fruitful relationships. It could be argued that it is therefore reprehensible to act in a way that damages the reputation of the profession. This is rather vague, though. Does it mean professionals should cover up for each other's mistakes? That does not appear to be ethical. Does it mean professionals should not criticize each other? That would surely depend on whether the criticism was justified and in the best interests of clients. Does it mean that professionals should be concerned about their reputations and always act in a way that is above reproach?

There is a concern that this places unjustifiable constraints on a professional's private life. When the profession of nursing was established for example, a nurse was expected to promise 'to pass my life in purity and to practice my profession faithfully' [21]. Whatever 'purity' might have meant then, it has no useful application now. More importantly, professional ethics requires the manifestation of virtues relevant to the profession rather than to private life.

The virtue of competence is important in a community-based approach to ethics. Clearly, the community expects competence in a professional. It is important that professionals not only exhibit competence in their specializations, but that they recognize the boundaries of their expertise. They should be willing to seek the advice and co-operation of other practitioners and should avoid professional jealousy.

Similarly, petty criticism of other professionals should be avoided. This should not prevent clients being informed of a range of opinions and alternative options. Nor should incompetent colleagues be protected at the expense of the client's welfare. Professionals have an obligation to report misconduct. Peer review and provision for registration are part of the obligations of the profession as a whole.

Using a community-based approach to professional ethics can provide guidelines to the perplexing questions about how professionals should treat other professionals. Since the profession has been set up by the community to provide for needs of clients, the first consideration should be the client's welfare. It would be wrong, therefore, to unjustifiably criticise other professionals upon whom the client relies and needs to trust. Of course, if another professional is incompetent, cannot be relied upon, and should not be trusted, then it would be best for the client if the incompetent professional stopped practising. This can be achieved through the processes of the profession's registration board. Reporting misconduct to the relevant authorities is the right thing to do, and is a professional obligation.

'Misconduct' should mean professional misconduct, not personal morals. The professional/personal boundaries work both ways. A registration board should not examine a professional's private life or behaviour that has no direct impact on clients.

Obligations of the profession

The profession as a whole (rather than individual professionals) has three obligations that can be derived from a community-based approach to ethics.

The first is to establish a professional body. This is to identify the members of its own professional community and communicate this information to the wider community. It does this by requiring qualifications and standards for membership of that body, and by establishing accreditation and registration protocols.

The second is to establish a code of ethics. The code serves as an expression of the profession's values, an agreement amongst its members, and a standard for professional behaviour. Breach of the code is grounds for expulsion form the profession. An excellent example of a code of ethics for the disability services profession is provided in the following chapter.

The third is to advise the wider community and its policy makers. This entails:
- Undertaking research into disability issues to provide a sound basis for practice and policy implementation.
- Calling for the provision of adequate and effective disability services.
- Advocating for justice for disabled people.

Justice – a community-based approach

Achieving justice for people with disabilities is a challenge for the profession and for the wider community. It is complicated by the fact that justice means different things to different people. There is a variety of theories and definitions of the term. Justice has to do with the distribution of resources, property, power and responsibilities. It may mean treating people equally, or conversely treating people according to their merits. It may mean entitlement to what a person has earned, or to what a person needs. Everyone wants justice, it seems, but there is no general agreement about what it means. Since the issue is so complex, I will discuss it separately in chapter ten and just mention a couple of ideas here that can be derived from a community-based approach to ethics.

In a community that values justice, what level of government services should be offered? Disability typically entails financial disadvantage. Should that burden be borne by the person with the disability, or by the family, or by the community through voluntary donations to charities, or by government through taxation? It can be argued that since disability is typically not anybody's fault, its concomitant disadvantages are not anybody's responsibility. The disadvantages are unfortunate, but not unfair. Opposing this, it can be argued that the whole point of community is for people to provide for each other's needs and we have a collective obligation to set up government agencies and social arrangements to achieve that end.

If we take a community-based approach, it seems plausible to argue that justice should mean a set of social arrangements that we would agree to because they were fair. In other words, the definition of a fair arrangement is an arrangement to which we would all agree. So far, so good.

The difficulty is finding a basis upon which we could agree. Any person's starting point in such a negotiation would presumably be influenced by their own circumstances. People doing poorly are likely to favour equality of outcomes, while people who are doing well are likely to favour individual entitlement. People in poverty may think it unfair that others are rich, while wealthy people may recommend recognition of individual responsibility, contribution and ownership.

The philosopher John Rawls has proposed a notion of justice which aims to provide a basis for agreement on what constitutes fairness[22]. We can adopt his theory to examine the ethics of providing disability services.

Let us imagine a situation in which people are setting up a new society. They know that some people in that society will have disabilities, but they do not know what their own personal circumstances will be, whether they will be one of the people with a disability or not. Would this original group agree that people with disabilities should be left to fend for themselves? Or, mindful that it could happen to anybody, would they agree that government services were justified? Surely the latter.

When the disability services profession calls for justice for people with disabilities and for the provision of adequate and effective disability services, Rawls' argument is a powerful tool. If it were accepted by the community at large and by policy makers, it would be reasonable to expect a significant improvement in the lives of people with disabilities.

The tool can also be applied to service providers. Do organization policies comply with this notion of justice? Are the arrangements for service delivery the sort of arrangements we would agree to if we did not know whether we would be the provider or the recipient?

Similarly, the tool can help us reflect on models of the professional-client relationship. If we contemplate the possibility of becoming a client, what sort of professional would we want? An agent? A parent figure to care for us? Someone we could trust? The question is not, of course, entirely hypothetical. Any one of us, including those of us who are currently professionals, could become clients through age, accident or illness.

Some illustrations in practice

In chapter one I described four instances that raise issues for ethics in disability. The four more described here are relevant to a community approach to ethics in that they provide illustrations of issues that arise from roles, relationships and community values.

Like most ethical challenges, they are more complex than may first appear. They provide an opportunity to apply the community-based approach to ethics. They also involve consideration of principles and consequences, approaches which will be discussed in subsequent chapters. The best practice is to use all three theories, apply, balance and use them to resolve the dilemma. At this stage it is appropriate to look at some instances that raise questions about ethical judgements made within the context of professional roles and community expectations. Subsequent chapters will discuss the other two theories.

Martha is warned against making friends

Martha has just started employment with an organization which provides supported accommodation to people with disabilities. She was somewhat taken aback when the manager told her 'not to get too friendly with the clients' and is uncertain what her obligations are concerning the manager's remark. Martha is not sure exactly what it means, or whether it was intended as advice or an instruction. Is it the policy of the organization, and if so, is the organization right to have such a policy?

During her university training, Martha has been on placement with a number of organizations and met many people with disabilities. Now, thinking about the manager's remark, she realises that people with disabilities face obstacles to socializing and making friends. She remembers an occasion a year ago when one young woman, Helen, who has a mild intellectual disability, talked about the issue. Helen had said, "I don't really have any friends. I'm not sure why. Maybe because I'm a bit weird. I like one of the ladies who comes in here to help. She's really nice and seems to be the only one who gets where I'm at. I only see her when she's here though. I'd like to see her other times but I don't think it's allowed".

Martha firmly believes that everyone needs friends, and is worried by the lack of opportunities people like Helen has. Martha is a nice person. She cares about people and likes to relate to them. That is why she has chosen one of the caring professions. She does not want to be cool and distant with her clients, but she is aware that she is new to the job and unsure what is expected of her.

Martha checks the policies of the organization. She finds no mention of prohibitions against friendships. She would have been surprised if she did. Surely, she thinks, we do not live in the sort of society where other people can dictate who your friends can or cannot be.

Martha is a registered member of a professional organization that has a code of ethics, so she checks what it has to say. The only clause she can find that seems to have any bearing on the question says:

Disability and Rehabilitation Professionals will not develop a relationship with current clients, families or their peers that may be detrimental to their provision of services or professional judgement [23].

She does not think the clause prohibits 'getting too friendly' but could a friendship relationship be detrimental to services or professional judgement? She asks her colleague, Alice, who has worked for the organization for some time.

Alice says, "I think there is a difference between being friendly and forming a relationship, and I don't think our manager expressed herself very well. If by being friendly, you mean being pleasant, being sympathetic, doing what ever you can to make your clients' lives better because you care, then sure, you should be friendly. Not everyone in this place is, mind you. Some just think they are here to provide exactly the services that are in the contract and caring is a tiresome extra. I don't work like that and I don't suppose you will. But I draw the line when it comes to forming a relationship, a friendship, call it what you like, with a particular client, especially if that includes seeing them outside of work.

Think about it. What does being friends mean? You can't be friends with someone who is not a friend in return, so friends are equal, and mutually dependant. They care about each other. But your clients are not in a position to care about you, or support you when times get tough. They are dependant on you, but you aren't dependant on them. What's more, all of them are dependant on you. How can you treat them fairly if one of them is your particular friend? Not to mention the potential for feelings of envy and rejection amongst those clients who are not your particular friend.

And what happens when you move on to a different job? Do you abandon your old friends and make new ones?

You have a professional role here. Stick to that and leave personal relationships out of it."

Martha can see that Alice is offering sensible advice but remains unhappy. She is not convinced that her employer should be able to tell her who her friends can be. On the other hand, if such restrictions are a justified expectation, should they not be made explicit in the organization's policies and contracts?

Alex allocates staff

Alex runs an Early Development Program at a suburban community centre. Bruce is a five-year-old child who attends the program once a week. Steven is undertaking a degree in Disability and Rehabilitation and as part of his training is working with Bruce in the Early Development Program.

Bruce has Fragile X Syndrome, with delays in his behavioural, physical, cognitive and language development. Bruce can communicate his needs to his mother through limited verbal use and gestures. He also attends pre-school. School enrolment is expected in a few months.

As well as Bruce, the Early Development Program caters for a number of children with physical, intellectual or multiple disabilities. As well as addressing developmental delays, it aims to optimise the child's social interactions, and assist the parents in meeting these goals.

Steven's work with Bruce has been very successful. Steven started his placement before the university year began, and has now been working with Bruce for six months. Bruce's mother is very happy with progress and hopes Steven can continue until Bruce goes to school.

Alex does not think this is the best arrangement. It is expected that Steven's training will expose him to a number of clients and professional challenges. Alex routinely changes the clients and tasks of practicum students. Since the program's goal is to improve social interactions, staying with one worker does not seem right for Bruce either. Alex decides to allocate Bruce to another worker, and Steven to other tasks.

Bruce's mother is upset by this decision. She points out that Bruce, though only five years old, has interacted with numerous specialists, carers, professionals and students. Each spent a short time with Bruce and then moved on. Steven has had the longest professional relationship that Bruce has experienced, and the results are pleasing. Bruce's concentration span has increased from less then 5 minutes to more than 15 minutes. The pre-school staff have noticed positive changes in Bruce's behaviour. Bruce's mother attributes this to Steven's excellent and continued work, but Steven is not so sure. It may be just that Bruce is maturing. He confidently predicts, though, that if he stops working with Bruce and works instead with one of his classmates, Bruce will not understand the change and will continue to seek out Steven and be disruptive if prevented.

Alex has a range of obligations to Steven and his training needs, to Bruce and his developmental needs, and to Bruce's mother. The obligations conflict and raise an ethical dilemma.

Jack looks for a home

Jack is a brilliant businessman. He is smart, healthy and energetic. He specialises in taking over small under-performing businesses and building them up. His latest project is in a small town which lies in a pleasant wooded valley in the countryside, some hours drive from the nearest city. He plans to turn a modest café into a bustling restaurant and tourist centre. The local townsfolk are enthusiastic about the idea.

Jack is confined to a wheelchair. Nobody in the town knows why and everyone thinks it is impolite to ask. He is temporarily staying at the local hotel, which has good access. The main street of the town is mostly public buildings, and typically are wheelchair accessible, including Jack's new business. The same is not true of the town's private houses. Jack wants to buy a home, but none of them has wheelchair access.

The exception is Delia's home. It used to be the post office. It is near Jack's business and like other public buildings on the main street, it is generously proportioned and has no steps. It is old, charming and solidly built, and when it ceased operating as a post office, Delia converted it into a private residence where she now lives. Jack would like to buy it from her. Delia understands Jack's position but does not want to move.

Delia is a teacher in a neighbouring larger town. Her school serves as a regional centre, offering special education to children with disabilities who live in the surrounding area. Both as a person and a professional, she feels committed to social justice for people with disabilities. She wonders whether selling her home to Jack is the ethical thing to do, even if she is reluctant to do so.

If she does sell, what price should she ask? Not only will she have to buy another place, but will have to bear the time and inconvenience costs of moving. She thinks it is fair to factor that in, and Jack is not short of money. On the other hand, she feels strongly that she should not take advantage of Jack's disability.

She wonders whether the rest of the townsfolk should be expected to help, either physically or financially, through volunteers or through the local government. Is it fair that she should be the only person to help Jack, if indeed she agrees to do so?

Government regulations require public buildings to have disability access, but not private homes. Both Delia and Jack now question the ethics of this. Should government legislate for disability access for new homes from now on? After all, people like Jack should be able to socialize in their friends' homes, and not be confined to public buildings. Legislation would, it must be acknowledged, place burdens on new home-buyers which would mostly be unnecessary.

In the meantime, how should Delia deal with Jack's request to buy her home?

Harry and George getting nowhere

Harry suffers debilitating anxiety. He has tried various therapists and various therapies. He has a history of treatments such as Cognitive Behaviour Therapy. He took medication for a while but loathed it and its side effects. Besides, neither the medication nor the Cognitive Behaviour Therapy has succeeded in restoring Harry to satisfactory functioning. He has been referred to George, a psychiatrist, for long term analysis. This is seen as Harry's 'last option' rather than trying again the treatments that he has undertaken without success.

Harry relates his history. He says he cannot understand why he becomes overwhelmed by debilitating anxiety. What he thinks might have been the initial trigger is long past, and he says he had an ordinary upbringing. George suspects otherwise, and says so. Together, George and Harry explore Harry's emotional issues to see if they can get an understanding of the causes of the symptoms and how they affect his life, family and work prospects.

This seems, at first, to work. Harry says he sees things in a new light now and it looks as if he is making progress. Against this, things go backward at times. This is not unexpected, as new events relating to past issues crop up and need exploring and analysing.

The analysis goes on for a considerable period of time, as analysis often does. Harry progresses, then regresses. Symptoms recede, then overwhelm him again. When this happens, Harry is dismayed, but feels he can understand them better and perhaps cope with them a bit more effectively.

George, though, slowly gets the impression that the process has stalled and the analysis is not really going anywhere. Much work seems to have been done, but fresh attacks continue to occur. Is there 'unfinished business'? Is success 'just around the corner'? Or is there realistically nothing more to be done? George expresses his concerns to Harry, who says he sometimes gets the same impression.

George discusses the problem with colleagues (without identifying Harry in any way), but they are unable to provide any helpful or specific advice.

George has a dilemma. Has his treatment of Harry failed, or is there something that might work if they just continue a little longer? Is George missing something, or has Harry developed a dependency? Harry thinks they are 'close to something' but George is doubtful that they will ever find it.

Should George stop treating Harry?

Features of a community-based approach to ethics

Not all approaches to ethical decisions start from a community basis. It may be useful at this stage to develop a list of the features that might identify a community-based approach. The left hand column of the table below lists some coherent features we might expect in this approach. The right hand column is not as coherent because it shows some examples of various alternatives, for illustrative purposes. I will discuss other approaches in subsequent chapters. In the meantime, we can do some comparisons and reflect on a community-based approach might influence the way individual people see themselves, and how professionals might organize their services, and how a society might develop a culture.

A PERSON who:

Has a community-based approach to ethics is likely to	Does **not** use a community-based approach to ethics may
See him/herself as primarily part of a community. Think fulfilment of the individual is to be achieved through social roles. Develop relationships. Develop a role in community. Care about others' positions. Sympathise with others. Appreciate others' contributions to community. Value others' roles. See the community as a way of serving individuals' needs.	See people primarily as individuals. See a community as nothing more than a collection of individuals. See individual rights as in conflict to community. See individual rights and wants as more important than community. See agreements between people as nothing more than trading between autonomous individuals.

PROFESSIONALS and ORGANIZATIONS that:

Have a community-based approach to ethics are likely to	Does **not** use a community-based approach to ethics may
Construct positive traditions and culture. Value professional ethics, roles and responsibilities. Provide clients with opportunities to contribute to community. Promote democratic processes for the construction of rules and arrangements.	Be authoritarian. See a primary need to manage conflict between individuals and community. Promote individual rights. Value consistency and stability over negotiation and agreement. Not differentiate between personal morals and professional ethics.

A SOCIETY that:

Has a community-based approach to ethics is likely to	Does **not** use a community-based approach to ethics may
Justify all social and political arrangements on the basis of agreements. Promote community. Value and facilitate individuals' contributions. Value democratic processes. Value public & community service. Provide a high level of government services.	Be authoritarian. Promote individual rights. Value consistency and stability over negotiation and agreement. See the government's primary role as managing conflicts between individuals and community.

Some limitations of community-based approach to ethics

The justification of a community-based approach to ethics relies upon the participation of its community members. This is a dangerous assumption with disability issues. People with disabilities can easily be left out of discussions.

Inclusion and exclusion

When people form a community, they categorise other people as either being members of that community, or as being outside of it. They adjust their behaviour and obligations accordingly. People accept more responsibility for their own families than for strangers. They acknowledge a bond with their fellow citizens that does not apply to people in foreign distant lands. The recognition of community is typically based on common language, common customs, and common appearance. The adverse side of this is discrimination against people who are not recognised as members of the community. This discrimination can manifest as xenophobia, racism and other prejudices. Because a disability can result in unusual behaviour or appearance, people with disabilities may suffer discrimination and prejudice.

Disabilities may also be practical barriers to community participation. Mobility may be an issue, as in Jack's case discussed above. Intellectual disability may prevent participation in decision-making and negotiating agreements. Ideally, community-based ethics involves discussion between equals, but in practice, this is rarely the case [17].

Many discussions of community, of ethics, of government and politics, assume that people are typically independent and self-determining, with similar aims and experiences. In a later chapter I will discuss how disability significantly challenges this assumption in theory and in practice.

Disagreements

As well as practical obstacles, there are theoretical limitations to a community-based approach. A community-based approach to ethics turns out to be inadequate theory when professionals face ethical dilemmas and need to make decisions about what is the right course of action. A community-based approach also struggles to define what constitutes justice in social arrangements and public policies. Certainly a professional can, and should, consult the relevant code of ethics, the terms of contract, the demands of the professional role, and the requirements of legislation and policy. The question remains, what is the ethical justification for *those* guidelines? A course of action may be deemed the right one because a community of affected people has decided it is right, but how did that community judge what is right and what is wrong?

Surely some communities simply get it wrong. Some fail to overcome obstacles to reaching agreement. They may be wracked by prejudice, racism, sectarian conflict or civil strife. Some are intractably dysfunctional.

The social norms of some communities differ significantly from what is acceptable in other societies. Relations between the sexes is one example, with views about marriage, monogamy, polygamy and chastity varying significantly from one community to another. Behaviour which is approved of in one society is severely punished in another. If one society is right and the other wrong, communitarian ethics seems unable to tell us which is which. If each society is right within its own borders, then what constitutes right and wrong seems to be arbitrary and lacking in justification.

Even within a harmonious, functioning society, there are disagreements about right and wrong. The stem cell and therapeutic cloning debate is an example. Some people argue that cloning is fundamentally wrong and should be prohibited. Others think that while there are some ethical problems with cloning, the benefits of stem cell therapy outweigh the objections. Others see no objections at all and recommend we pursue stem cell experimentation vigorously. A community-based approach to ethics cannot settle such a dilemma except perhaps to accept whatever the majority decides. But how does the majority reach a decision?

Agreements within a community change over time, as well. The sterilisation of people with disabilities for eugenic purposes used to be thought acceptable, but is not now [24]. How could a community-based approach to ethics justify or even explain changes in community attitudes?

A need for standards

A fundamental difficulty for Communitarian ethics is that it offers little guidance to ethical debates in a community. If Communitarian ethics relies upon the adoption of negotiated and agreed social norms, on what grounds are agreements reached? Indeed, how could negotiations even begin? If anyone is going to propose a set of social arrangements because they are worthwhile, there needs to be some justification of their worth in order for a community to even start considering whether to adopt them.

So we need to go beyond community agreements and look for ways to discuss what is right and wrong, what is ethical and unethical, what is the best way for us to treat each other. Two major ethical theories propose ways of judging the rightness or wrongness of decisions, policies and social arrangements. They are an approach based on principles and an approach based on consequences, and will be examined in following chapters.

Conclusion

A community-based approach to ethics comes from the notion that people naturally form communities, share values and goals, and care about each other's welfare. The theory has useful applications to ethics in disability provision.

Social arrangements can be seen as the expression of our community values. These arrangements include legislation, public policy, government services, the establishment of provider organizations and the establishment of professions.

We find ourselves having to make ethical decisions as we design, construct and implement social arrangements. Communitarian ethics recommends that the decision- making process involves consultation and negotiation, and be reflective of community values. Justice is a significant community value, as is caring for people's needs.

A community-based approach to ethics has important inputs to professional ethics in disability provision. Professions are social institutions set up by the community to respond to human needs. Professionals have roles and responsibilities that derive from their clients' circumstances.

When making ethical decisions, professionals involved in disability provision should have as their primary consideration the needs and circumstances of their clients: that is, people with disabilities. These considerations, put together with the professional's role and expertise, will define the appropriate professional-client relationship, and the professional's obligations.

The professional-client relationship is set within a web of community interactions.

When making ethical decisions, professionals need to consider the effects for other involved parties, such as families.

Professionals should be mindful of the terms of contract with employers, and with the goals and policies of organizations they work for or with. Relevant parts of contracts and policies should be explained to affected parties.

Professionals should adhere to a professional code of ethics.

Professionals should work within legislative constraints.

Professionals should advocate for justice for people with disabilities. This includes working against prejudice and working for adequate provision of services.

Professionals should promote positive values in the community, including international agreements such as the United Nations Convention on the Rights of People with Disabilities.

A community-based approach to ethics provides a justification for the above obligations. It needs to be supplemented with further ethical theories, such as a principles-based approach, and the calculation of consequences. These approaches will be discussed in subsequent chapters.

Chapter 3
A Consequences-Approach to Professional Ethics

A consequences-approach in a nutshell

This ethical theory starts from the idea that people experience pleasure and pain, happiness and distress, fulfilment and frustration.

People should treat each other in ways that produce the best outcomes for all concerned. The best outcomes are the maximum of pleasure, happiness and fulfilment, and the minimum of pain, distress and frustration.

In a society that is influenced by a consequences-approach to ethics, the citizens' welfare is of prime importance. The policies of government (and its agencies) should be evaluated according to outcomes. Similarly, professionals should consider the consequences of their decisions, the impact they have on their clients and on others whose welfare is at stake. They should act in such a way as to maximise their clients' welfare and minimise any undesirable effects.

Adding consequences and principles to a community- based approach to ethics

In the previous chapter, I examined a community-based approach to ethics, applying it to disability issues and professional decision-making. In answer to the fundamental ethical question "How should people treat each other?" a Communitarian might reply, "In whatever ways the people involved have

43

agreed to treat each other. They should recognize our bonds and relationships with each other. They should empathise with others and care about their needs and circumstances. They should construct shared values and cooperate in realising them. Professionals have obligations and responsibilities which are a result of their roles, their relationships with clients, and community expectations".

This response is fine as far as it goes, but it is insufficient. It does not provide guidelines on how a community might go about constructing shared values and mutual expectations. It is true that communities develop shared values. It is useful to conceive of legislation, professional codes of ethics, social arrangements and conventions as expressions of community values. But community values change over time. Some traditions are conserved while others are discarded. New social arrangements are proposed and constructed. How does a community judge whether proposals are good ones? Some members of a community might be enthusiastic proponents of a welfare state, whilst others might advocate minimal government intervention. Some people may be optimistic about the benefits of stem cell research, whilst others might worry that such research constitutes serious ethical violations of respect for human life. When people are attempting to negotiate with each other, or to persuade others to adopt shared values and ways of doing things, what ethical theories can be used to inform and guide the discussions?

There are two ethical theories that are prominent in such discussions. One looks to consequences and the other to principles.

When we make an ethical judgement according to consequences, we say that a decision (or a policy, or a social arrangement) is right if it has good results, if it makes people happier, if it increases the welfare of those affected by the decision.

When we make an ethical judgement according to principles, we say a decision (or a policy, or a social arrangement) is right if it conforms firmly to principles, if it respects people and their rights and if it is impartial and consistent.

Much of the time, these two approaches work in harmony with each other. Treating people with respect generally increases their welfare. Treating people disrespectfully makes them unhappy. Sometimes, though, the two strategies clash, and there are many ethical dilemmas that are a result of conflicts between them. Most people, whether they are consciously aware of it or not, use a combination of the two strategies, though they are likely to lean more towards one or the other. This is true of societies as well. While a combination is common, the two approaches are fundamentally quite different and need to be disentangled in order to examine their strengths, weaknesses, and application to disability issues. Principles will be the subject of the next chapter, and the consequences-based approach will be explored in this one.

The obvious appeal of consequences

If we are faced with some competing choices of action and we are considering what is the best thing to do, an obvious strategy is to calculate the consequences of our decisions. We might decide that a decision is the right one because it will result in desired consequences [1].

When defining ethics as the way people should treat each other, it is important to note that when we make ethical decisions, we are not calculating what the consequences will be for *ourselves*, but what effects there will be for *others*.

If we ask the fundamental ethical question "How should people treat each other?" a Consequentialist might reply "In whatever way is good for them." This consequence-based approach is associated with the seminal philosophers Jeremy Bentham and John Stuart Mill and known as Utilitarianism. According to them, the rightness of a decision should be judged by its utility, that is, its usefulness in bringing about an increase in people's happiness [2]. Their ethical advice is that we should make decisions, adopt policies, and set up social arrangements that increase people's pleasure, happiness and welfare. We should aim to decrease pain, misery and distress [3]. We should think about all the people who will be affected and try to maximise the benefit for as many of them as we possibly can. As I discuss this idea, it will be convenient to use the terms 'Utilitarianism', 'Consequentialism', and 'maximising benefits' as meaning much the same thing.

This ethical decision-making strategy is so obviously sensible that it needs very little further justification. The entire domain of ethics exists because people have wants, needs and interests, and they co-operate with each other to fulfil them. That is why we need to figure out how to treat each other. We form relationships, set up social arrangements, adopt conventions, develop policies and enact legislation because these are the means by which we co-operate to produce the outcomes we consider preferable. We prefer pleasure to pain, happiness to misery. We want to avoid the depredations of crime, poverty and sickness. We tackle material and social ills by developing and applying professional expertise.

Disability service provision is clearly a response to human needs. The drive to make the world a better place by improving clients' circumstances is a characteristic of disability professionals. It follows that they would accept Utilitarianism as a sound ethical strategy. Although Utilitarianism, or to use ordinary language, the consideration of consequences, is an obviously appealing strategy, there are a surprising number of objections to it [4].

Some people object to the very starting point, which is that pain is a bad consequence and pleasure is a good one. Is ethics really about pleasure and pain? Surely there is more to life and goodness and morality than pleasure and pain? To some people, calculating consequences seems a shallow approach which reeks of expediency, rather than looking for a meaningful way to lead one's life. In response, a Consequentialist could retort that ethics should be a practical affair, not a highfalutin set of abstract ideals. We are dealing with real people, in real circumstances and the only thing that really matters is their welfare.

Other critics are concerned with the proposal that we should aim for the best consequences. Obviously, this must mean that some consequences are better than others and we can calculate the differences. But how could we possibly do that? Are we supposed to put a number on how much pleasure we get from some experience, so we can measure it against some other experience? How many pleasures are worth what degree of pain? Again, a Consequentialist could retort that this is a practical matter, and that we do in fact make such calculations all the time in our daily lives.

Some critics point out that the problem is even worse. Not only are we supposed to calculate pleasure over pain, but getting a good set of consequences for some people can result in bad consequences for others. So not only do we have to measure the good over the bad, we also have to measure the good for some number of people over the bad for some other number of people. Even if we maximize good consequences, how should we distribute them? And if maximizing good consequences for a lot of people comes at the cost of sacrificing an unfortunate few people, is that all right? In response, a Consequentialist might admit that distribution is a real problem, but point out that it is a real problem for any theory of ethics and for any set of social arrangements. It is just something we have to keep working at.

Other people worry about taking on the responsibility for doing the calculations and making decisions about other people's lives. If ethics is about how people should treat each other, then Consequentialism seems to demand that *I* make decisions about what is good for *you*, that professionals make decisions about what is good for clients, that governments make decisions about what is good for citizens. There seems to be a lot of scope here for being patronizing, or for basing decisions on personal preferences and prejudices, or for simply making errors. People are simply not equipped to 'play god' with other people's lives. A Consequentialist might retort that, once again, this is how life is in practice. The decisions we make *do*, in fact, affect others. Professionals do have the responsibility of looking after clients' welfare. We might not like to 'play god', but we cannot, in fact, avoid it. The best thing to do is be reflective, be sympathetic and consult a lot.

Those objections, and their application to disability issues, will form the content of the remainder of this chapter, but first, let us look at some instances where thinking about the consequences is an important part of making ethical decisions.

Some dilemmas concerning consequences

Bob and Betty discuss their dreams

Bob and Betty have each acquired brain injuries through car crashes. Bob has short-term memory loss and some cognitive impairment. As a result he becomes confused and distressed. He is frustrated by his disability and has developed an unrealistic ambition to become a politician in charge of government disability services. He talks constantly about this ambition to the extent that other people avoid him. Jane is a disability services professional who has been allocated to him in order to assist him to re-acquire social and interpersonal skills. Inevitably, he talks to Jane a lot about his political dreams and ambitions. Jane is unsure how to respond. She recognizes the importance of ambitions in anyone's life, and does not want to distress Bob by crushing his dreams. She cannot truthfully treat them as realistic, and she does not believe that continually evading the issue is either practical or honest.

Betty is another client who has short-term memory loss and impaired cognitive function. Her ambitions are less extreme, though still unrealistic. She is being assisted to develop computer typing skills and hopes to be able to get them to the level where she will be employed. She has not been in paid work since her accident and cannot remember people's names or agreed tasks. Despite this, she feels that she is making progress and seeks assurance that she will become employed in the future. Again, Jane wonders how honest she should be with Betty.

Latimer House develops a restraint policy

The residents of Latimer House have intellectual disabilities and challenging behaviour. From time to time, staff respond by restraining residents physically. Sometimes this risks injury to the resident or to the staff member, or both. Challenging behaviour which is not restrained can also present risks of injury. Medication, with or without clients' consent, is sometimes used to moderate residents' mood swings and behaviour. There is a high turnover of staff.

The management of Latimer House is considering adopting a policy of no restraint, either physically or chemically. It recognizes that physical restraint has a number of negative consequences, such as injury risk, psychological trauma, panic and anger, and loss of dignity for the resident. It is aware of the argument that using medication as a chemical restraint results in residents being 'happier' but is concerned about side effects and about the temptation for staff to over-use medication as an easy way out.

Some staff have said that a blanket 'no restraint' policy is unworkable. They agree that the well-being of residents is of prime consideration, but point out that the interests of the staff are also important and that there are occasions when restraint is necessary for the safety of residents and staff. Management is contemplating an arrangement whereby staff can make application for exceptions to a 'no restraint' policy. Staff say that requiring applications is unrealistic and predict that such a policy will result in the high turnover of staff becoming significantly worse.

Steven wants a cigarette

Steven has physical disabilities and requires support workers to assist him in his daily needs. He is thirty years old and has been a smoker since he was a teenager. He recently decided to quit and announced his intention. He has not had a cigarette now for three days. One of his support workers, Mark, hates the smell of cigarettes and is very pleased that Steven has quit, remarking how much more pleasant it is to work with him now than previously.

Steven, however, is finding it very difficult to cope with his nicotine cravings and asks Mark to supply him with a cigarette.

Mark does not want to comply. He points out that if Steven continues to abstain from smoking, the cravings will eventually fade. He reminds Steven that smoking causes cancer, and has bad consequences for fitness and for health generally. He does not want to be a passive smoker himself, nor assist Steven in actions that are predictably harmful.

Steven responds that a significant proportion of the population smokes and that most of them do not get cancer. Due to his disabilities, he is not particularly interested in physical fitness, and if he did not have disabilities, he would not need anyone's permission or assistance to smoke. He thinks that the dangers are exaggerated, and anyway, as a rational adult, it is up to him to calculate the consequences for himself.

Mark retorts that the rational decision is not to smoke and the only reason Steven wants a cigarette is that he is addicted. Steven concedes that might be true, and that he still intends to give up eventually, but that right now he wants a smoke. Mark cannot decide whether he should comply with Steven's demand.

Concerns about the consequences approach, and responses to concerns

The greatest good for the greatest number

The consequence-based approach calculates the results of a decision, measuring its impact on the people it affects. This raises a number of very difficult questions.
- How do we know who will be affected?
- What do we do if we think that a decision will have good effects for some people and bad ones for some others?
- How could we know what the effects will be? Making predictions is very difficult.
- How do we know how many people will be affected? The number might be very large and impossible to estimate.
- Is each one of us really responsible for our life's potential impacts on every other person around, including those we have never met? Surely this is an impractical burden.

A focus on the client

If we apply the theory to professional ethics, it becomes much more manageable. A professional is required to consider the needs of the client in particular, rather than the interests of everybody in the community. When we apply the consequences-approach to disability issues we need to modify the theory significantly. We need to discard a universal calculation in favour of a particular focus, which is limited to the professional sphere. That is in the nature of professions. If the focus is disability service provision, then policies and professional services should be judged according to their efficacy for the people with disabilities who are accessing the service. As discussed in chapter two, other parties may be affected, and merit consideration, but a professional prioritises the client.

Utilitarianism requires us to calculate 'the greatest good for the greatest number' [5]. There are some difficulties with this. It could be taken to condone appalling misery for a small group as long as it makes most people better off. Even without such an extreme example, a calculation of consequences does not provide any guidelines about the distribution of the consequences. A decision or a policy which is in the interests of some people may not be in the interests of others. Taxation is an example. We might think that taking a small amount of tax from most people in order to provide for a small minority who are in desperate need is justifiable policy, but how much is small? Consequentialism does not provide any means of calculating what level of service provision is right, except, of course, to point out that an inefficient provision is not as good as an efficacious one.

A practitioner's decisions are not usually so difficult. Practitioners do not normally have to balance the interests of many people over many other people. They focus on the client. This makes the calculation of consequences much more realistic and practical. Admittedly, sometimes the needs of one client will conflict with another's and both cannot be met satisfactorily, so a practitioner might need to make some difficult judgements. Calculating and balancing consequences is a professional's job. When decisions are easy and the results obvious, we do not need professional advice.

As discussed in chapter two, the profession as a whole has an obligation to advocate for people with disabilities and to call for effective government policies. Calculating, measuring and evaluating consequences is part of this obligation.

In the discussion of justice in chapters two and six, I discuss a proposal by the philosopher John Rawls. Rawls is not a Utilitarian [6]. But if we add his suggestions to Utilitarianism, we may improve the theory.

A focus on the worst circumstances

The defect we might improve is that Utilitarianism could condone appalling misery for a small number of people on the grounds that a large number were thereby better off. Rawls suggests that such an arrangement would never be chosen by people who were in a position to design a just society, and also suggests that if a redistribution of resources is being contemplated, then the worst off should be considered first. The 'maximin' strategy proposes that good consequences should be maximised for those people who have the minimum resources [7].

It seems plausible that Rawls' hypothetical social engineers would:
- approve of social arrangements that had good consequences
- would see the benefit of setting up professions with particular responsibilities
- would provide professional expertise to the people who needed it most and
- would avoid extreme maldistribution of resources.

Adding in Rawls' ideas about justice improves a consequences-approach to ethics.

The difficulty of calculating consequences

Another criticism of a consequences-approach is that consequences cannot be calculated. To do so requires making predictions about what will result, and we have no way of telling what the future will bring.

This criticism has little merit. People do in fact make predictions all the time. It is an essential and unavoidable demand of everyday life. When we drive a car or decide what to eat, we make predictions. If we get them wrong, the consequences can be disastrous. Our own lives depend on making predictions and calculating consequences and we do so continually. We also calculate the predicted impact of our behaviour on other people. The success of our social lives depends on our ability to do so. A criticism of Consequentialism based on the claim that we cannot predict fails because we do, in practice, predict consequences all the time.

Another criticism is that we cannot make calculations because happiness cannot be quantified [8]. 'Calculation' implies using numbers. We cannot talk sensibly of '10 units of happiness', let alone compare it with a completely different type of unhappiness. How could we measure physical pain and subtract it from an 'amount' of aesthetic pleasure?

This objection also fails, ignoring the facts of everyday life. We all routinely make these sorts of judgements. We might, for example, consider the alternatives of going to a restaurant, going to the movies, or meeting with friends. This everyday decision requires us to make judgements about which will be most enjoyable including a calculation of the amount of time, money and effort each entails. We daily make evaluations of very disparate pleasures, be they aesthetic, physical or social, and compare them with costs. We also make evaluations that require long-term predictions. We might hate going to a dentist, but predict we will suffer even more distress in the long term if we do not.

Calculating consequences, making predictions and evaluating different outcomes are an ordinary part of life. It is unfortunate that life is not entirely predictable and our calculations are not always realised. Constant adjustment and re-evaluation is necessary. Skills and experience help.

Professionals are expected to develop skills and experience that make their calculations and predictions more reliable. It is for this very reason that professionals are typically engaged in the first place. Clients ask for advice especially when they do not know enough to make sound predictions. A professional who shrugged and said "Future outcomes can neither be foretold not evaluated" would be quite rightly criticised for avoiding professional responsibility.

The same can be said for policies, government interventions and legislation. The entire point of these stratagems is to predict and bring about outcomes that are calculated to improve the circumstances of those who are affected by them. Again, miscalculations or unexpected events can occur. Policy outcomes should be monitored and adjustments made if required.

It must be acknowledged that predictions have some uncertainty and even that the level of uncertainty is itself difficult to calculate. We are always calculating what will probably transpire, but do not know precisely what the probability is. This applies to individual decisions and to large-scale policies. Where possible, the range of potential outcomes and their likelihood should be discussed with those people who will be affected.

Unfortunately, there is a tendency for the fear of miscalculation to paralyse some professionals and policy makers so that they refuse to make any decision at all, or to initiate any intervention. They may attempt to justify this by saying "We should not play god". However, deciding not to intervene has consequences, just as much as an intervention has consequences. Making predictions and decisions is a human challenge, not a divine prerogative. Applying care and expertise to bring about the best probable outcomes is a professional responsibility. Shirking that responsibility is not ethical.

Defining good consequences

We do not have a precise agreement concerning what is meant by 'good' consequences. The theory of Utilitarianism began, reasonably enough, by defining pain as bad and pleasure as good [9]. Its originator, Jeremy Bentham, was scornful of any claims that some pleasures, such as reading fine literature, were in any way 'higher' than others, such as mindless games [10]. He maintained this was just a matter of personal taste. Human life is, however, somewhat more complex. It is true that while people have different tastes, we all share an aversion to pain. It is also true that there is a good deal more to happiness than an absence of pain, and that people will tolerate pain to achieve other consequences, including quite abstract feelings such as a sense of fulfilment, or self-esteem or even serving the needs of others.

Despite the difficulty of definition, people typically know whether they are happy or unhappy, whether they are experiencing a sense of well-being or not.

The client as an expert

Professionals should therefore be cautious when deciding what is good for the client. We each value or own sense of personal taste, and it is only too easy to define good consequences in terms of our own personal preferences.

Ethical and practical challenges arise when a professional and a client have conflicting views about what constitutes good consequences. A client may want to eat food which is inadvisable given his disability, like Jim in chapter one. A client might have imprudent spending habits, or might avoid medication with unpleasant side effects. If calculating and evaluating consequences is a guide to ethical decision-making, what should happen if the client and the professional make different calculations? Who should decide? Can the theory of Utilitarianism resolve such dilemmas? A version of Utilitarianism that tackles this problem is 'Preference Utilitarianism'.

Preference Utilitarianism

There is a proposal in Utilitarian theory that good outcomes should be defined as *the outcomes preferred by those who are affected by the ethical decisions*, that is, the people experiencing the outcomes [11]. This strategy of Preference Utilitarianism has much to recommend it. It seems eminently reasonable that the people experiencing the consequences of a decision are best placed, and most entitled, to report on whether they are good consequences. There is nothing quite as reliable as direct experience. If I report that I am in pain, it does not make sense for another person, no matter how expert, to tell me I am mistaken. Preference Utilitarianism is also compatible with the Communitarian strategy discussed in the previous chapter. In order to decide how people should be treated, it is best to ask them.

Difficulties with Preference Utilitarianism

Despite its plausibility as a general ethical theory, Preference Utilitarianism falters when applied to professional ethics and to disability service provision. Some clients are not able to report on their experiences. Others are not able to competently calculate consequences, especially when the nature of their disability compromises their capacity to make decisions. Indeed, it is plausible to say that all clients lack in some way the knowledge and expertise to make the best decisions. That is why the professional has been engaged in the first place. A professional is, by definition, someone with the skills and qualifications to make good decisions, and it is therefore arguable that the professional's judgement should be given priority when there is a difference of opinion.

This argument is dangerous on both practical and ethical grounds. The picture of an incapable client and a professional expert is seriously incomplete. On the contrary, the relationship should be seen as one between two experts. There is a professional who is an expert in disability service provision, and a client who is an expert on the client. Only the client has detailed knowledge about his of her life style, pain-tolerance, relationships, ambitions, and most importantly, personal preferences [12]. By adding the two areas of expertise together, the best results are likely to be obtained. It can be argued that the client is in the best position to evaluate the consequences, or it could be argued that the client's preferences define 'good' consequences. Both propositions counter the notion that the professional knows best.

Actual instances of clients making bad choices might lead us to question this, and some theorists have attempted to distinguish between 'a person's manifest preference and his true preference' [13], but this is confusing consequences with the ways of achieving those consequences. Clearly a client might be mistaken or misinformed about the effectiveness of some means, that is, ways of achieving well-being. A professional might be mistaken about the acceptability of some means. But when it comes to results, only clients can judge whether the consequences are satisfactory, whether well-being is the result, and whether the means were acceptable. It would be an over-confident professional or an insensitive organization that, lacking the intimate knowledge of a client's perspective, attempted to enforce insufficiently informed interventions.

This view of the client as an expert who develops a relationship with an advising professional is quite compatible with the Communitarian approach. Furthermore, it is likely to be preferred by Rawls' hypothetical social engineers discussed in chapter two. People would be unlikely to agree to a society in which their decision-making was over-ruled if they consulted an expert. Disability professionals and service providers have a great deal of practical power. They should, when exercising that power, take pains to empathise with the position of their clients who are experiencing the impacts of decisions made on their behalf, which includes loss of control over one's life.

The client-as-expert view is also compatible with the 'agency' model of relationship described in chapter one. It is least compatible with the Paternalism model.

Paternalism

There is a concern that a consequences-approach encourages and justifies Paternalism.

As discussed in chapter one, whether agency or Paternalism is the appropriate model depends upon the capabilities of the client. Paternalism is decision making by experts on behalf of and about people who do not have the skills, knowledge or maturity to make decisions for themselves. Some clients are simply not good decision-makers. Some indeed, make no decisions at all. Professional judgement should prevail when the client cannot make sound judgements.

The challenge is to ascertain the level of a client's decision-making capability. An all-or-nothing approach should be resisted. If a client is competent, then the professional and client will presumably agree about what is in the client's best interests and no ethical challenges present themselves.

If the client disagrees, the professional might be tempted to take this as evidence that the client cannot make sound decisions, but that temptation should be resisted [12]. Its logical result is to put all the power back in the hands of the professional and ignore the client's inputs. It risks over-riding the client's needs and circumstances with the professional's personal perspective, tastes and preferences. It denies that clients have levels of expertise.

Almost all clients have some degree of ability to assess and report upon whether their experiences are satisfactory or not. The only exception would be people in a coma, who would not be accessing disability services anyway. Even Baby Charlotte in chapter one had some experiences and preferences which could be ascertained. The level of a client's competence should not be judged simply by the amount by which they coincide with the professional's views. The effectiveness of their decision-making can be measured in other areas of their lives, such as their ability to communicate, socialize and look after their daily needs. Even if these abilities are severely compromised, clients still experience the results of others' decisions and care should be taken to ascertain whether their experiences are the best that can be obtained.

Paternalism advises that a professional has an obligation to make expert decisions on behalf of clients who are not capable of making them for themselves. Preference Utilitarianism advises that clients, who experience the effects of decisions and have to live with the consequences, are best placed to evaluate and report on their experiences. It follows that the extent that Paternalism is justified depends on the decision-making capability of the client, and even high levels of Paternalism should be guided by the consequent experiences of the client.

Paternalism is also an issue in a principles-based approach, which will be the subject of the next chapter. Deception of clients for their own good violates principles. Is it justified when it results in good consequences?

Deception

A worrying objection to Utilitarianism is that it can be used to justify telling lies. Surely lying is simply wrong. At any rate, people are outraged and distressed when they discover they are being lied to. Whatever the excuses might be for deception, the end does not justify the means. It is reprehensible for cynical professionals to adopt an expedient attitude towards their clients which recommends that what they don't know won't hurt them – just keep them quiet and happy.

This objection has several strands which need untangling.

It is true that Utilitarians do not agree that lying is *simply wrong*. While some people might have an intuitive sense that some actions are simply right, or wrong, because of the sort of actions they are, Utilitarians argue that this is mistaken [14]. Things are not good or bad in themselves but only in context, judged by their effects. Typically, the *effects* of lying are bad, and this is what makes it wrong according to a consequences- approach.

Utilitarians would agree that people are outraged and distressed when they find they are being lied to. This is a good argument against lying, and on these grounds, Utilitarianism does not condone deception. Of course, lying is typically to the advantage of the deceiver and to the disadvantage of the people being deceived. Someone selling a car might lie about its defects to a prospective buyer. This is wrong because it has bad consequences for the buyer. Admittedly it has good consequences for the seller, but ethics is about deciding how best to treat others, rather than the selfish pursuit of one's own ends.

But what about lies that actually are intended to advantage the person being lied to, perhaps even to the disadvantage of the person telling the lies?

An everyday hypothetical scenario can serve as an illustration. Imagine a teenage girl who has just finished school and has been offered a place at university. She likes pop music, though, and has applied for a job in a local music store. The store manager telephones to say she has the job, but the call is taken by the girl's mother, who informs the manager that the girl is no longer interested. The mother tells the girl she did not get the job. The girl goes to university, achieving a successful and happy life. Years later, her mother confesses her deception and the daughter is outraged. Is she right to condemn her mother, or did her mother do the right thing?

Once again, there are a number of tangled strands in the ethical analysis of this story.

The long-term consequence of the daughter's successful life does outweigh the brief distress the daughter feels when she discovers the deception, so on those grounds the mother's action was ethical, according to a calculation of the consequences. This calculation, though, should also consider whether it would be possible to achieve the desired result *without* telling the lie. Utilitarianism seeks the *maximum* benefit with the *least* harm.

There is, too, the consideration of trust. Is the mother in the habit of telling lies, so the relationship between mother and daughter is not in the long run conducive to a happy life? Is the daughter unable to make prudent decisions for herself because she cannot rely on what her parents tell her? Does she find herself in an insecure environment where she lies in turn to her parents?

The parallels to a professional relationship are obvious. Manipulative lies to clients for their own good may be a short-term expediency, but providing for their needs may become impossible if there is no trust in the relationship.

The daughter's outrage indicates a dispute about the proper use of Paternalism (which perhaps should be called Parentalism, since the root meaning of 'paternal' relates to 'father' rather than both parents). It is unlikely that the daughter has any issues about her parents' stories about Santa Claus or tooth fairies, but as children develop they expect parents to relinquish Paternalism. Teenage years are usually difficult precisely because relations with parents need to be renegotiated.

Clients are not children (although obviously some happen to be children as well as being clients). Paternalism and deception are not typically justified in a professional - client relationship. It can still be argued, though, that where clients do have a diminished capacity to handle information and make prudent decisions, deception and manipulation may be an ethical and practical necessity.

The ends do not justify the means

It is often said that the ends do not justify the means. If we accept that, then it would be a serious objection to Utilitarianism. A hypothetical example, though, shows that the objection has little merit and is easily refuted. Imagine that your child is being chased by a murderer. To your relief, you see your child managing to evade the murderer and to hide. The murderer demands to know where your child is hiding. Are you obliged to tell the truth? Surely not [15].

The extreme consequences of telling the truth in these circumstances justify the lie. Ordinarily, though, a society, or a professional relationship, in which people who habitually lied and shrugged off complaints with "Ah well, the end justifies the means" would predictably be unworkable. As a rule, lying is wrong.

Act Utilitarianism and Rule Utilitarianism

Perhaps calculating consequences would be more practical and reliable if we set up general rules of behaviour, rather than agonizing over every individual act. This proposal is known as Rule Utilitarianism, as contrasted with Act Utilitarianism [16].

Act Utilitarianism advises us to always act in a way that will maximize the benefit to everyone affected by that action.

Rule Utilitarianism advises us to construct and conform to rules of behaviour which are calculated to maximize the benefit of everyone affected.

As previously discussed, applying these notions to professional ethics requires modifying 'everyone affected' to everyone affected within the professional context, prioritising the client.

Five advantages of Rule Utilitarianism

1. It is more practical and less burdensome. Instead of the tiresome process of estimating consequences for an endless series of decisions and actions, we can draw upon our experiences and habitually apply general rules instead. We do this in other areas of our lives, such as choosing our food or driving to work. Instead of wrestling with the fine details of exactly how truthful to be in every conversation, we can recognize that 'honesty is the best policy' and be straightforward all the time. Calculations based on many instances are likely to be more reliable than single estimates. Long-term consequences can be factored in more effectively. Perhaps we know, either from logic and experience, that a community in which people frequently lie to each other is less likely to be a happy than one where people trust each other.

2. Rule Utilitarianism avoids the concern that the end justifies the means. While we recognize that some ends justify some means, it is not the case that any ends justify any means. Rules allow us to openly debate, negotiate and adopt procedures which are justified by their effects.

3. Rules allow people to predict what others will do and thereby arrange their own lives accordingly. The wrong done by liars and thieves is not confined to the damage of a particular theft or lie, but destabilizes the co-operative arrangements of the community. Even amongst people of goodwill, trustworthiness, reliability and consistency are easier to work with than unpredictable whims. This is particularly true for clients who are dependant upon the behaviour of professionals.

4. Disability service provision relies upon organizations and procedures, rather than *ad hoc* decisions and responses to individual cases. Governments have legislation, organizations have policies and professions have codes of ethics. If we apply Rule Utilitarianism to the formulation and implementation of policy, then a good policy would be one that resulted in benefits for those whom it was meant to serve. The actual results of a policy should be measured and compared to predicted results, with adjustments made to the policy as necessary.

5. Rule Utilitarianism can be taken further than constructing individual rules such as 'be honest' or 'public building codes require disability access'. Rule Utilitarianism can be seen as an entire ideal moral code adopted by everyone in the community [17]. Honesty, caring for the needy, promoting and protecting the freedom of individuals, and other ideals can be expressed in social norms, policies and legislation. As such, Rule Utilitarianism is not only compatible with Communitarianism, but can provide the community with much-needed advice concerning what the community's negotiations and agreements should rest upon. That advice would be to adopt agreements which are calculated to maximize benefit to the members of the community. It might advise that there would be specific benefits to be gained by setting up professions to provide particular benefits, say to community members with disabilities. If the justification of social norms and arrangements is based on the calculation of their consequences, community debate will presumably be less divided by relativism or ideological differences.

Despite these advantages, dilemmas remain. Even those rules, policies and conventions that have excellent justification overall will occasionally falter when applied to individual cases. If it is calculated that sticking to a rule will produce bad consequences in a particular case, should the rule be broken? A rule that has exceptions, and is only honoured when it is expedient to do so, is not much use as a rule. If exceptions are taken into account and the consequences calculated each time, then Rule Utilitarianism may as well be abandoned in favour of Act Utilitarianism. On the other hand, it is implausible that any rule can predict the circumstances and consequences of every case, so exceptions are inevitable.

If absolutely binding rules were desirable and feasible, then there would be no need for professions. It is precisely because human needs and circumstances are complex and varied that professional judgment, based on expertise and experience, is needed to deal with real cases.

Features of a consequences-approach to ethics

Not all approaches to ethical decisions are characterised by calculating the consequences. Some other approaches are discussed in other chapters. It may be useful at this stage to develop a list of the features that might identify a Consequentialist or Utilitarian method of making ethical decisions. The left hand column of the table lists some coherent features we might expect in a consequences approach. The right hand column does not need to be coherent because it notes some examples of various alternatives, for illustrative purposes. The table can usefully be compared with similar tables in the chapter on Communitarianism and the chapter discussing Principles.

A PERSON who:

Has a consequences-approach to ethical decision making is likely to:	Does **not** use a consequences-approach may:
Care about others' welfare. Sympathise with others. Aim to make people happy. Calculate the consequences of his/her actions. Strive to maximise good outcomes.	Not care primarily about people's welfare. Not believe he/she is responsible for other people's happiness. Make or stick to decisions regardless of consequences.

PROFESSIONALS and ORGANISATIONS that:

Have a consequences-approach to ethical decision making are likely to:	Do **not** use a consequences-approach may:
Be committed to caring for clients. Be concerned about clients' welfare. Calculate the consequences of decisions. Adjust to circumstances. Take responsibility for the results of their decisions. Design policies to maximise benefit and monitor the results of their decisions.	Believe there are more important considerations than clients' well-being. Stick to decisions and rules regardless of consequences. Not monitor the impact of their operations and procedures. May apply a variety of considerations (such as terms of contracts, efficiency, rights) rather than just client benefit.

A SOCIETY that:

Has a consequences-approach:	**Does not** have a consequences-approach may:
Justifies all social and political arrangements on the basis of good outcomes. Promotes people's welfare. Cares for the needy. Defines justice in terms of distribution of resources. Favours significant government responsibility and intervention in social welfare.	Believe that if misfortune happens to some people, society does not have an obligation to care for them. Believe that government should not interfere in people's lives. Believe government is only responsible for maintaining order. Apply rules strictly without regard to circumstances. Favour individual freedoms, rights and responsibilities over all other approaches.

Some limitations of a consequences-approach to ethics

We have been working with a definition of good consequences as happiness, well-being, pleasure and related positive feelings and experiences. Similarly, we have taken bad consequences to be pain, distress, and unhappiness. But are these the only consequences that matter? Are they the only outcomes that we do or should value?

We could examine this question by considering a hypothetical case. Imagine that a promising young pianist has injured her hands in a car accident and will never play again [18]. Clearly we could say that this is a bad consequence because she will experience frustration at not being able to play, and we will never again have the pleasure of hearing her wonderful music. But perhaps this is the wrong way round. We take pleasure in her music because it is wonderful. It is not wonderful music just because we take pleasure in it. There is more to the loss than we can balance simply by cheering her up. One limitation of Utilitarianism is that pleasure is not the only value. Music has value, and that is why we enjoy it. By simply considering the pleasure music produces, Utilitarians are missing the point.

An absolute Utilitarian would be unfazed by this criticism, and point out that there is in fact no standard of how wonderful music is *except* for how much people appreciate it.

We do not need hypothetical cases to realise that pleasure and the absence of pain are frequently not the over-riding concern of people's lives. A narcotic-induced permanent daze, no matter how blissful, is not the ultimate goal in life for most of us. Some people will go further and refuse painkillers that alleviate results of illness or injury, preferring independence and self-control. Some terminally ill patients will struggle to extend their pain-filled lives, perhaps so that they can continue to be with loved ones. On the other hand, different people have different values, and make different decisions about what constitutes their welfare. If Utilitarians only measure pleasure, they misread human nature. People value other things.

A Preference Utilitarian would be unmoved by such a criticism, recommending that good consequences be defined as those consequences that are preferred by the people affected.

Preference Utilitarianism is persuasive when people know what their preferences are and how to achieve them, but this is frequently not the case in a professional context. A lack of knowledge, skills and expertise is typically the reason people seek professional guidance in the first place. In disability provision, the difficulties multiply if the nature of the disability compromises the client's ability to make effective decisions.

Some clients may not be able to make sound judgements about their own welfare, and some may not be able to express their preferences to their providers. Some policy makers may not be in direct contact with those who are affected by the policies. The professional application of Utilitarianism in disability provision requires quite a lot of hypothesizing about the relative desirability of consequences. Sympathetic and effective professionals will attempt to place themselves in their clients' shoes, but the process may not be easy or error free. The distribution of power, authority and responsibility remain a professional issue. Who should decide what constitutes good consequences? Some combination of client and professional is needed, but what combination remains an open question.

As discussed above, the distribution of consequences themselves is another unresolved issue. The maxim of the greatest good for the greatest number appears to condone sacrificing the few for the benefit of the majority – hardly a proposition acceptable in the ethics of disability issues. Professionals need to focus on the needs of their clients rather than on masses of people, so in that sense their decisions are simpler. The profession as a whole has a role in advocating for its clients, who, being in a minority, risk being abandoned.

The notion of rights is an attempt to prevent the worst excesses of Utilitarianism by setting minimum standards for how people should be treated [19]. Indeed, many ethicists argue that it is rights and not consequences that should drive decisions, an argument that will be taken up in the next chapter. In their view, respect for persons, the right to life, freedom and self-determination are fundamental principles that should be maintained regardless of consequences.

The right to privacy is valued by many people. This does not seem to be because they calculate that it has clear beneficial consequences. On the contrary, the free flow of medical information, for example, would be of considerable benefit to the community. It would assist research, help measure the impact of therapies and policies, and facilitate efficiencies. Despite this, most people seem to value privacy for its own sake.

Many ethical dilemmas result from a conflict between principles and rights on the one hand, and consequences on the other. Both sides influence the Communitarian approach, but neither has won the debate. Social norms require that promises should be kept, obligations should be met and contracts should be honoured. If you have borrowed money and you are on your way to return it as promised, you might chance upon a beggar who is in dire need. Perhaps the person from whom you borrowed the money is both forgetful and wealthy, and will not miss it if you give the money to the beggar. Nonetheless, the social expectation is that you keep your promise and return the money. Many people would argue that there are some behaviours that are simply the right thing to do in principle.

It could be argued in response that asserting rights and principles is actually a defence of Preference Utilitarianism. Self-determination is the best way of achieving the results we prefer, and we sensibly do not trust others to make decisions on our behalf. For self-determination to be effective, we need to rely upon others to keep their promises, trust them not to lie to us, and demand respect for the freedom to make our own choices.

Conclusion

It is obvious that a consequences-approach is applicable to ethics in disability. Professionals have responsibilities for the welfare of their clients. The very reason for the existence of professions is to cater for the needs of clients. Professionals utilise their knowledge, skills and experience to make recommendations, give advice and apply interventions in order to produce beneficial results.

Legislation and policy similarly should be beneficial. Laws that worsen citizens' circumstances should be criticised. Policies that do not have beneficial impacts should be reviewed.

Utilitarians recommend that the consequences of a decision should be calculated, measuring the outcomes for everybody affected by the decision. Professional ethics has a narrower focus. Professionals have particular responsibilities for the needs of their clients, and should prioritise those.

The consequences-based approach has limitations.

There may be disputes about what counts as good consequences. There may be disagreements about who decides what are good consequences – the client or the professional. Preference utilitarianism can help here, with an alliance being formed between the client's preferences and the professional's expertise. Where a client's decision-making ability is impaired, a professional may need to make careful and finely-judged decisions.

Good consequences can be used to justify actions which are wrong by other ethical standards, such as deception. The stance that 'the end never justifies the means' is clearly not viable, but there is no formula in Consequentialism that can calculate which ends justify which means. Still, professional expertise is about making judgements in real circumstances, not about applying formulas.

The Utilitarian maxim of 'the greatest good for the greatest number' raises concerns that a minority might suffer appalling treatment in the interests of the majority. The addition of Rawls' theory of justice, where the worst circumstances are to be avoided, or failing that, to be ameliorated, improves the Utilitarian approach. It may still be prudent, though, to institute some basic rights and principles in the interests of justice and to guard against the excessive application of Utilitarianism. Rights and principles are the subject of the next chapter.

Chapter 4
A Principles-Based Approach to Professional Ethics

A principles-based approach in a nutshell

This approach starts from the idea that some actions are right and some are wrong in principle, simply because of the sort of actions they are. The most influential theory using this approach proposes that there are two tests to determine whether an action is right. One test asks whether the action could be applied universally, that is, consistently, impartially and in all circumstances. The second test asks whether the action treats people with respect, rather than manipulating or exploiting them.

This line of reasoning can lead to the principle that people should respect each other and their rights.

It can be applied readily to Professional Ethics. Professionals should recognise clients' rights, should promote clients' self-determination and should be open, honest, reliable and impartial.

Respect for persons

In this chapter I will examine the idea that there are fundamental ethical principles. This powerful idea has a lot of influence in ethical debates. It is worth discussing the background of this approach, its strengths and weaknesses, and how it can be used to guide ethical decisions in disability provision.

By *principle* I mean a fundamental idea, something that requires unswerving commitment, something we should stick to even when the circumstances make it difficult.

One fundamental ethical principle is a respect for persons. This does not just mean we should be polite to people. It means we should recognise that each individual person has intrinsic value and dignity, that each person has intentions and purposes and a unique life to lead. Respecting people implies respecting people's rights, treating them impartially and consistently.

This idea could be expressed as two rules:

Rule 1: Treat persons with regard for their individual value and dignity. Respect their rights.

Rule 2: Be consistent. This means being impartial, being reliable, and being committed to doing the right thing because it is the right thing to do.

The opposite to these two rules would be to manipulate people, exploit them, make decisions based on convenience, expedience, emotion or personal whims.

Like the consequences approach, the principles approach appears obviously right. Of course we should respect people and their rights. The difficulty is that consequences and principles sometimes conflict. Many ethical dilemmas, when examined, turn out to be a clash between respecting individual rights on the one hand and getting the best overall results on the other. The restraint policy of Latimer House, discussed in the last chapter, is an example. Restraining people demeans them, compromises their dignity and their freedom. Not restraining them results in people being harmed. A further difficulty is setting out what 'respecting persons and their rights' means in practice. An attitude of respect is a good starting point, but more is needed. If professional ethics is about how professionals should treat clients, then respect must be about how clients are actually treated, not merely about how professionals think or feel. Similarly, respect for people's rights requires setting out what those rights actually are, responding to those rights, and preventing violations of them. There is not much point in having a right if nobody has a responsibility for making sure it is realized in practice. If a child with a disability has the right to an education, then the state has a corresponding right to provide education that is appropriate and accessible. So we need to sort out what rights people have (and do not have) and whether people with disabilities have the same rights or different rights.

Deontology

The idea that we should use principles when making ethical decisions is sometimes known as Deontology. *Deon* is a Greek word meaning duty or something you are obliged to do [1]. So Deontology proposes that one has a duty to do the right thing simply because it is the right thing to do. An example is that a promise should be kept because it is a promise. A promise is simply the sort of thing that should not be broken, in principle.

This is a different approach from calculating that breaking a promise might cause mistrust or distress. Aiming to produce a particular consequence is sometimes called a teleological approach. *Telos* is a Greek word meaning end, or purpose. So being guided by sticking to principles (Deontology) is a different approach to calculating consequences (Teleology).

The Deontological approach is associated with the philosopher Immanuel Kant. The terminology he used does not sound familiar in contemporary language, but his ideas have had a considerable influence, so it is worth considering what he said, and how his ideas are applicable to discussions of disability ethics. The two rules that begin this chapter are derived from his proposal. He put them the other way around, with consistency first and respect second.

Kant proposed two maxims, that is, two rules of conduct:

Always act in a way that is consistent with what could be a universal rule.

Never treat other people as just means to an end, but rather as ends in themselves.

Following these maxims, he said, is a *categorical imperative*[2].

Before I explore how these ideas might be applicable to ethics in disability provision, some explanations and illustrations of them are necessary.

Universal rules

A 'universal rule' is one that could rationally be applied universally: that is, under all circumstances. A rule that says "Always tell the truth" makes sense. A rule that says "Always tell a lie" does not. A society of people who always lied to each other is unimaginable. A rule that says "Sometimes tell the truth and sometimes lie" is no use as a rule.

According to this approach, if you are trying to decide whether a decision is right or wrong, you should ask yourself whether the decision conforms to a universal rule, whether it is in principle the right thing to do. 'Do unto others as you would have them do unto you' is a useful test. If you treat other people one way, but would want to make an exception for how you would like to be treated, you are not conforming to a universal rule. The universal rule is even stronger than this, though, because it does not rely upon mere personal preference. Some sorts of behaviour, such as deception, are simply wrong.

Means to an end

People use tools, a knife, say, as a 'means to an end'. A person might have a goal of cutting open a package, and the intention of using a knife to achieve that end. That would be a rational thing for a person to do. The knife itself, of course, has no intentions of its own, so a person does not have to consider what the knife might think about being used this way. Other people, however, are also rational beings, have their own intentions and should be respected accordingly. Deception is typically used to manipulate people, so it is wrong. When you tell a lie, you are perverting your victim's behaviour, influencing it towards your purposes rather than theirs. This is usually to your benefit, but not necessarily. Even if you deceive someone because you think it is for their own good, it is still your judgement, your purposes and your intentions that they are serving, not their own. So deception is one example of treating people as means to an end. It is wrong, because it violates the maxim 'Never treat other people just as a means to an end, but rather as ends in themselves.'

The categorical imperative

Kant used the term 'categorical imperative' to mean an obligation to do something simply because it is the right thing to do. It is different from a 'hypothetical imperative' which means "Do x if you want y". An example of a hypothetical imperative is "If you want to be trusted, always tell the truth". A categorical imperative is "Always tell the truth, because telling the truth is the right thing to do."

Applying the concepts

There are numerous books and ongoing discussion about Kant's ethical theory, with much debate about its validity and how best to interpret it. My purpose here is not to contribute to that debate, but to explore how the notion of principles might be applied to ethics in disability provision, and what might be gleaned from Kant's proposals in that regard. A consideration of the 'universal rule' idea may help us develop principles of consistency and impartiality. Consideration of the 'people as ends' idea may support the recognition of the rights of people with disabilities.

The principles-based approach and the consequences-based approach are in theory rivals and mutually exclusive. In the real world of professional ethics and policy construction, both need to be accommodated.

The principle of respect for human rights

Respect for persons, for their dignity and their intrinsic worth is a bit abstract. A more concrete and practical approach might be to respect people's rights. To do this, we need to decide what rights we will recognize and respect. We need to make them explicit so that we can forge agreements about what these rights are and how to protect them in practice. We need to set up social arrangements and legislation to make sure people are not denied their rights.

What fundamental rights do people have? What formal agreements, codes of practice and legislation recognize and protect these rights?

If we ask the fundamental ethical question "How should people treat each other?" a reasonable answer would be that we should recognize each other as fellow human beings and respect each other accordingly. The very existence of ethics flows from the undeniable fact that human beings make decisions, exercise choice, have goals and values, form relationships with other people and co-operate with them. It is an inescapable part of human life that we not only make decisions about our own lives, but that we make decisions about how to treat others. At the same time, we care deeply about others' attitudes to ourselves and how they treat us. We each want to be respected not merely for the practical reason of helping us advance our interests but also because it influences our identity and self-esteem. In order to be a flourishing human being, any one of us needs a sense of self worth and a sense that our intrinsic worth is recognized by others.

Human beings also value their own freedom. Because we each have our own goals and preferences, we value the freedom to pursue those goals. To do this, we need personal and political freedoms. We want to be able to decide for ourselves how to live our lives, express our preferences and our opinions. Social policy, legislation and political arrangements simultaneously constrain and empower us, so we need to be able to comment on them and participate in their construction.

In practice, we cannot exercise freedom or pursue our life goals if we are debilitated by illness, or if we lack education, skills and knowledge, or if we lack material resources like property and income. It is reasonable, therefore, to set up political arrangements that do not deny us access to health services, access to education, opportunities for employment or ownership of property.

Since it is human nature to want respect, freedom and opportunity for ourselves, it follows that we should acknowledge that everybody else does likewise, and that we should recognize everyone's rights to respect, freedom and opportunity.

Formal agreements, codes and conventions

A recognition of these fundamental rights is the justification for specific legal and political rights, such as the right to vote or the right to fair and equal treatment by the law. Professional Codes of Ethics, social policies and legislation often make specific reference to rights.

The Universal Declaration of Human Rights

The Universal Declaration of Human Rights begins with a statement about the inherent worth of each human being [3]. It goes on to say that everybody has a right to:
- Liberty
- Property
- Freedom of thought
- Freedom of expression
- Political participation
- Social security
- Choice of employment

- Leisure
- Health care
- Education
- and everybody has duties to the community so as to make it possible for people to flourish.

Legislation

The principle of respect for persons is the justification of much legislation. For example, people may legally refuse medical treatment. Doctors are required to provide information to patients about the risks, benefits and side effects of medical treatment. In this way, legal procedures recognize people's right to make their own decisions about their lives and preferences. People value their own privacy, so the right to privacy has recently become enforced through legislation. There is much legislation that affirms people's inherent worth and prohibits discrimination, and there is legislation that provides for access to the services that people need in order to flourish. Legislation covers such issues as:

Aged care

Disability discrimination

Disability services

Human rights and equal opportunity

Racial discrimination

Social security

Property

Building codes

Child protection

Criminal law

Education

Elections

Family and community services

Guardianship

Mental Health

Transport [4].

All of this legislation is influenced by the ethical principle that people should be respected as human beings, should be able to exercise their freedoms, and should be protected against discrimination and exploitation.

Professional code of ethics

A Disability Professionals Code of Ethics is provided in chapter five. It is influenced by a principles-based approach. It states a belief:
- in the worth, dignity and uniqueness of all persons
- in the right of all people to live and participate in community life
- in the empowerment of individuals to maximise their self determination through access to information, choice, informed consent and/or advocacy in all decision-making.

United Nations Convention on the Rights of People with Disabilities

Unfortunately, people do not always recognize each other as people just like themselves. I noted in chapter two that this could be a problem in a community-based approach to ethics. Somebody who looks or behaves differently from the norm may not be recognized as a member of the community. Exclusion is a common experience for people with disabilities. The Convention on the Rights of People with Disabilities reminds people of this danger and re-affirms that people with disabilities have the same rights as others, as well as facing barriers to their flourishing. The Convention affirms eight general principles:

(a) Respect for inherent dignity and individual autonomy, including the freedom to make one's own choices, and independence of persons;

(b) Non-discrimination;

(c) Full and effective participation in society;

(d) Respect for difference and acceptance of persons with disabilities as part of human diversity and humanity;

(e) Equality of opportunity;

(f) Accessibility;

(g) Equality between men and women;

(h) Respect for the evolving capacities of children with disabilities and respect for the right of children with disabilities to preserve their identities [5].

Countries agreeing to the Convention accept that they have a number of ethical obligations, including to:

Support the above principles through social policy and legislation;

Avoid practices that are inconsistent with the principles;

Promote research, and development of goods, services, equipment and facilities which are designed to be universally accessible to people including persons with disabilities;

Promote technologies that suit the needs of persons with disabilities;

Promote awareness of the capabilities and contributions of persons with disabilities;

Enable persons with disabilities to live independently, eliminating barriers to accessibility in buildings, roads, transport, schools, housing, medical facilities and workplaces;

Reaffirm that persons with disabilities should enjoy legal capacity on an equal basis with others and have equal access to justice;

Protect the privacy of persons with disabilities;

Ensure an inclusive education system directed to the full development of human potential and sense of dignity, with reasonable accommodation of the individual's requirements;

Provide persons with disabilities with the same health care as provided to other persons, plus services needed specifically because of disabilities;

Prohibit discrimination in employment and promote opportunities for self-employment;

Provide State assistance in situations of poverty;

Guarantee political rights and participation;

Ensure access to cultural participation [6].

The capabilities approach

The philosopher Margaret Nussbaum proposes that we should take a positive, affirmative and explicit approach. The principle of respect for persons starts with the recognition that each person has a unique life, with their own intentions, purposes and preferences. These are not just characteristics that people *have*, it is what human beings *do*. People make decisions, engage with others, value their freedom to fulfil themselves. People are capable of expressing themselves, forming relationships with others and engaging with their physical and social environments. If we are serious about respecting persons, their rights and their freedoms, then we should make sure that they can flourish as human beings.

Nussbaum proposes that there are some characteristics of human beings that make them human beings. They are capable of acting in ways that we recognize as being essentially human. A respect for persons involves a respect for human capabilities. It involves setting up human communities in ways that protect and promote human capabilities. If our social arrangements prevent any person from exercising their basic human capabilities, then we do not in practice have respect for persons.

What are people capable of? What are the capabilities of people that are the essential characteristics of being human? What capabilities must we respect and promote if we respect humans, their intrinsic worth their dignities and their rights? Nussbaum proposes the following.

Capabilities

1. ***Life.*** Being able to live to the end of a human life of normal length; not dying prematurely, or before one's life is so reduced as to be not worth living.

2. ***Bodily Health.*** Being able to have good health, including reproductive health; to be adequately nourished; to have adequate shelter.

3. *Bodily Integrity.* Being able to move freely from place to place; to be secure against violent assault, including sexual assault and domestic violence; having opportunities for sexual satisfaction and for choice in matters of reproduction.

4. *Senses, Imagination, and Thought.* Being able to use the senses, to imagine, think, and reason - and to do these things in a "truly human" way, a way informed and cultivated by an adequate education, including, but by no means limited to, literacy and basic mathematical and scientific training. Being able to use imagination and thought in connection with experiencing and producing works and events of one's own choice, religious, literary, musical and so forth. Being able to use one's mind in ways protected by guarantees of freedom of expression with respect to both political and artistic speech and freedom of religious exercise. Being able to have pleasurable experiences and to avoid nonbeneficial pain.

5. *Emotions.* Being able to have attachments to things and persons outside ourselves; to love those who love and care for us; to grieve at their absence; in general to love and to grieve, to experience longing, gratitude, and justified anger. Not having one's emotional developing blighted by fear or anxiety. (Supporting this capability means supporting forms of human association that can be shown to be crucial in their development.)

6. **Practical reason**. Being able to form a conception of the good and to engage in critical reflection about the planning of one's own life. (This entails protection for liberty of conscience and religious observance.)

7. *Affiliation.*

A. Being able to live with and towards others, to recognize and show concern for other human beings, to engage in various forms of social interaction; to be able to imagine the situation of another. (Protecting this capability means protecting institutions that constitute and nourish such forms of affiliation, and also protecting the freedom of assembly and political speech.)

B. Having the social bases of self-respect and non-humiliation; being able to be treated as a dignified being whose worth is equal to that of others. This entails provisions of non-discrimination on the basis of race, sex, sexual orientation, ethnicity, caste, religion, national origin.

8. **Other Species**. Being able to live with concern for and in relation to animals, plants, and the world of nature.

9. *Play.* Being able to laugh, to play, to enjoy recreational activities.

10. **Control over one's environment**.

A. *Political.* Being able to participate effectively in political choices that govern one's life; having the rights of political participation, protections of free speech and association.

B. *Material.* Being able to hold property (both land and movable goods), and having property rights on an equal basis with others; having the right to seek employment on an equal basis with others; having the freedom from unwarranted search and seizure. In work, being able to work as a human being, exercising practical reason and entering into meaningful relationships of mutual recognition with other workers [7].

The idea here is not, of course, that people should be *required* to exercise all these capabilities all the time in order to merit our respect. The idea is that they should be *free* to do so. If we ask our fundamental ethical question 'How should people treat each other?' we could answer that we should set up social arrangements that allow people to be what people are capable of being. If our social arrangements provide barriers to accessing health and education needs, or prevent people having the opportunity to laugh and play, then we are not treating people ethically.

Five advantages of a principles approach in ethics

If we are confronted with the necessity of making a difficult ethical decision, there are a number of advantages to using a principles-based approach. These advantages apply whether the decision is one that needs to be made by the community as a whole, or whether it has to do with managing an organization, or whether it is the responsibility of a particular professional person.

1. **Efficiency**. A principles approach is simple compared to the complex calculations of the consequences approach. Calculating consequences requires taking into account all the circumstances, all the people affected and their preferences, the balance of long term and short-term outcomes and the predictions stretching into guessed-at and indefinite futures. Then the calculations have to be done all over again as circumstances change. In contrast, a principles approach lays down a few rules and conforms to them. It lets people get on with their own lives and make decisions for themselves.

2. **Consistency and reliability**. If everybody conforms to well-known and agreed principles, people know where they stand and can manage their lives accordingly. It is much easier to work with someone who consistently tells the truth, for example. Trying to second-guess whether someone is lying in order to effect what they perceive to be a good outcome is unsettling and tiresome. Human relations work better if they are based on trust. Social arrangements work better if they are stable and predictable.

3. **Moderation**. Protecting basic human rights prevents extremely bad treatment of disadvantaged people. The ethics of calculating the best consequences for the greatest number of people does not appear to prevent the exploitation of a minority for the benefit of the majority. If calculating overall consequences is the only ethical strategy being used, then fairly ordinary provisions such as disability access to buildings can be ruled out as impractical or expensive. It can be argued that consequences merely require us to do what is expedient, whereas principles requires us to do what is right.

4. **Justice**. Respect for persons leads to fair and equal treatment and rules out discrimination on arbitrary grounds such as gender, race or disability. There are different sorts of justice. There is justice before the law and justice in the distribution of resources. Principles works better in both. Rights and principles can be made explicit and protected by legislation. Social arrangements, public policy and government services can ensure that people have sufficient resources to exercise their basic rights. The capabilities approach is a positive variant of the principles and basic- rights ap-

proach. It maintains that social justice requires us to recognize and provide for the fulfillment of the basic human capabilities.

5. **Rationality and impartiality**. If people's ethical decisions are based upon respect for persons and their rights, then those decisions will be reasonable and impartial, rather than being swayed by emotion, circumstances or personal preferences. People can exchange their reasons for decisions, justify them and correct errors that are drawn to their attention. People cannot exchange emotions in the same way, nor can they come to agreements if they happen to prefer different outcomes.

Combining the principles approach with the community approach

The purpose of this book is to examine general ethical theories and apply them to issues encountered in the provision of disability services. Applying general ethical theories to the specific challenges of disability issues is not straightforward. Some work needs to be done. Some theories, as I discussed in chapter one, are less relevant to this task than others, so I selected the most promising. This led me to concentrate on the community-based approach (chapter two), the consequences-based approach (chapter three), and the principles-based approach (this chapter). Each of these approaches has its strengths and weaknesses. Each is inadequate, on its own, to provide a complete ethical framework for policy makers, providers and professionals. Some adaptations of the theories, and combinations of their best features, are required to achieve practical and effective decision making.

Given a working definition of ethics as the study of how people should treat each other, the community-based approach provides a useful starting point. It recommends that people should recognize their relations with each other, should come to some agreements about how they should treat each other, should establish professions to address specific needs, and should have expectations concerning proper professional conduct. Some agreements will be expressed formally in legislation, social policy and codes of ethics; others will be in less formal conventions and traditions.

So far, so good, but more is needed. On what basis do people in a community seek agreements with each other? Are they aiming for mutual advantage? Are they agreeing not to violate each other's rights?

To be fruitful, community discussions need to work from a basis of some shared values and goals. The consequences-based approach recommends that the aim should be to maximise good outcomes for everyone concerned. Social arrangements, government interventions, organizations' policies and professional decisions should be evaluated according to their actual impact. Good policies are those that produce good results. Ethical decisions are those that maximize happiness, alleviate distress and promote client welfare.

To maximise benefits is good advice, but perhaps not sufficient. It does not tell us what to do when good results for some entail bad results for others. Perhaps we should add some basic human rights to prevent sacrificing a minority for the benefit of the majority. A consequences-based approach also appears to leave out other ideas we value, such as respect for persons, freedom, integrity, impartiality and equality. A principles-based approach, in contrast, covers these issues.

I have proposed in this chapter that there are a number of advantages to the principles-based approach. It promotes consistency and reliability. It respects people and their rights. It is relatively easy to write into legislation and into international agreements. It is difficult to imagine how the United Nations might produce a convention in which the nations of the world agreed to calculate the best consequences. Such a document would be very short and of little use.

Difficulties with the principles approach

Despite the obvious merits of respecting persons and their rights, there are some serious flaws in the principles approach.

Consistency regardless of consequences

As I have discussed, making decisions based on principles is a different approach from making decisions based on consequences. Acting on principles requires us to do the right thing because it is the right thing to do. Principles do not change according to the circumstances. Principles can be thought of as universal rules. Lying is wrong in principle. To say that lying is wrong some of the time and right some of the time, depending on the circumstances, is not a principle and is not a rule. Similarly, it makes sense to say that people have rights. It does not make sense to say that some people have some rights some of the time. If people have a right to equality before the law, then denying them equal regard because of, say, gender or disability, is a violation of that right.

So the principles approach demands that ethical decisions must be consistent and applied regardless of the circumstances and consequences. There is something seriously wrong with this position, as a hypothetical example easily shows. This example is a standard objection to the principles approach. It was raised in the previous chapter because it is a powerful argument that proponents of the consequences approach use to criticize the principles approach [8].

Imagine that a crazed axe murderer is chasing your young daughter. Fortunately you see her evade the murderer and successfully hide from him. The murderer confronts you and demands to know where she has hidden. Do you tell the truth or do you lie? The principles approach demands that you tell the truth, but surely in these circumstances you should lie.

Perhaps we could try to rescue the principles approach by pointing out that the crazed murderer was himself wrong in principle and was attempting to deprive your daughter of her rights. This argument does not work for two reasons. One is that you are not entitled in principle to do the wrong thing just because someone else is doing the wrong thing. The second is that there is no hierarchy of principles. When two principles clash, there is no list saying which one is more important. When the rights of one person conflict with another, there is no way in principle of deciding whose rights should be respected and whose violated.

This is also the case in the capabilities approach, where it is proposed that each and every capability is important and none should be disregarded in favor of the others.

In the real world, circumstances sometimes force us to choose between competing principles, or conflicting rights, or various capabilities. The principles approach lets us down when this happens.

In the real world, principles sometimes conflict with consequences. There is no simple method for dealing with these conflicts. Sometimes we should respect a person's decision even if we predict the consequences will be undesirable. Sometimes we should take steps to avoid disastrous outcomes, even if that requires manipulation or deception.

Intrinsic rights or agreed rights

Where do rights come from? Are they a feature of being human? Do people just *have* intrinsic value, dignity and natural rights, and it is therefore our duty to respect them?

Alternatively, are rights properties we grant to each other? Do we have rights just because we live in a community that lists them in a constitution and legislation? Should we respect each other because we each value ourselves and therefore agree to value and respect each other?

Each of these alternative theories poses problems for disability issues.

Proponents of the first position maintain that people have a defining characteristic that demands respect. The characteristic is that they are rational agents. Ethics depends upon this feature of human nature. People make decisions, have reasons for those decisions, manage their lives and have preferences. If they did not do so, there would be no discussion of ethics. Of course, people have other features too. They have unique fingerprints. People are valuable to each other, for reasons of friendship, perhaps, or for economic reasons. But the foundation of their intrinsic worth and dignity is that they are rational agents.

The difficulty this presents for ethics about disability issues is immediately apparent. What if a person is not, in fact, a rational agent? Any disability compromises being able to act as an agent. Somebody who is a free, independent agent who acts for themselves is not likely to be a subject of disability ethics. Some disabilities compromise rationality. If recipients of disability provisions are not rational agents, do they therefore have no rights and merit no respect as persons? Surely not. If that were so, then the United Nations Convention on the Rights of Persons with Disabilities would be a contradiction in terms.

It seems then, that asserting that people merit respect because they have intrinsic worth as rational agents puts us in a very difficult position if we want to apply this approach to disability issues.

The United Nations Convention is a convention, that is, it is an agreement. So perhaps the second position is more sound. People merit respect and have rights because people in a community have agreed to grant each other rights and respect. There are two difficulties with this position. One is that a community may not respect human rights. Does this mean that people in that community have no rights and merit no respect? Is it all right to enslave people unless there is a community agreement to prohibit it? The other difficulty is that some people may not be recognized as members of the community, perhaps because of their ethnicity or because they have disabilities.

In practice, the difficulties of the second position can be overcome. People can agree to respect all the members of their communities and to recognize universal human rights. They can make doubly sure that this applies to people with disabilities by agreeing to a convention on the rights of people with disabilities. Many societies have done exactly that.

Proponents of the capabilities approach propose that any community that wishes to be just and ethical and treat its members appropriately as human beings should set up social arrangements that guarantee the freedom for people to exercise these capabilities.

Some cautions about the terms 'principles' and 'rights'

In much of this chapter I have been discussing 'principles' in a quite narrow sense, with a focus on two guidelines drawn from Deontology. The two notions are respect for persons, and being consistent. There are other approaches that use the term more widely. The term 'rights' is also often used loosely. Some people talk about 'rights and responsibilities'. Medical ethics has its own set of principles. Utilitarians say there is only one principle. All three of these uses are different from the way I have been defining principles and rights in this chapter.

Rights and responsibilities

It is often said that 'you cannot have rights without responsibilities' [9]. This is not correct, at least in the way it is usually meant. A small baby has no responsibilities, but presumably has rights.

If somebody has a right, this implies that somebody *else* has a responsibility. If a child has a right to an education, somebody must accept the responsibility of providing an education. If people have a right to equality before the law, then judges and legislators have a responsibility to ensure that people are treated equally.

Some responsibilities are positive, such as providing education. Some are negative, such as not compromising a person's freedom. If we are to apply principles to ethical decision making, if we are serious about respecting persons and their rights, we should recognize what responsibilities this entails and who has the obligation to take on which responsibilities.

In the general community, the term 'rights' can be over-used. People sometimes assert that they have rights when they are merely expressing desires. The right 'not to be offended' is one example.

The Utilitarian principle

Utilitarians say there is actually only one principle, the principle of utility, that is, ethics consists of maximising benefit. This single principle is in contrast to the two deontological principles I have been examining.

Four principles in medical ethics

Medical ethics quotes four principles – autonomy, beneficence, non-maleficence and justice [10]. The principle of autonomy is much the same as the approach from principles I have been examining here. It views people as self-determining and considers that they have the right to make decisions for themselves. The principle of beneficence proposes that health workers should be altruistic and should act in a way that produces good results. The principle of beneficence is a mixture of aiming for good consequences, which was examined in a chapter three, and virtue, which was mentioned in chapter one of this book. The principle of non-maleficence says that health workers should avoid doing harm. This notion is simplistic and unworkable, particularly in medicine. Surgery often does harm. Medicines often have nasty side effects. Their ethical justification, of course, lies in calculating that they do more good than harm. Calculating consequences is a better approach than having two principles of non-maleficence and beneficence. The last principle, that of justice, needs definition. As we have seen earlier, there are differing opinions about what constitutes fair and just treatment.

The principles of medical ethics are not the same as deontological principles. They take circumstances into account and do not demand unswerving commitment. Besides this, disability services and medical services are provided by different professions dealing with different clients and working with different issues. The principles of medical ethics are not very useful for issues in disability provision.

Some dilemmas involving a principles approach

The following ethical dilemmas illustrate the usefulness, and difficulties, in applying a principles-based approach to disability issues.

Kathy wants to vote

Abigail has a responsible position working in the Australian Electoral Commission. She administers voting procedures for government elections and provides advice about voting rights and registration requirements. Australia has an unusual arrangement that citizens are required to vote, unless they have an exemption or are excluded for some reason.

Kathy is a 21-year-old woman who has a moderate intellectual disability. She works in supported employment. She completed high school when she was 18, in supported education. There has recently been a federal election, and Kathy has talked about it to Carl, a support worker. She has an interest in elections and has some opinions about some of the candidates and their parties. Although voting in Australia is compulsory for adults, Kathy does not vote, and is not on the electoral roll. She tells Carl that she would like to vote.

Carl talks to Kathy's family and makes an appointment with Abigail.

Abigail explains to Carl that generally all adults are required to vote, but that some are not entitled to. They are:
- people under 18
- people who are of unsound mind (incapable of understanding the nature and significance of voting)
- people serving a prison sentence of more than three years
- people who have been convicted of treason or treachery and have not been pardoned [11].

Carl tells Abigail that Kathy's parents telephoned the Australian Electoral Commission when Kathy turned 18. The Commission sent Kathy's parents an exemption form which was signed by Kathy's doctor, as required.

Carl asks Abigail if this is common, but Abigail does not know. He asks if the exemption can be reversed, but again Abigail has not come across the situation before and does not know what the procedure would be. She says to Carl that she supposes that Kathy would need a psychological examination to prove she was of sound mind. Carl points out that he has never had to have a psychological examination in order to get on to the electoral roll, and he doubts that Abigail has, either. Abigail agrees that this is so, and says she will look into the matter and get back to him.

When she does so, Abigail is surprised to discover there is no procedure in place to reverse the exemption position. Neither can she find any information on how many people are exempted from voting on the grounds of cognitive impairment. It appears that information is not recorded anywhere.

Abigail is not sure what to do. She could just quietly let the matter drop in the expectation that Kathy will lose interest. She could tell Carl that she cannot discuss Kathy's circumstances with Carl because it would breach Kathy's right to privacy, and hope that Kathy will not pursue the matter. On the other hand, she could try to find some way of getting Kathy on to the electoral roll as an individual case. She could go further. She could write a report on the issue to the Commission and recommend that procedures be reviewed and amended.

Abigail believes that everyone has the right to vote. It is, however, something she takes for granted, not something she has had to strive for. She also accepts the rules about traitors, criminals and people of unsound mind who do not understand. She thinks writing a report on Kathy's case might stir up a lot of difficulty for the Commission and for people with disabilities. It might even result in Kathy being pestered by the media.

On the other hand, Abigail does not want to discriminate against Kathy or deny her rights to vote. So Abigail realizes she faces a dilemma. What are her responsibilities? What course of action should she take and how vigorously should she pursue it?

Mr. and Mrs. Ellers want a (Deaf) baby

Joe and Jasmine Ellers meet the eligibility criteria for *in vitro* fertilization to conceive their first child. Mr. and Mrs. Ellers are both profoundly deaf. They have requested a 'preimplantation genetic diagnosis' (PGD) but rather than use it to rule out any genetic traits, they want the PGD used to screen *in* the genetic trait for deafness. This would ensure a high probability of having a baby who is deaf.

Daniel is a board member of the Reproductive Technology Authority. This is an independent statutory body set up to regulate the practices of assisted reproductive technology. Daniel's task is to advise the board whether it would be ethical or unethical to grant Mr. and Mrs. Ellers request for IVF treatment that is intended to result in their having a deaf baby.

Joe and Jasmine Ellers identify themselves as members of the Deaf culture, and describe themselves as Deaf with a capital 'D' to indicate that affiliation. They argue that the Deaf culture is comparable to other groups characterized by ethnicity or shared linguistic minority. The Deaf community welcomes warmly the birth of a deaf baby as a new member of the community. Rather than just a disability, deafness is part of the rich diversity of society. The Ellers further argue that refusing them the opportunity to have a child with their preferred characteristics, that they can bring up as members of their cultural group, is a denial of their rights. What is more, it is an example of the majority defining what is 'normal', demeaning people on account of their differences, and discriminating against minority groups. This majority attitude is not only disrespectful of the Deaf culture but could eventually wipe it out.

Daniel accepts the Ellers' assurances that they would be good parents and would bring up a deaf child within a supportive culture. He understands that preventing their access to reproductive technology could be seen as discriminating against them on the basis of disability. He is familiar with the Capabilities theory of ethics and justice, and is particularly mindful of Capability 7.

7. *Affiliation.*

A. Being able to live with and towards others, to recognize and show concern for other human beings, to engage in various forms of social interaction; to be able to imagine the situation of another'. (Protecting this capability means protecting institutions that constitute and nourish such forms of affiliation, and also protecting the freedom of assembly and political speech.)

B. Having the social bases of self-respect and non-humiliation; being able to be treated as a dignified being whose worth is equal to that of others. This entails provisions of non-discrimination on the basis of race, sex, sexual orientation, ethnicity, caste, religion, national origin [7].

He wonders whether, in all fairness, disability should be added explicitly to the final sentence, but at any rate, he understands the Ellers' claim that the Deaf culture is analogous to groups based on race, ethnicity or national origin. As a professional in the field of reproductive technology, he is, of course, in favor of 'choice in matters of reproduction', which he knows is in Capability 3.

> 3. *Bodily Integrity.* Being able to move freely from place to place; to be secure against violent assault, including sexual assault and domestic violence; having opportunities for sexual satisfaction and for choice in matters of reproduction.

There is, though, the rights and capabilities of the baby to consider, not just the parents. Even though the baby's deafness will be genetic, and not the result of violence, is the deliberate selection of the genetic trait a violation of the baby's 'bodily integrity'?

Furthermore, as the child develops, surely in practice many of the Capabilities will be compromised by deafness. Deafness is not just a cultural difference. It is, in fact, a disability. Even if the Deaf culture is like an ethnic or linguistic group, the Ellers' baby will not, as an adult, be free to decide whether to remain in the group or leave it. The ability to make that decision will already have been taken away. The Ellers do not seem to be respecting their child's right to self-determination. Of course, in practice, people rarely move in or out of ethnic groups. Although this might occasionally be possible, people's ethnicity is generally determined by their birth. Nobody would think it odd if Jasmine was a member of a minority ethnic group, had married Joe because he was of the same ethnic group, and hoped that their offspring would value their cultural heritage and continue to associate with their relatives. On the other hand, in a multicultural society, many people do move away from the minority ethnic culture of their parents. Typically they become bilingual in their parents' language and the majority language. This opportunity would be denied to the Ellers' deaf baby.

Still, Daniel muses, even if Deafness is a culture, being deaf is still a disability. Disabilities compromise self-determination. Is denying the Ellers' request right or wrong in principle? Is it impartial, just and consistent? Does it respect the persons involved?

Special needs school children wearing high visibility clothing

Ms Illings has a problem. She is the principal of a primary school. The school has an Inclusive Special Class, and on the school's website is the stated aim 'to provide for particular students to access the full range of curriculum areas.' The particular students that Ms Illings' school makes a special effort to cater for include children with mild disabilities, developmental disorders and some with undesirable behaviours, such as running away or violence.

Last week, one such child did run away, or at any rate, left the school grounds and strayed on to the moderately busy road that runs along one of the school boundaries. There is a fence, but it is not really childproof. The school has an internal quadrangle that is secure, but the rest of the grounds are extensive, and children play over a wide range of the grounds at recess and lunch times.

Ms Illings was shocked and very worried by the incident of the escaping special needs child. She has put in a request for a secure fence around the entire school, but she does not know if the funds will be granted, and if they are, how long it will take to install the fence, or even if it will turn out to be effective. The teachers on yard duty point out how difficult it is to spot a potential absconder over the large areas of the school grounds, not to mention identifying and dealing with children who have other undesirable behaviours. One teacher has suggested that the special needs children be confined to the quadrangle, but that seems unnecessarily restrictive to Ms Illings. So she has come up with a bright idea. The school owns a number of high visibility vests which the children sometimes wear when going out of the school on excursions. Ms Illings has ordered that the special needs children should wear these vests at play time. This will make it easier for the teachers to keep an eye on them, identify them even when they are quite a distance away, and make it easier to predict and prevent undesirable behaviour, including absconding. Furthermore, if a child does stray outside the school grounds and on to the road, the high-visibility vest will make being hit by a car less likely.

But now matters have become more complicated. Ms Illings has received a letter from Mr. Caldwell, the father of one of the special needs children. He is furious that his child is required to wear an identifying vest. He says that social interaction and play is an essential part of schooling. The vests significantly damage integration, he argues. They remind children with mild disabilities that they are different from other children, and they point out the differences to the other children as well. The vests are demeaning and discriminatory. They remind Mr. Caldwell of the Nazi demand that Jews wear a yellow star.

Mr. Caldwell accepts that Ms Illings is trying to reduce risk, but he maintains that is often an excuse for oppressive restrictions. Against this risk there is the certainty that children's self-esteem and social skills will be damaged. The vests do not respect the children who are made to wear them, do not promote respect in others, and do not facilitate the development of the child into a self-determining person.

Ms Illings is in a dilemma. She is shocked by being compared to a Nazi. She is trying to do the best for the school children, but is she guilty of discrimination?

Features of a principles approach to ethics

Not all approaches to ethical decisions are characterised by the application of principles and universal rules. Some other approaches are discussed in other chapters. It may be useful at this stage to develop a list of the features that might identify a principles-based approach to ethical decision making.

The left hand column of the table lists some coherent features we might expect in a principles-based approach. The right hand column does not need to be coherent because it notes some examples of various alternatives, for illustrative purposes. The table can usefully be compared with similar tables in the chapter two on community and chapter three discussing consequences.

A PERSON who:

Has a principles-based approach to ethical decision making is likely to:	Does **not** use a principles-approach may:
Make decisions rationally.	Change decisions depending on circumstances.
Make decisions independently.	Be swayed by emotions.
Treat others as independent.	Be swayed by pressure from others.
Respect others' rights.	Manipulate other people.
Stick to decisions despite the consequences.	Not respect other people or their rights.
Be impartial.	Worry about consequences.
	Favour some people rather than others.

PROFESSIONALS and ORGANISATIONS that:

Have a principles-based approach to ethical decision making are likely to:	Do **not** use a principles-based approach may:
Encourage autonomy.	Treat people differently according to circumstances.
Provide reasons.	Demand unthinking respect for authority.
Be open and transparent.	Discourage questions.
Define 'fairness' as equal treatment.	Promote conformity.
Stick to rules despite consequences.	Be secretive.
Respect rights.	
Recognise responsibilities.	
Provide clients with opportunities to be independent.	

A SOCIETY that:

Values principles:	Does not prioritise principles:
Provides citizens with opportunities to be self-determining.	Considers welfare more important than rights.
Promotes people's independence.	Considers outcomes more important than processes.
Provides reasons for political decisions.	Favours some citizens more than others.
Is open and transparent.	Has a secretive government.
Respects rights.	
Promotes the rule of law.	
Is impartial.	

Conclusion

When we are making decisions about how to treat each other, or how to resolve ethical issues, it is reasonable that we should look for some fundamental principles to guide our decisions and discussions. If there are some simple, straightforward principles that we can commit to, and that we can rely on others to follow, then we can make decisions about our own lives, exercise our freedoms and treat other people likewise.

This idea has a great deal of influence in professional ethics and in public discussion of ethical issues. Two principles are prominent. One is that we should respect others and treat them as self-determining persons, and not treat them just as means to our own ends. The other is that we should make decisions that can be applied universally, that is, consistently and impartially, rather than expediently.

Legislation, codes of ethics and formal conventions are ways of expressing a commitment to respect for persons. Typically a respect for persons leads to a statement of people's rights. Legislation can be used to enforce a respect for people's rights.

The Capabilities proposal is an alternative approach to the fundamental principle of respect for persons. This approach recommends we should adopt social arrangements that allow people to exercise the capabilities that are characteristic of self-determining humans.

The most striking feature of a principles-based approach is that it is uncompromising. A community-based approach to ethics uses negotiation and agreements. There are dangers with this approach. Agreements can change. Community moods and values can swing without rational justification. Majority agreements can oppress minorities. Adding a commitment to principles alleviates these dangers and protects vulnerable people. Principles are therefore valuable generally in community ethics and particularly in professional ethics concerning disability. Similarly, a consequences approach has dangers. It can be used to justify benefits for a majority at the expense of a minority. It can be used to oppress vulnerable people 'for their own good'. A principles-based approach can limit the potential excesses of Consequentialism. A commitment to principles can lead to a recognition of fundamental rights which protect vulnerable people.

The best approach then appears to be for communities to come to agreements about social arrangements that are expected to promote everybody's welfare, with the proviso that they do not violate fundamental human rights. This combined approach is just as applicable to professional ethics and to the provision of disability services.

Chapter 5
A Code of Ethics

This chapter comprises a code of ethics for disability professionals. It comes from a Disability and Rehabilitation Professionals' Association, so it is an example of a community-based approach [1]. It is also influenced by the approaches that refer to consequences and to principles, although it does not necessarily use those terms. 'Principle A' in this code actually refers to a community-based approach. 'Principle B' is the same fundamental ethical principle discussed in chapter four. 'Principle C' uses a consequences-based approach and 'Principle D' reflects, once again, the Communitarian chapter of this book. This code reflects other professional codes listed in its bibliography [2].

The code is as follows:

A Code of Ethics and Practice for Disability and Rehabilitation Professionals

Preamble

The need to provide clear ethical guidelines for Disability and Rehabilitation Professionals is essential. This document developed from the earlier work of the DEA and attempts to encompass professionals working in a wide range or areas and with a range of backgrounds and professional qualifications [3].

An attempt has been made, however, to keep statements about ethical issues concise and clear under the assumption that statements about ethics cannot replace good professional judgement. This document is seen as a tool to guide professionals in their practice with regard to
- What is acceptable professional conduct and standards of practice, and
- The value base and principles of DARPA [4].

Vision statement of Disability and Rehabilitation Professionals' Association

What we are aiming for:

To enhance the quality of life for people with a disability or rehabilitation needs by supporting Disability and Rehabilitation Professionals in their various roles.

Mission statement of Disability and Rehabilitation Professionals' Association

Our mission statement describes the role of the association:

- to provide a professional association for Disability and Rehabilitation Professionals
- to support the highest standard of professional conduct of members
- to advise on the professional standards for entry into the profession
- to promote the continuing professional education of members
- to promote the role played by trained Disability and Rehabilitation Professionals
- to promote a national association network in Australia.

Beliefs of Disability and Rehabilitation Professionals

Our beliefs influence the way we approach our works. We believe:

- in the worth, dignity and uniqueness of all persons
- in the right of all people to live and participate in community life
- in the empowerment of individuals to maximise their self determination through access to information, choice, informed consent and/or advocacy in all decision making
- that Disability and Rehabilitation Professionals, in terms of their professional skills and expertise, have a vital role to play in the facilitation of optimum quality of life opportunities

General Principles: Overview

Disability and Rehabilitation Professionals endeavour to maintain high standards of competence in their work. They recognise the boundaries of their particular skills and expertise. Disability and Rehabilitation Professionals provide only those supports and use only those techniques for which they are qualified by education, training or experience.

Disability and Rehabilitation Professionals are aware of the fact that competencies are required when serving, teaching, training or supervising individuals with support needs, or providing services to individuals or their families and relevant others. Consideration is given to the diversity and unique nature of a person's support needs, methods of communication, learning and life style.

In their dynamic professional roles Disability and Rehabilitation Professionals will endeavour to exercise careful judgement, maintain knowledge of relevant professional information related to services they provide and recognise the need for ongoing professional development. In doing so, Disability and Rehabilitation Professionals make appropriate use of academic, professional, technical and administrative resources as well as to consult when necessary.

Principle A: Integrity and Professional Responsibility

Disability and Rehabilitation Professionals seek to promote integrity in the practice of supporting people with a disability or other support needs. Disability and Rehabilitation Professionals are honest, fair and respectful of others in all aspects of professional work, such as, supporting, training and research. Disability and Rehabilitation Professionals attempt to develop an awareness of their own beliefs, values, needs and limitations and the impact this may have on their work.

Disability and Rehabilitation Professionals uphold professional standards of conduct, clarify their professional roles and obligations, accept appropriate responsibility for their behaviour and are flexible in order to meet individual client needs. Disability and Rehabilitation Professionals consult with, refer to, work in cooperation with other professionals and organisations in order to serve the best interests of people with a disability or other support needs.

Disability and Rehabilitation Professionals are aware of their professional and academic responsibilities to the community in which they work and live. Disability and Rehabilitation Professionals should participate in service planning and the development of service standards at local, national and international levels.

Disability and Rehabilitation Professionals are concerned about professional and academic conduct. To achieve this we agree to accept responsibility and accountability for our actions and encourage the development of practice, policy and law that serve the best interests of clients and the public. Disability and Rehabilitation Professionals are encouraged to voluntarily contribute a portion of their time to assist in community and/or professional development

Principle B: Respect for People's Worth, Dignity and Uniqueness

Disability and Rehabilitation Professionals show appropriate respect to the fundamental rights, dignity and worth of all people. They respect the rights of individuals to privacy, confidentiality, self determination and autonomy.

Disability and Rehabilitation Professionals are aware of cultural, individual, and role differences, including those due to age, gender, race, ethnicity, national origin, religion, sexual orientation, disability, socioeconomic status, marital status, political belief or any other preference or personal characteristic. Disability and Rehabilitation Professionals attempt to eliminate the effect of such biases on their work.

Principle C: Concern for Others' Wellbeing and Empowerment

The professional objective of Disability and Rehabilitation Professionals is to contribute in a positive manner to those with whom they interact professionally. Disability and Rehabilitation Professionals are sensitive to real and ascribed differences in power between themselves and others, and they do not exploit or mislead others during or after professional relationships. Also, Disability and Rehabilitation Professionals value the promotion of an environment that enhances a person's quality of life. Disability and Rehabilitation Professionals uphold the provision of quality services for all people.

Principle D: Community Education

Disability and Rehabilitation Professionals seek opportunities to communicate to the wider community the fundamental values of the professional as supported by this Code of Ethics. This includes; seeking opportunities to advocate and inform the wider community regarding aspects and issues relating to disability or support needs and the role and function of Disability and Rehabilitation Professionals. Disability and Rehabilitation Professionals should be proactive about promoting their profession and are asked to acknowledge their specific expertise in the Disability and/or Rehabilitation areas by using the titles as follows:
- Disability Professional - for those with professional training focussing on disability studies.
- Rehabilitation Professional - for those with professional training focussing on rehabilitation studies

Where an individual has particular generic training, it is seen as appropriate to acknowledge this and examples are given below
- Psychologist and Disability Professional
- Physiotherapist and Rehabilitation Professional
- Social Worker and Disability Professional

It is suggested that the title given to a person's position within an organisation is not incompatible with this approach. For example
- Options Coordinator (Social Worker and Disability Professional)
- Manager (Disability Professional)

Ethical and Professional Principles

1. Ethical and Professional Statements

The Association recognises the diversity and complexity of the roles and settings in which Disability and Rehabilitation Professionals work. The following statements are a guide for the professional conduct of Disability and Rehabilitation Professionals.

1.1 Parameters of Expertise

(a) Disability and Rehabilitation Professionals provide services, educate, train and conduct research only within the boundaries of their competence based on education, training, and their supervised or professional experience.

(b) Disability and Rehabilitation Professionals provide services, educate, train or conduct research in new areas or involving new methods only after first undertaking appropriate study, training, supervision and/or consultation from persons who are competent in those new areas or methods.

(c) Disability and Rehabilitation Professionals take reasonable steps to ensure the competence of their work and protect clients, research participants, peers and others from harm, in those emerging areas in which generally recognised standards for training do not yet exist.

(d) In maintaining expertise, Disability and Rehabilitation Professionals who provide assessment, programming services, specific therapies, counselling, behaviour management, evaluation, education and training, research, organisational, consultative or other professional activities maintain a reasonable level of awareness about current and professional information in their fields of activity. This includes partaking in ongoing efforts to maintain competence in their skills.

1.2 General Awareness of Legislation

(a) Disability and Rehabilitation Professionals need to be aware of, and familiar with the content and implications of Commonwealth and State legislation relating to disability, human services and areas relevant to their professional roles (Refer Appendix A and Appendix B).

(b) Disability and Rehabilitation Professionals need to keep abreast of legislative changes that relate to their professional roles.

1.3 General Awareness of International Statements, Treaties and Alliances

Disability and Rehabilitation Professionals need to be aware of, and familiar with the content and implications of International statements, treaties and alliances and their impact upon government policy and service provision to people with a disability and the community (Refer Appendix C).

1.4 Respecting Differences

(a) Disability and Rehabilitation Professionals do not engage in unfair discrimination based on age, gender, marital status, political belief, race, ethnicity, national origin, religion, sexual orientation, disability, socioeconomic status or any other preference or personal characteristic.

(b) Should differences of age, gender, race, ethnicity, national origin, religion, sexual orientation, disability, socioeconomic status, marital status, political belief or any other preference or personal characteristic significantly affect a Disability and Rehabilitation Professionals work concerning particular individuals or groups, that professional should make a commitment to obtain the training, experience, consultation or supervision to ensure the competence of their services.

(c) In their work related activities, Disability and Rehabilitation Professionals should respect the rights of others to hold values, attitudes and opinions that differ from their own.

(d) Disability and Rehabilitation Professionals will respect the cultural background of individuals and families and familiarise themselves with relevant cultural protocols whenever necessary.

1.5 Respecting Choice

Disability and Rehabilitation Professionals must respect the rights of individuals to make informed choices in relation to their life.

1.6 Undue Influence

(a) Disability and Rehabilitation Professionals do not exercise undue influence over people with whom they may provide placement, supervision, evaluation or an exercise of authority, such as clients, students, subordinate personnel or research participants or personnel under Disability and Rehabilitation Professionals direct supervision.

(b) Disability and Rehabilitation Professionals recognise that their professional judgement and intervention may affect the lives of the client, their families and carers and ensure that this influence is not misused to cause detriment or exploitation.

1.7 Harassment

Disability and Rehabilitation Professionals will not knowingly engage in behaviour that is harassing or demeaning to persons with whom they interact in their work, based on factors such as age, gender, marital status, political belief, race, ethnicity, national origin, religion, sexual orientation, disability, socioeconomic status or any other preference or personal characteristic.

1.8 Personal Issues

Disability and Rehabilitation Professionals recognise that their personal issues may interfere with their effectiveness. Therefore, they should avoid undertaking an activity when they know that their personal issues are likely to lead to, or have a detrimental impact upon a client, family, student, research participant or peer or other person to whom they owe professional obligation.

This obligation includes identifying the need for, and seeking assistance for their personal issues as early as possible in order to ensure their professional performance is not significantly affected.

1.9 Duty of Care

(a) A duty of care is owed by a Disability and Rehabilitation Professional to a client, family or peer . If harm is suffered by the individual that was "reasonably foreseeable" a breach of duty of care may be deemed to have occurred. What is "reasonably foreseeable" would be determined in the context of the circumstances.

(b) The level of duty of care owed by a Disability and Rehabilitation Professional is related to their education, training, and experience.

(c) When a Disability and Rehabilitation Professional is uncertain regarding a situation, advice or guidance should be sought from appropriate professionals, peers and/or organisations with relevant expertise.

1.10 Duty to Inform

Disability and Rehabilitation Professionals need to inform consumers, consumers' families and carers, colleagues and other professionals:

(a) about the parameters of their qualifications, and any ethical considerations, and

(b) the philosophical and service delivery boundaries of the agency for which they work that may affect their interaction as a professional.

1.11 Duty to Report

Disability and Rehabilitation Professionals have an obligation under duty of care to report any breaches of the law particularly in respect to abuse, neglect and exploitation of people who have disabilities, their families and carers.

1.12 Conflict of Interest

Disability and Rehabilitation Professionals will identify where there is a potential conflict of interest based on personal, financial, social, organisational or political factors which may create a risk of harm or exploitation. If a conflict arises a Disability and Rehabilitation Professional should take all reasonable steps as necessary to resolve the issue with due regard for the best interests of the persons involved and maximum compliance with the Code of Ethics.

1.13 Consultation, Collaboration and Referrals

(a) As transdisciplinary professionals, Disability and Rehabilitation Professionals recognise the need to collaborate with colleagues and other practitioners.

(b) Disability and Rehabilitation Professionals arrange for appropriate consultations and referrals based on the best interests of their clients with appropriate consent and subject to other relevant consideration including legal and contractual obligations.

(c) When indicated and professionally appropriate, Disability and Rehabilitation Professionals cooperate with other professionals in order to serve clients effectively and appropriately.

(d) Disability and Rehabilitation Professionals liaise with and for people with disabilities and support needs with mainstream, generic, and specialist service providers to obtain relevant services for their clients.

1.14 Delegation and Supervision

(a) Disability and Rehabilitation Professionals provide proper training and supervision to their employees, students, research assistants, team members, peers and other Disability and Rehabilitation Professionals they are deemed to have a supervisory capacity over, and take reasonable steps to see that such individuals perform services responsibly, competently and ethically.

(b) Disability and Rehabilitation Professionals should make an attempt to negotiate and modify their role or correct the situation of organisational policies, procedures or practices that prevent fulfillment of this obligation.

1.15 Documentation of Professional Work

(a) Disability and Rehabilitation Professionals should document their professional work appropriately to ensure accountability and meet legal or organisational requirements.

(b) Disability and Rehabilitation Professionals should recognise and acknowledge the clients' rights to access documented information about themselves. In this context Disability and Rehabilitation Professionals should ensure that information is documented in a manner that is sensitive and comprehensible given the person's abilities.

1.16 Records and Information

Disability and Rehabilitation Professionals create, maintain, disseminate, store, retain and dispose of records and data relating to their research, practice and other work in accordance with legal requirements, organisational policy and this Code of Ethics.

1.19 Financial Negotiations

As early as is practicable in a professional relationship the Disability and Rehabilitation Professional and client of the services must reach an agreement specifying the fee for service and payment arrangements if applicable. When negotiating fees, Disability and Rehabilitation Professionals should give consideration to the client's ability to pay and any financial negotiations should be documented and consistent with legal requirements.

2. Assessment and Evaluation

2.1 Assessments and Evaluation in Professional Context

Disability and Rehabilitation Professionals who undertake evaluations, assessments and interventions do so only within the context of a defined professional relationship. Any assessment recommendations, reports or evaluative statements are based on a consultative model. This consultative model involves using appropriate techniques or processes which include the involvement of the individual with a disability and relevant others.

2.2 Effective Use of Assessments

Disability and Rehabilitation Professionals who implement interventions and/or other outcomes, recommendations or planning goals based on assessment, do so in line with current disability service standards and legislation. Disability and Rehabilitation Professionals are committed to ensuring no misuse or overt misunderstanding of assessment information or processes.

2.3 Consumer Friendly Material

(a) Disability and Rehabilitation Professionals are committed to fully inclusive consultative practices, which includes ensuring outcomes and processes are accessible to clients, families, advocates and relevant others.

(b) Disability and Rehabilitation Professionals have a responsibility to have and develop a sensitivity to the communications skills, of clients, families, advocates and relevant others.

(c) Consumer friendly material relates to the responsibility of Disability and Rehabilitation Professionals to have a sensitivity to the educative and cultural experiences of clients, families, advocates and relevant others with whom they professionally interact.

3. Advertising and Presentations

3.1 Public Statements

Public statements include, but are not limited to paid and unpaid advertising pamphlets, printed matter, personal resumes, curriculum vitae, interviews or comments for use in the media, statements in legal proceedings, lectures, seminars, public oral presentations and published materials.

3.2 Ensuring Accurate Statements

(a) Disability and Rehabilitation Professionals will endeavour to ensure statements made by others with regard to Disability and Rehabilitation Professionals and services they provide are correct. Disability and Rehabilitation Professionals will maintain this by providing correct information, taking responsibility for public statements made by themselves, and to make honest efforts to correct deceptive or incorrect statements.

(b) In their roles Disability and Rehabilitation Professionals will not make deceptive, misleading or false public statements related to their training, experience, academic degrees, credentials, current or past roles.

3.3 Public Presentations

When presenting information by means of lectures, seminars, articles, materials or other means, Disability and Rehabilitation Professionals will be required to ensure this information is correctly based on practical experience, theoretical experience, documented evidence or sound research, consistent with this Code of Ethics.

4. Professional Relationships

4.1 Relationships and Service Provision

(a) Disability and Rehabilitation Professionals will not develop a relationship with current clients, families or their peers that may be detrimental to their provision of services or professional judgement.

(b) Disability and Rehabilitation Professionals will not exploit persons over whom they have supervision, authority or to whom they owe a duty of care. This includes: clients, students, peers, employees, families, advocates or others to whom they owe a professional obligation.

(c) Disability and Rehabilitation Professionals will provide information to service users about the basis of their relationship, their role, and the role of the service user in a manner that suits the individual's abilities.

4.2 Relationship Framework

Disability and Rehabilitation Professionals will provide their clients, families, and peers with informed choices about the service they will provide, particular approaches to be used, programmes, time frames, goals and anticipated outcomes. Disability and Rehabilitation Professionals will ensure this is presented in a manner that suits individual abilities and ensures understanding about the basis of the relationship.

4.3 Consent for Services

(a) Disability and Rehabilitation Professionals will ensure consent for services or information is obtained from the appropriate person or persons. This should be achieved by;

    i) considering, the person's capacity to consent

    ii) using sensitive and appropriate communication methods

    iii) informing the person or persons of service choices

    iv) ensuring that consent is recorded and documented correctly

(b) It is the responsibility of a Disability and Rehabilitation Professional to be aware of issues relating to consent. Giving consideration to legislation, the individual's abilities, and the possible involvement of State or Commonwealth authorities or administrators such as a 'Guardianship Board'.

4.4 Continuity of Services

Disability and Rehabilitation Professionals will use appropriate data and information recording methods and maintain these throughout their service provision. This will ensure that services to their clients are continued with minimal disruption in the case of unforseen circumstances.

4.5 Closure of Professional Relationship

Disability and Rehabilitation Professionals will provide suitable notice and information when a service or professional relationship will be ceased. Disability and Rehabilitation Professionals will cease a professional relationship when the current service being provided is no longer required, or no longer benefiting the client. Disability and Rehabilitation Professionals will investigate and suggest alternative services, where appropriate, to the client prior to cessation of services. This will be provided in a manner that ensures that the client understands and, where possible, is able to contribute to and choose alternative services.

5. Privacy and Confidentiality

These standards apply to the professional and academic activities of all Disability and Rehabilitation Professionals.

5.1 Limits and Maintenance of Confidentiality

(a) Discussion should be initiated by the Disability and Rehabilitation Professional with persons or organisations that they have a professional or academic relationship with, about any possible infringements of confidentiality as well as potential uses of information and records created.

(b) Except where not possible, Disability and Rehabilitation Professionals should discuss confidentiality and related issues at the commencement of the relationship or as altered circumstances require.

(c) Disability and Rehabilitation Professionals should be familiar with the legal rights afforded to persons they have a professional or academic relationship to, and anticipate requirements for the maintenance of these rights to confidentiality.

5.2 Privacy

(a) When preparing or keeping, records, reports, assessments or other information (be they: oral, written or any other communication) Disability and Rehabilitation Professional's should only use or keep information pertinent to the matter at hand. Any confidential information acquired via professional or academic relationships must only be revealed to people for whom the information is imperative or to confer with an appropriate professional.

(b) To maximise privacy Disability and Rehabilitation Professionals should only include in their written/oral reports information relevant to the purpose for which the communication is required.

(c) See Principle 4.3, 'Consent for Services'.

5.3 Records Storage

Disability and Rehabilitation Professionals should ensure that systems of record storage do not allow for breaches of confidentiality as set out in this Code of Ethics. Regardless of methods used for storage, (written, electronic or other) records should be kept and disposed of using legally permitted methods and in line with this Code of Ethics.

5.4 Disclosure of Confidential Information

(a) Disclosure of confidential information by a Disability and Rehabilitation Professional cannot be made without the consent of the person from whom the information originated. Exception is only allowed where legally required (e.g., Mandatory Notification Legislation) or where failure to disclose information would breach the professional's duty of care. In these instances, the extent of disclosure is to be no more than necessary to accomplish the purpose.

(b) Disability and Rehabilitation Professionals may disclose confidential information with the appropriate consent of the client, or another legally authorised person on behalf of the client, unless it is not legally permitted.

5.5 Consulting with Appropriate Professionals

Disability and Rehabilitation Professionals can confer with an appropriate professional where;

> i) the information presented could not lead to the person from whom the information originated being identified
>
> ii) the person has agreed to specific information being discussed
>
> iii) disclosing information is necessary

In each instance the extent of disclosure is to be no more than necessary to accomplish the purpose.

5.6 Shared Databases

Where a Disability and Rehabilitation Professional shares database(s) with others, strategies need to be in place to ensure that those with access to the database(s) are not able to identify the person from whom the information originated. This is not required where the person from whom the information originated or an authorised other has granted permission for all users of the database(s) to access information that might identify them.

5.7 Public use of Confidential Information

Information provided by a Disability and Rehabilitation Professional that is publicly presented, such as via lectures, seminars or circulated articles should not contain material that may lead to the identification of a person, unless that person or an authorised other has agreed to the specific information being discussed.

5.8 Continuity in Case of Change of Circumstances

To ensure the continuance of confidentiality of records, a contingency plan should be made by the Disability and Rehabilitation Professional to cover the possibility that they may;

i) die

ii) become impaired and unable to continue professional practice

iii) leave or change their workplace

iv) encounter a conflict of interest

v) take extended leave

5.9 Holding of Records

Disability and Rehabilitation Professionals should take honest and lawful steps to ensure that records and data remain available to the extent needed to serve the best interest of clients, research participants and relevant others.

6. Programming, intervention / therapy and support

6.1 Design of Programmes

(a) Disability and Rehabilitation Professionals involved in educative /training/ support programmes must ensure programmes are competently designed and genuinely focused on the support needs of the individual or group, provide positive and enhancing experiences, and meet professional requirements for accountability as well as service provider standards and policies.

(b) Disability and Rehabilitation Professionals responsible for programmes/ specific therapies need to ensure an accurate description of programme/therapy content, the educative/ training/ support goals, objectives and criteria are documented to ensure effective implementation. This information must be made accessible to all relevant parties.

(c) When engaged in implementing programmes, Disability and Rehabilitation Professionals need to present information accurately and with objectivity.

6.2 Closure of Programmes/Therapy

Disability and Rehabilitation Professionals are responsible to ensure closure of programmes and/or support is planned and documented appropriately considering the needs and obligations of all relevant parties.

7. Supervision of students

7.1 Support and Supervision of Students Undertaking Tertiary Studies

(a) Disability and Rehabilitation Professionals assigned to support and supervise students ensure they present as a professional and appropriate role model. This includes demonstrating the ethical principles of this code in daily work practices and procedures.

(b) Disability and Rehabilitation Professionals provide suitable opportunities for the student to achieve course and personal learning objectives.

(c) In academic and supervisory relations, Disability and Rehabilitation Professionals establish an appropriate process for providing feedback to students.

(d) Disability and Rehabilitation Professionals evaluate students on the basis of the actual performance on relevant and established programme/therapy requirements.

(e) Disability and Rehabilitation Professionals are encouraged to provide opportunities for placement and supervision of students of recognised tertiary qualifications majoring in the particular professional's area of expertise.

(f) Where Disability and Rehabilitation Professionals provide placement and supervision to students from disciplines other than their own area of professional training, the Disability and Rehabilitation Professional has a responsibility to familiarise themselves with the necessary protocols, ethics and standards of practice for the relevant profession.

8. Research and Publication

8.1 Obtaining Approval

(a) Prior to conducting research, Disability and Rehabilitation Professionals consult with and obtain approval from relevant committees, boards or organisations.

(b) Disability and Rehabilitation Professionals design, implement and report research adhering to the professional standards and research protocols of the approving committee, board or organisation.

8.2 Conduct of Research

(a) Disability and Rehabilitation Professionals design, implement and report research that is viewed as ethical under this Code of Ethics.

(b) Disability and Rehabilitation Professionals seek to resolve any ethical issue that is unclear via consultation with appropriate committees, boards or organisational management.

(c) Disability and Rehabilitation Professionals plan and conduct research in a manner consistent with Federal and State laws and regulations as well as professional standards governing the conduct of research.

9. Resolving ethical issues

9.1 Awareness of Code of Ethics

Disability and Rehabilitation Professionals have an obligation to be familiar with this Code of Ethics, other applicable codes of ethics and their application to Disability and Rehabilitation Professional's work. Lack of awareness or misunderstanding of an ethical standard is not itself a defence to a charge of unethical conduct.

9.2 Management of Ethical Issues

(a) Disability and Rehabilitation Professionals have the requisite knowledge and skills to identify ethical issues and respond to them appropriately.

(b) When a Disability and Rehabilitation Professional is uncertain whether a particular situation or course of action would violate this Code of Ethics, the Disability and Rehabilitation Professional should consult with their appropriate management, the Disability Services Office and/or peak advocacy agencies.

9.3 Ethics and Professional/Organisational Demands

If the demands of an organisation with which Disability and Rehabilitation Professionals are affiliated or employed, conflict with this Code of Ethics, Disability and Rehabilitation Professionals should clarify the nature of the conflict, make known their commitment to the Code of Ethics, and to the extent feasible, seek to resolve the conflict in a manner that permits the fullest adherence to the Code of Ethics.

9.4 Informal Resolution of Breaches of Ethics

(a) When Disability and Rehabilitation Professionals believe that there may have been an ethical violation by another Disability and Rehabilitation Professional, they should attempt to resolve the issue by bringing it to the attention of that individual if an informal resolution appears appropriate and the intervention does not violate any confidentiality rights that may be involved.

(b) If there is no capacity to informally resolve a breach of ethics there is an onus on the Disability and Rehabilitation Professional to seek out the appropriate complaints organisation and submit a professional complaint.

(c) When there is no appropriate complaints mechanism it is in the interests of all involved parties for the Disability and Rehabilitation Professional who has determined there may be a breach to complete a written report on the incident to be kept in their personal files for future reference.

9.5 Inappropriate Complaints

Disability and Rehabilitation Professionals do not lodge or encourage the lodging of ethics complaints that are trivial and are intended to harm the respondent rather than protect individuals with a disability and/or other related parties.

APPENDICES

Appendix A - Commonwealth Legislation - Guidelines

- Disability Discrimination Act (1992)
- Disability Services Act (1986)
- Home and Community Care Act (1985)
- Occupation, Health, Safety & Welfare Act (1986)
- Privacy Act (1988)
- Social Security Act (1991)
- Veteran Entitlement Act (1986)
- Freedom of Information Act (1982)

Appendix B - State Legislation - Guidelines

- Mental Health Act (1993)
- Guardianship and Administration (1993)
- Equal Opportunity Act (1984)
- Privacy Act (1991)
- Disability Services Act (1993)
- Consent to Medical Treatment and Palliative Care Act (1995)
- Children's Protection Act (1993)

Appendix C - International Statements, Treaties & Alliances - Guidelines

- United Nations Declaration of Human Rights (1946)
- United Nations Declaration Standard Rules on the Equalisation Opportunities for Persons with Disabilities (1993)

*Please note that the above is not an exhaustive list. Refer to SA Law Handbook for more relevant legislation.

Chapter 6
Making Ethical Decisions

The project of this book is to develop ethical guidelines to help professionals, practitioners and policy makers to make decisions about disability issues. Drawing on three foundational ethical theories, it seems reasonable to accept the following:

Ethics is the study of how people should treat each other.

Some ethical decisions are personal, some are social and some are professional.

People live in communities. They associate with each other and form relationships.

People should (and do) come to agreements about how to treat each other. These agreements should respect people and their rights, and should produce good consequences for all concerned.

People have needs which influence how they should be treated. Some needs are common to all, such as education and security. Some people have particular needs such as those resulting from disabilities.

Communities set up social policies and government agencies to meet people's needs.

Communities also set up professions so that specialists can develop expertise in providing for specific needs. Various professions provide services in such areas as medicine, education, law, and disability.

Professional decision-making and social policy should respect people and their rights. It should provide for their capabilities and advance their welfare.

It is unfortunately the case that issues in professional ethics present much potential for conflicts and dilemmas. Principles may conflict with each other. Some people's rights may clash with other people's rights. Good consequences for some people may entail bad consequences for others. Respecting the rights of people may result in bad outcomes for them. In short, principles can clash with principles, consequences can clash with consequences, and principles can clash with consequences.

Much of the time, ethical decision making is simple, but sometimes it can be dauntingly complicated. There is no hierarchy of principles, no simple algorithm for calculating consequences, and no formula for resolving conflicts between them. Human judgement is required. Professionals and policy makers need ethical expertise to make those judgements.

In this chapter I will discuss how we could apply the theories in practice, to help us make ethical decisions, and to frame good policy.

A methodical approach to an ethical issue

We could envisage having to make an ethical decision as professionals in the field of disability services in the following typical circumstances.

We notice an ethical issue. We wonder what we should do about it and consider our options. We think about who will be affected by our decisions. We recognize our responsibilities to our clients. We consider what consultation and co-operation with our colleagues is required in the circumstances. We formulate a precise plan of action. We examine that plan in the light of ethical theories to see if it is the right thing to do or not. We decide to implement the plan because it is ethical, or alternatively to reject it on the grounds that it is unethical and there is a better course of action available.

In this chapter I will examine this process methodically. This will allow a strategic approach to ethical challenges. The decision-making process comprises a series of steps and an examination of what is required in each of these steps.

A particular case example will help as an illustration. I have chosen an issue which is not a desperately serious one. Big issues, or matters of life and death, can obscure the details of the decision-making process just because they are so weighty. There are plenty of day-to-day ethical issues in the life of disabled people and disability professionals, so I will use one of those to illustrate a decision-making process. I will examine some big-picture issues in subsequent chapters.

A strategy for making ethical decisions

1. Identify the issue.
2. Gather the facts.
3. Consider options.
4. Identify and prioritise the stakeholders.
5. Identify other involved parties.
6. Precisely draft a decision/recommendation.
7. Examine the draft decision using a community approach.
8. Examine the decision by calculating its consequences.
9. Examine the decision using a principles approach.
10. In the light of the examination, confirm the draft decision or reject it.

A strategy for making ethical decisions – expanded

1. Identify the issue

What is an *issue*? An issue arises when circumstances call for a response but it is not clear what action (if any) should be taken, or what is the best response. If there is obviously a best course of action to take, or a bad course of action to avoid, then there is no issue. Issues present competing alternative courses of action. A *dilemma* arises when there are two competing alternative courses of action [1]. Choosing amongst the alternatives requires thought, examination, reflection, discussion and expertise.

Some issues are *ethical* issues, that is, they are about whether people are being treated well or badly. An ethical issue arises when what is at stake is someone's welfare, or someone's freedom and fulfilment, or some set of agreements between people about their welfare or rights.

Professional ethics is concerned with issues that arise within the context of professionals providing services to clients. It has to do with clients' welfare and rights, and professionals' roles and responsibilities.

An example of an ethical dilemma: Cleaning up Julie's room

Imagine that we work for an organization that provides community housing and associated services to people with mild intellectual disabilities. One of the residents is Julie, a woman in her twenties who is keen on arts and crafts. Her room is messy because she keeps a lot of her craft materials in it. Staff have also on occasion found containers of rotting food there. The CEO of the organization and our team leader have consulted with each other about this and have instructed us to clean up Julie's room while she is not there. The organization has provided us with a key that will unlock her room.

Julie has been asked before to clean up her room but its condition still concerns our team leader. She will be distressed if we clean it up, hence the instruction to do it while she is out. The fact that she will be distressed immediately makes this an ethical issue, as well as concerns for her right to privacy. Against this are risks to her health and the health of other residents, and our responsibilities towards her and them.

2. *Gather the facts*

When making decisions that affect other people's welfare it is, of course, important to know the facts. This might require making careful observations, talking to the people themselves or consulting with experts. In the Baby Charlotte case (chapter one), the judge required the expert advice of doctors [2]. Similarly, the speech pathologist's assessment of Jim's condition is vital in his case.

Facts by themselves cannot provide an ethical decision [3]. Human judgement is required. But humans should not make judgements when they are ignorant of the facts.

Facts about Julie

Julie's room is untidy and crammed with craft materials. On occasion there have also been containers of rotting food.

There have been no illnesses or pests as a result of Julie's untidiness.

There have been no complaints from other residents.

Julie has a mild intellectual disability. She is competent at ordinary daily tasks. She generally eats healthily and dresses in clean clothes.

In Julie's case, it appears we have all the necessary facts and do not need any expert advice.

3. *Consider Options*

There may be a number of possible responses to an ethical issue, each with its own advantages, or worse, each with its own disadvantages. Professionals are accustomed to considering options, to solving problems and to consulting with colleagues about the best way to proceed. Ethical decision-making is no different from other professional challenges in this respect. Reflection, creative thinking, and seeking the advice of experts, including the client, are all part of the ethical decision-making process.

Sometimes ethical dilemmas can be resolved by removing the problem. Successfully persuading Jim (in chapter one) to be careful when eating would be a desirable outcome. Sometimes, however, *whatever* we do will have a serious flaw, in which case we need to make a decision and choose the *least worst* course of action, or the best course of action all things considered. When the issue is difficult, choosing to do nothing may appear attractive.

This in itself is an option, but the decision to do nothing is itself an ethical decision and needs justification like any alternative ethical decision.

Some people have personalities that are averse to making decisions. They may view making and implementing ethical decisions as 'arrogant' or 'playing God'. Some people respond to ethical dilemmas by transferring the responsibility to other people. In some circumstances, this is an acceptable option, but it is still a decision. Professionals should canvass various alternatives (including the alternative of not intervening), examine them on their merits and be able to justify their decisions.

Options concerning the dilemma of Julie's room

One obvious option is to comply with the instruction and clean up Julie's room.

Another option we should consider is not intervening in Julie's room and informing the team leader that we do not consider cleaning her room is the best course of action.

A third option is an attempt to persuade Julie to clean up the room herself to a level acceptable to the team leader. This however has been tried before, without success.

4. Identify and prioritise the stakeholders

The stakeholders are the people whose welfare or rights are at stake [4]. Their well-being will be enhanced or compromised by the professional's ethical decision and they are thereby vulnerable.

In professional ethics, the stakeholders are, of course, the clients. While this is obvious it is important to realize that fellow professionals or the employing organization are not stakeholders. They may have opinions and advice. They may even have preferences concerning outcomes, but they are simply not vulnerable to professionals' decisions in the same way a client is. A professional may be *accountable to* a range of people, but is *responsible for* the client, and should make decisions in the client's best interests.

Sometimes the family of the client is a recipient of services, and is therefore vulnerable to the professional's decisions and have a significant vested interest in the outcomes. There may be conflicts between the client's best interests and the family's. In Baby Charlotte's case (chapter one) the doctors argued that operating on their patient Charlotte was not in her best interest. The parents clearly were also deeply affected by the prospect of Charlotte's death and wanted her life prolonged. The judge in that case had to prioritise the people affected by the decision.

Generally, it is in the nature of a profession that the interests of the client should be prioritised over other people's. Of course, the interests of one client may conflict with another.

Julie as a stakeholder

Clearly, the client in this case is Julie and she is the prime stakeholder. The team leader and the CEO of the organization are not stakeholders.

The other residents are stakeholders if they are vulnerable to the decision. Thus they would be stakeholders if the state of Julie's room was detrimental to their health or posed significant risks. On the other hand, they would also be stakeholders if cleaning Julie's room represented a threat to their rights and their privacy as residents.

The other residents are clients on an equal footing with Julie, but will probably be less affected by the decision.

5. Identify other involved parties

Besides the stakeholders, there are likely to be other people who have connections to the issue. The expert advice of other professionals may be critical. Parents may be significantly affected. Members of the wider community may also be involved. Consulting with a wide range of people may be useful. In Jim's case (chapter one), the professional advice of the speech pathologist is clearly vital. Is Jim at slight risk, moderate risk or in severe danger? The people who run the community group, and those who attend will be affected to some degree by the decision, too.

On the other hand, attempts to please everyone should not detract from a focus on the client as the prime stakeholder. Wide consultation may provide useful insights, but the professional is not accountable to everyone involved, and is certainly not responsible for the welfare of everyone involved, either. The professional is primarily responsible for making decisions regarding the welfare of the client.

Other parties affected by the dilemma of Julie's room

The other residents in Julie's house are stakeholders too, and their rights and welfare should be considered. Parties who are involved but who are not stakeholders appear to be limited to the other professionals who provide support services, including the team leader and the CEO of the organization.

6. Precisely draft a decision/recommendation

It is tempting to avoid or defer difficult ethical decisions indefinitely. This, though, amounts to a decision in itself, since the issue, whatever it is, will presumably continue to have ramifications for those concerned. Postponement might not be a bad thing, but the impacts of postponement should be considered as carefully as the impact of decisive action. Baby Charlotte's situation is a clear example. To provide her with surgery is one alternative. To refrain from surgery is the opposite alternative. To postpone the decision is in practice the same thing as the second alternative, that is, to refrain from surgery. In another example given in chapter one concerning Angela at the shops, there is a similar situation. Either Angela goes to the shops or she does not.

Another way of avoiding difficult decisions is to be vague about what the decision actually is. It might be tempting to say that we should not be too strict with Jim or Angela, but what does that mean in practice? What is too strict, what is correctly strict, and what is too liberal? Similarly, it might be tempting to say that medical decisions concerning Charlotte should be made by medical doctors. But which medical decision is the most ethical?

The next step after framing a decision is to measure it against the three standards of ethics used in this book. They are community ethics, the calculation of consequences, and the standard of ethical principles. In order to make that evaluation, it is necessary to consider precisely what decision is being contemplated or recommended. If it is precise, then its opposing alternative will also be clear. Providing Baby Charlotte with a tracheostomy is a clear recommendation. If tracheostomy is not undertaken, precisely what therapies or support will be provided?

Deciding whether or not to clean up Julie's room

In Julie's case, the decision is precise and straightforward. We need to decide whether or not to clean up Julie's room. If after considering the ethics of this course of action, we decide that it is justified, then we would go ahead and clean up the room. If we decided that such a course of action would be unethical, then we do not clean up the room and the circumstances stay as they are. In that case, we may need to justify to our team leader and our employing organization why, on ethical grounds, we did not clean up the room.

7. Examine the draft decision using a community approach

A community-based approach to professional ethics would evaluate a course of action according to whether it is appropriate to the professional's role and relationships. This approach is discussed in detail in chapter two on the community approach to ethical decision-making.

Roles and relationships can be at several levels and with a number of people.

At an informal level, we might ask whether the course of action is a result of the professional caring for the client and being sympathetic to the client's circumstances, feelings, wishes and welfare. We might also ask what are the expectations of the client, and of the wider community.

At a more formal level, we might consider the terms of the professional's employment or contract. The employing organization may have policies specifying its role and the role of the professionals it engages.

The professional code of ethics provides guidelines against which the contemplated course of action could be measured.

There may be relevant legal obligations which are an expression of the community values regarding the ethical issue being examined.

We might ask whether the course of action is just or fair. There is a hypothetical test of justice and fairness [5]. We could imagine we were members of a community that was about to set up a society. To make sure we are being fair, we imagine that we do not know what our own circumstances are going to be in this society. We do not know if we will be healthy or frail, rich or poor, professional or client, or anything else about our lives. Then we can ask ourselves if the contemplated course of action is the sort of thing that would be agreed to by a community of individuals, including ourselves, bearing in mind that we do not know what our own circumstances will be. We could consider Jim's case (from chapter one) as an example. The issue is whether Jim should be prevented from attending the community group because of his swallowing difficulties. Do we think that people with swallowing difficulties should be so restrained, given that there is some possibility that we might find ourselves in our new hypothetical society, to be people with swallowing difficulties? If there were some possibility that we would find ourselves in Baby Charlotte's circumstances, would we prefer that nature take its course, or would we favour surgery to prolong our lives but concomitantly prolong our distress?

We might also apply the 'sunlight test'. Would we be happy for our decision to be out in the open and visible for all to see? Would we be happy to explain it and justify it to the rest of the community?

Applying the community approach to whether it is ethical to clean up Julie's room

Presumably we care about Julie and are concerned about her health and welfare. We are also concerned about the health and welfare of the other residents in Julie's home. We have the expertise to judge whether the state of Julie's room puts her and others at risk and, as professionals, we are in a position to make a prudent decision. It would be a reasonable expectation of our employing organization and the community in general that we keep Julie safe, especially in areas where her intellectual disability compromises her capacity to look after herself.

Does Julie understand our role in this? Perhaps she would not be at all surprised if we cleaned up her room in her absence. After all, we have spoken to her about the need for a clean-up. Or would she consider such an action to be a shocking betrayal of trust? Would the other residents become insecure and suspicious of us if we invaded Julie's room when she was not there?

What does our professional code of ethics advise that is relevant to this situation? If we check the code provided in chapter five, we see a number of clauses that are relevant.

The code requires us to be sensitive to Julie's individual preferences and life style.

> Consideration is given to the diversity and unique nature of a person's support needs, methods of communication, learning and life style.

> Disability and Rehabilitation Professionals show appropriate respect to the fundamental rights, dignity and worth of all people. They respect the rights of individuals to privacy, confidentiality, self determination and autonomy.

> Disability and Rehabilitation Professionals value the promotion of an environment that enhances a person's quality of life.

It also requires us to be honest with Julie.

> Disability and Rehabilitation Professionals are honest, fair and respectful of others in all aspects of professional work.

But it does require us to take care that her health is not at risk.

> A duty of care is owed by a Disability and Rehabilitation Professional to a client, family or peer. If harm is suffered by the individual that was "reasonably foreseeable" a breach of duty of care may be deemed to have occurred.

In law, tenants have some protections against their homes being invaded, even by people who are well-intentioned. Do those protections apply here? If so, can they be over-ridden by health concerns?

Hypothetically, would an ideal community agree that people like Julie should be protected by professionals' interventions? If we were to contemplate a future in which we were in Julie's circumstances, do we think that such intervention is warranted? Or would we consider that our privacy rights were more important?

Does cleaning Julie's room pass the 'sunlight test'? If we clean up Julie's room, would we be happy for the community to know we had done so? If we decide not to intervene, would we be happy for the community to know that we had decided to leave the state of Julie's room as it is? As the Code of Ethics points out:

> Disability and Rehabilitation Professionals are aware of their professional and academic responsibilities to the community in which they work and live.

Our decision should depend a great deal on our relationship with Julie and the other residents. If Julie accepts that it is part of our role to supervise the cleanliness of her room and intervene when necessary, then doing so would be justified. If, on the other hand, she considers it a breach of trust, then we need to balance that against our other responsibilities, including our role in keeping her safe and preventing risks to her health. How great is the risk to her health? This leads us to the next step in our decision making process, that of calculating consequences.

8. Examine the decision by calculating its consequences

Calculating the consequences of a course of action is essential when deciding whether or not we should proceed with it. According to this approach, if a course of action maximises the welfare of those affected by it and minimises harm, then it is ethical. In the professional context, the effects on the welfare of clients are the focus. This approach is discussed in more detail in chapter three on calculating consequences.

The welfare of clients includes their physical conditions, their psychological states, their health, their general well being and their opportunities to flourish. Long term effects and short term effects need to be calculated and balanced.

When calculating consequences, we might ask the following:

Have we collected the facts we need in order to calculate the likely consequences of the action being contemplated?

Is there pain or discomfort that can be alleviated?

Is there distress that can avoided?

Is there a sense of self-esteem, or security, or happiness, that can be promoted and maximised?

Are there dangers that can be averted?

Does the course of action affect the general circumstances in a positive way?

Does it have potential to improve the social or physical arrangements?

Is the course of action a single isolated decision, or does it set a precedent that will have longer lasting effects?

Does the course of action conform to practices that we already know generally have good results?

Do the people affected by the course of action, especially the clients, have the opportunity to provide information about how they are being affected, and whether the effects are positive or negative?

The last question relates to Preference Utilitarianism. The consequences approach requires us to aim for good outcomes. What counts as a *good* outcome? What yardstick do we use to decide whether an outcome is good, or whether it is better than an alternative outcome? What defines 'good'? Importantly, *who* defines 'good'? Using the Preference Utilitarian strategy, we could define a good outcome as the outcome that is preferred by the people experiencing the outcome. In this way, the two questions concerning what is a good outcome and who decides what is a good outcome get bundled together. Ideally, the person or people affected by the results decide what count as the best results. In professional ethics, though, the process is not that straightforward. The professional is in a better position to decide what counts as best results and what is the best way of achieving them. Professionals have greater expertise in making decisions and better access to facts and effective strategies. That is why they are professionals and have professional responsibilities. Clients, by definition and in actual fact, rely upon professionals' skills in decision-making. When people have all the knowledge and skills they need to calculate the consequences and make decisions for themselves, they do not need professional advice and are not clients. Professionals have the demanding responsibility of making decisions that are calculated to be in the clients' best interests. Hopefully the client and the professional will concur, but if the client lacks competence, the professional may need to make a decision on behalf of the client or even contrary to the client's stated preferences.

The consequences of cleaning Julie's room

The primary purpose of the instruction to clean Julie's room is to avert the health dangers to her and the other residents. Her untidiness includes leaving containers of food that can rot and thereby provide a health hazard and an opportunity for pests. This has the potential for very poor consequences for Julie and for our other clients living in the same house.

Tidying up the room may also demonstrate to Julie how pleasant it can be to live in neat, tidy surroundings, and she may then take it upon herself to maintain her room in a better state.

These are foreseeable good consequences. In contrast, though, there is the predictable distress that Julie will experience if we invade her room when she is not there. It will impact on her sense of security and self-esteem and change her surroundings contrary to her preferences. It will predictably have similar effects on the other residents and may contribute to a sense of distrust between clients and professionals. As well as the immediate psychological distress involved, distrust may have long term poor effects, compromising the professional/client relationship.

Preference Utilitarianism would recommend that it should be Julie, and the other residents, who decide which is the better outcome. How seriously do they object to the intervention of cleaning Julie's room while she is not there? How risky do they consider the untidiness and health issues? Attempts have been made to persuade Julie that cleanliness and tidiness are desirable outcomes, but without success. It is important that, as professionals serving Julie's needs, we should make a serious effort at achieving an agreement with her about the issue. If we do not succeed, then Julie's preferences have to be considered in the light of her competence to make decisions. When we gathered the facts surrounding this issue, we discovered that Julie does have a mild intellectual disability. She is, though, competent at ordinary daily tasks. She generally eats healthily and dresses in clean clothes.

The rotting food may present an objective danger. The general untidiness, though, may simply run counter to the personal preferences of the professionals. Professional ethics is about the preferences of the client, rather than the professional [6].

There may be predictable poor consequences for the professional for not complying with instructions from the organization's management to clean up the room. This is a factor, but only a minor one. In professional ethics it is the consequences to the client that are important, rather than to the professional. Furthermore, a professional, by definition, makes decisions and is responsible for them, rather than blindly following routine instructions.

Our decision depends on our calculation of the risks to Julie's health compared with the distress that will result form our intervention in her room.

9. Examine the decision using a principles approach

To be ethical in principle we must respect people and their rights. We should also be consistent and impartial. We should be unswervingly committed to principles rather than expediency, or being swayed by circumstances, emotion, pressure or self-interest. This approach is discussed in detail in chapter four on principles.

We should respect other people as people, that is, as persons with their own lives to lead and their own decisions to make. We should avoid deception, coercion and manipulation.

We should promote people's flourishing and fulfilment. We should set up arrangements that allow them to exercise their capabilities.

We should pay attention to the rights that our community has acknowledged formally. Some of these are mandated in legislation. Some are expressed in the Universal Declaration of Human Rights [7]. To remind us that these rights apply to people with disabilities, there is the United Nations Convention on the Rights of People with Disabilities [8]. Professional codes of ethics also formally acknowledge the rights of clients.

The fundamental human right to self-determination is a significant issue in disability ethics, because disability inevitably compromises self-determination.

So, when evaluating a course of action against ethical principles, we might ask the following:

Does the course of action respect the client as a person?

Does it have the client's consent?

Is the decision effectively being made by the client, with the expert advice of the professional?

Is the client fully informed? Are secrecy, manipulation and deception being avoided?

Are the rights of the clients being respected, as laid down in the professional code of ethics, in legislation and in international conventions?

Is the client's flourishing being promoted? Does the course of action allow the exercise of the client's capabilities?

Is the course of action one that could be applied consistently, rather than just an expedient reaction to a particular set of circumstances?

Julie, her rights, and her room

Invading Julie's room against her wishes, without her consent, and when she is not there, is clearly disrespectful of her and her rights.

If compulsory room-cleaning is applied consistently, it also threatens the rights of the other residents in the house.

It may be in breach of Julie's rights as a tenant that are mandated in legislation. It runs counter to the rights expressed in the United Nations documents on fundamental rights and rights of people with disabilities.

On the other hand, these rights flow from respecting other people as self-determining persons. Julie's self-determination is compromised by her intellectual disability. The presence of rotting food in her room is the result of her lacking the ability to make sound, rational and prudent decisions.

Furthermore, if she becomes ill as a result of her room's condition, her self-determination will be further compromised by her illness. Her potential to exercise her capabilities, to express herself through her arts and crafts, and to fulfil herself generally, will be restricted in practice if she is physically debilitated by sickness. Furthermore, she is disregarding the rights of her fellow residents by putting them at risk of debilitating illness.

Certainly, being ill will compromise her capabilities as discussed in chapter four. Capability 2 is:

> 2. ***Bodily Health***. Being able to have good health, including reproductive health; to be adequately nourished; to have adequate shelter.

Julie's room is messy partly because of her dedication to her craft work. Capability 4 is important in this context.

> ***Senses, Imagination, and Thought***. Being able to use the senses, to imagine, think, and reason ... Being able to use imagination and thought in connection with experiencing and producing works and events of one's own choice, religious, literary, musical and so forth. Being able to use one's mind in ways protected by guarantees of freedom of expression with respect to both political and artistic speech and freedom of religious exercise. Being able to have pleasurable experiences and to avoid nonbeneficial pain.

We should take care that intervening in Julie's room does not make her insecure and anxious. Capability five includes,

> Not having one's emotional developing blighted by fear or anxiety.

Capability 9 is:

> ***Play***. Being able to laugh, to play, to enjoy recreational activities.

Capability 10 includes:

> ***Control over one's environment.***
>
> B. *Material*. Being able to hold property (both land and movable goods), and having property rights on an equal basis with others... having the freedom from unwarranted search and seizure.

Again, our decision turns on whether we should protect Julie from foreseeable and significant risks to her health, or whether we should protect and promote her rights and capabilities.

10. In the light of the examination, confirm the draft decision or reject it

Sometimes, examining a course of action leads to a clear conclusion about what is the best thing to do. It may be the case that the contemplated action will yield good results for all concerned and respects their rights. Under such circumstances, the people involved, and the wider community, would no doubt agree that it is the best thing to do. Such a course of action would therefore be ethical by all three standards. The calculation of its consequences comes up with positive results. In principle it is satisfactory, and by community standards it is acceptable.

A satisfaction of all three standards would not be surprising. Respecting people often yields good results. Manipulating and deceiving them often has bad consequences. People typically co-operate in communities to satisfy their needs and understand the value of respecting each other.

So when we examine a course of action to see if it is ethical, finding a decision that meets the requirements of all three theories would be ideal. This is not uncommon. Much human interaction is in fact ethical and is negotiated with such little difficulty that it is not recognised as presenting ethical issues.

Ethical issues arise when the three approaches conflict. Producing good consequences for one person may result in bad consequences for another. Actually, there may be a mixture of good consequences and bad consequences for the same person. There may also be good short-term consequences and bad long-term consequences, or vice versa. Similarly, principles can conflict with other principles. The rights of one person may be incompatible with the rights of another. Then there is the challenge of reconciling principles and consequences. If principles are to provide us with reliable rules for conduct and social arrangements, they must not be cast aside when circumstances make them inexpedient. Principles should be stuck to, regardless of the consequences. The counter argument is that only consequences matter. Principles are just rules of thumb that facilitate good consequences. This conflict appears to be so embedded in the two theories that ethical dilemmas will always be with us.

As a result, people in general, and professionals exercising their expertise, must make difficult judgements in complex circumstances. When we calculate the consequences, we need to do more than identify good and bad outcomes. We need to calculate how serious they are, how good and how bad they might be. When recognizing an infringement of human rights, we need to judge how seriously people's self-determination is being compromised. When reflecting on professional roles, we need to consider the differing expectations of the various parties and the wider community.

Resolving the matter of Julie's messy room

Clearly a good resolution would be to persuade Julie to clean up her room or at least consent to that being done. However, this has been tried, and failed. So now the decision is stark. Is it ethical to clean up her room against her wishes, or not? How do we balance the three strategies of the community approach, the consequences approach and the principles approach?

Applying community standards to the issue of what to do about Julie's room does not help much in resolving the ethical dilemma. Professionals would be failing in their responsibilities if they were negligent about threats to Julie's health. At the same time, there is an expectation that the professional/client relationship will be characterised by respect, and that Julie's fundamental and legal rights will be preserved and protected.

The issue is therefore a standard one of conflict between principles and consequences. Cleaning Julie's room while she is not there looks to be quite disrespectful of her. It is possible she would not regard it as a serious breach of her rights, but then, why do it when she is not there? It runs counter to the spirit, if not the letter, of tenants' legal rights. These considerations would pale into insignificance though, if all the residents became seriously ill as a result of Julie's mess.

So how serious is the health hazard? There has been no illness yet, and no evidence of pests. The consequences need to be quite bad to over-ride the breach of principles. It is likely that untidiness is a personal preference of the staff involved. The health hazard may be just an association made in the minds of the staff rather than an objective calculation of consequences.

If there is insufficient reason to predict dire consequences, Julie's room should not be cleaned against her wishes.

Chapter 7
Confidentiality

Confidentiality presents a complex ethical challenge. From a community-based perspective, it appears that in contemporary society people value confidentiality and privacy highly, but they are ambivalent about exceptions and limits. From a principles-based perspective, confidentiality and privacy are aspects of autonomy, and a rights-based approach values them [1]. There are mixed results when consequences are calculated. Dilemmas arise when honouring the confidentiality rights of clients involves risks to other people. In addition, there is no general agreement about what sorts of information should be categorised as private and what sorts can reasonably be accepted as public.

In this chapter, I will explore this tangled issue and discuss the obligations concerning confidentiality that are borne by professionals. There are important legal obligations about which professionals should seek legal advice. Unfortunately, laws vary from place to place and, even in a single jurisdiction, legal judgements conflict with each other. Legal uncertainties reflect the ethical complexity of the issue. Using an ethical framework, I will consider issues from the perspective of the individual professional with a client, and also from the big-picture perspective of government agencies and national databases. I will use the establishment of a national autism register as an illustration of the ethical issues inherent in databases.

Confidentiality and privacy are prominent issues in modern society, made particularly pressing by the power of the Internet. Privacy is not quite the same thing as confidentiality, though they are related. You have privacy when you can live your life without being observed by others, such as in the privacy of your own home. Issues of confidentiality arise when there is information about you that is available to other people but that should not be available publicly, for a variety of reasons. Professionals typically have and need information about their clients, and some of this information should not be made available publicly. Professionals face the challenge of recognizing what information about clients should be kept in confidence and what can be shared, with which other persons it should or should not be shared, and how information should be obtained, stored and used.

Confidentiality is an important and complex issue in professional ethics. There are competing considerations around the what, when and how of information usage, and these considerations are significant for the client, and for the community. Juggling these competing forces is an on-going challenge [2]. Besides communitarian considerations, confidentiality is also an issue for other approaches to ethics, such as a consequence-based approach or a principle-based approach, but the consideration of principles and consequences does not meet the challenge any more satisfactorily than a community based approach.

The word 'confidential' connects to a community-based approach to ethics in that it is related to 'fiduciary'. Fiduciary is one of the models of professional-client relationship discussed earlier. The common origin of both words, fiduciary and confidentiality, is the Latin word 'fidere', meaning to trust [3]. Clients need to trust professionals. Clients need to be confident that information they entrust to professionals is kept in confidence.

When a professional in any field provides services to a client, the professional needs information about the client in order to give expert advice and to make decisions. There are obvious and powerful reasons why a client would not make some of this information generally available publicly. People are understandably cautious about information concerning their financial position, but need to make this information available to their accountants, and, more worryingly, to large anonymous government departments such as those handling taxation and welfare. There are large numbers (and, it seems, ever-increasing numbers) of criminals attempting to access people's financial information that they can use for theft, or for selling to confidence tricksters. Confidence tricksters are so named, of course, because they are the very people who should not be trusted. Accountants and government departments therefore have an important obligation to keep information in confidence, if only for the practical reason of limiting potential for theft. Disability professionals working in large government departments and agencies therefore have obligations to make sure information about the people they service does not fall into the wrong hands.

The default position – all information is confidential

Disability professionals working with individual clients have a different perspective from large government agencies. They may not need to take precautions against their database being raided by cyber criminals. The information they have about their clients is typically not specific financial details (though it may include these) but will cover a wide range from the innocuous and commonplace to the significant and highly personal. When professionals survey all that they know about their clients, which parts should they assume are by their nature confidential, and which parts do they not need worry about?

Of course, a lot of information about people is publicly known, rather than being private details, including significant personal details. We are all accustomed to the fact that our gender and age are readily apparent to other people that we mix with, and we accept that, even if we are sometimes tempted to lie about our age. We express personal opinions, boast about our children's achievements and join clubs with others who have similar interests or aspirations. Parts of our lives contain confidential information, but much is lived openly in public. What parts of a client's life should a professional regard as confidential and what parts should be regarded as just ordinary daily public life?

The starting point, arguably, is that *all* information about clients should be considered confidential unless there are good reasons otherwise.

This may appear to be a bit extreme as a starting point. We are accustomed to some taboos in ordinary conversations, such as questions about sexual preferences and activities, although amongst friends such information is often freely available. Information that a client likes cats, say, is surely not in the same category as financial details or sexual preferences. If, by some quirk it was, surely a client could say "I'm telling you this in confidence".

Despite the fact that some information is either public or of no great import, there are a number of good reasons why the starting point for information should be that all of it is confidential unless known to be otherwise.

The power of the professions

Professions are, by definition, populated by people who have a great deal of expertise and so have the ability to do great good, and, correspondingly, the potential to do great harm. A client is vulnerable to professional decisions. Clients and professionals are not partners who need each other equally. A client is not in a position to consider the risks of each piece of information that is coming into the professional's hands. Professionals are licensed by the community to use information. The license, the mandated qualifications, and the code of ethics are ways in which a community recognizes the potential effects of professionals, and at the same time puts constraints on them. Information is power. The community at large and the individual client both need to be confident that the power will not be abused.

Significance of the information

Even if clients did take on the task of considering the risks of divulging each piece of information, clients are not in a position to judge what information professionals need and what is irrelevant [4]. Are a client's moods and feelings irrelevant, or are they possible indicators of a significant physiological process linked to the disability? Are the education achievements of their siblings irrelevant, or are they useful indicators to hereditary factors (perhaps in the diagnosis of an autism spectrum disorder)? Clients may think that some of their experiences are unique to themselves, without realizing that they are common to other people with similar needs. The reverse may happen, where they attribute significance to events which are coincidental rather than cause and effect. If a child is diagnosed with autism soon after an inoculation, is that significant information as some parents believe, or an irrelevant coincidence? Clients do not have the expertise to make these sorts of judgements, only professionals do. Clients therefore need to be able to reveal all information, including that which is intimate or embarrassing, in the confidence that the professional will use that information for the clients' benefit or not use it at all.

Correspondingly, professionals should gather only that information which is relevant to their decision-making and provision of services. Admittedly, this can be a wide variety of information for disability professionals, in comparison to, say, accountants.

The Code of Ethics for Disability and Rehabilitation Professionals (see chapter five) advises that

> When preparing or keeping, records, reports, assessments or other information (be they oral, written or any other communication) Disability and Rehabilitation Professionals should only use or keep information pertinent to the matter at hand

Clients therefore need to feel comfortable about divulging any and all information so that professionals can select what is relevant, based on their professional knowledge.

Individual sensitivities vary

While a client may not be able to tell in advance what the professional needs to know, the professional may not be able to tell what information is considered by the client to be sensitive and what they are happy to publicly reveal. One client may be keen to declare a sexual preference to the world, but be embarrassed by their taste in music. Another client's attitude may be exactly the reverse. Professionals will no doubt have their own intuitive personal attitudes. Some may think it obvious that sexual preferences are sensitive and music tastes are not. Other professionals may not think it obvious at all. Importantly, the judgement should not be driven by the professional handling the information, but by the client whose information it is. It is not practical to expect a client to label some information by saying, "I'm telling you this in confidence", nor to decide what information is best withheld or what can be safely revealed. Certainly, clients can be asked which information they are happy to reveal. Permission can be sought for passing on information or waiving confidential provisions. If a client is explicitly unconcerned that some information need not be treated in confidence, then, generally speaking, that resolves the ethical issue, at least from the perspectives of autonomy, rights and legal obligations. Otherwise, the default position should be that all information is confidential.

This is difficult to manage in practice. Even the fact that a person is a client at all may be sensitive information in some circumstances. Clients receiving services related to mental illness, for example, may consider that fact to be sensitive information that should be kept confidential. It should not be assumed that this is the only sort of service which is *prima facie* sensitive and confidential. Again, because individuals vary, their perception of what is sensitive cannot be assumed. In practice, clients typically access the services of professionals at facilities designed for that purpose. They may go to an accountant's office for financial advice, go to hospital or doctors' rooms for health services, or live in supported accommodation, so the fact that they are clients may not be confidential in practice. Neither, though, should it be freely available. Professionals have an obligation of discretion.

Cultural Sensitivities

Using a community-based approach, confidentiality is an ethical obligation for professionals simply because the community deems it is. Whether a professional sympathizes with a client's particular sensitivities, or, in contrast, thinks they are unnecessary and irrational, is beside the point. Certainly, dealing with information and making expert decisions in the light of that information is an essential feature of being a professional, so a restriction on information access can be irksome, counter-productive to effective practice, and in some ways the antithesis of what being a professional is all about. Perhaps society has taken the wrong approach to the issue anyway. Maybe we would all be better off in practice if we simply abandoned the idea of privacy and confidentiality. With the advent of credit cards, security cameras, Facebook and other Internet functions, we seem to be heading in that direction anyway. Against this, the emergence of laws protecting privacy is a strong indication that the community does not favour abandoning privacy and confidentiality. Professions are created by the community to serve people's needs, so professions have an obligation to respect confidentiality because the community demands that they do.

Some cultures do not have the same perspective of an individual's right to privacy. Sometimes being part of a family is seen as more important than individual privacy rights. The notion of confidentiality grows from philosophical assumptions that are particular to western culture. It is rooted in notions of individuality and autonomy, notions which are elevated to a much higher degree in Western culture than in any other [5]. If the members of a client's family have cultural traditions that do not elevate individual autonomy above family relationships, then they may expect and even demand information. Professionals do not work in isolation. They relate to clients, to clients' families and to the community at large. If the client's own family and culture do not prioritise confidentiality, should the professional do so, or be guided by that family's preferences and cultural values?

Again, the decision about what is confidential must rest with the client. Although it may be desirable for professionals to be expert in the variety of cultural sensitivities of a multicultural population, it is not practical. Nor would it be practical to figure out how the individual/family balance resolves in particular cases. A particular culture's traditions may elevate the family, but there is no way of knowing the extent to which particular clients subscribe to their traditions or have moved away from them [6]. Professionals therefore need to respect their individual client's wishes, prioritising them over others' concerns. This may be seen as prioritising western culture, but then the existence and the roles of the professions are also an expression of western culture. At any rate, accommodating the range of sensitivities, be they cultural or individual, is not within the expertise of disability professionals, and so must be driven by the client.

Of course, the family role is quite different if the client is a minor, or for other reasons is not an autonomous adult. If a client has a substitute decision-maker, then clearly the decision-maker needs information in order to make sound decisions. If parents have the responsibility of making decisions about and for their children who are receiving the professional services, then they need to be taken into the professional's confidence. Community and legal standards concerning autonomy do not apply to children as they do to adults. There will inevitably be difficulties as children move into adulthood, or where an adult client has diminished capacity for self-determination.

Some of the reasons that people have for valuing confidentiality are practical, such as the need to protect themselves from financial predators. Some of the reasons are to do with their perception of their personal reputation and standing in the community. They may be embarrassed or fearful of what others might think of them. On this account, they may even wish for confidentiality to be maintained after their death. Normally the community and the law only concern itself with living persons. Laws about defamation, that protect people's reputations, do not apply once the person is dead. Using a consequence-based approach, harm cannot be done to someone who is dead. Their reputation could be harmed, perhaps, but consequences should be calculated for actual persons, not for abstractions. From a principles-based approach, the dead have no autonomy and exercise no capabilities, so there is no reason to afford them any rights. Despite this, some people do care about their standing after death, which the community recognizes to some extent, for example by honouring wishes expressed in their wills. Some professional codes of ethics concerning privacy and confidentiality do extend after death, though not the Disability and Rehabilitation Professionals' Code provided in chapter five of this book [7].

Some people, with justification, are concerned about stigmatising and stereotyping. It is unfortunately true that a stigma may frequently be associated with disability. In some sense, information about a person is inextricable from the formation of that person's identity (see the discussion in chapter nine on Identity). A person's identity can be seen as a combination of characteristics including gender, culture, occupation, physical features, achievements, group membership and so on. In order for people to define themselves, even if they accept that needs to be done through negotiation with others, they need to exercise some control over what information is available about themselves to others.

Control of information is the significant issue. If clients release information to professionals they do not know, or to bureaucracies, they may justifiably wonder where it will go, how far it will spread and to what use it will be put. Although confidentiality is a *prima facie* ethical obligation for professionals, there are a number of exceptions. So many exceptions, actually, that it is a continuing ethical challenge.

Exceptions to confidentiality

Professionals work with other professionals, with clients' family members, in the community at large and within legal obligations. Each of these relationships may require the exchange of information.

Client consent

As discussed, some information about a client is confidential, some is not. If a client deems that some information is not of a confidential nature, then it is not, by definition. It is the client's decision that determines the status of the information. If the client consents for information to be freely available, then the ethical barrier to disclosing it is removed. This assumes of course, that the client is competent to make and give an informed decision. If the client is not competent, then typically decisions are made by a parent or guardian who has that responsibility.

For information that a client deems is confidential, the client may give consent for its limited release to particular people and other professionals. Confidentiality remains, but applies to a wider pool of people than a single professional. A client may even waive all restrictions of confidentiality.

There may be situations in which information is legitimately required by other parties with or without the client's consent, but even here the client's consent should be sought and obtained if possible.

Other professionals

Although it is convenient to talk about a professional-client relationship, the reality is that professionals frequently work in teams, rather than solely with a client. Information needs to be shared by the team. The confidentiality provisions may typically be at the level of the team or the organization, rather than entrusted to a single professional. Hospital data is an illustration. The confidentiality expectations and obligations apply to the records the hospital keeps. They are not renegotiated by the patient with each and every doctor, nurse and administrator who deals with the patient. Similarly, a disability service organization may be the holder of confidential information which is available to each of the professionals involved with a specific client. It should be clear to the client whether this is the case.

A professional might need to discuss a client with another professional. Clearly, the second professional has a confidential obligation in these circumstances. Again, where practical, the client's permission should be sought. This might be specific permission or as part of an understanding that the professionals are team members in the organization which holds the confidentiality obligation.

Professionals sometimes need to seek advice from other professionals outside the team, in order to get expert opinion or a fresh perspective. Some such discussions may even be for the professional's benefit rather than for the client, because the professional is feeling over-burdened, or stressed, or too close to a troubling issue. In these cases, the professional can avoid an ethical issue of confidentiality by discussing the issue, rather than the client, and by removing from their story any information that identifies the client.

Risk to others

A client may reveal information to a professional which, if kept confidential, can result in harm to large numbers of people. Clearly, in such circumstances, a calculation of consequences is called for.

The community may place a formal obligation on professionals to breach confidentiality where there is significant risk to others. Professionals may be required to report infectious diseases. Hospitals may be required to report to police the level of alcohol in patients involved in road accidents.

As well as the consequences to large numbers of people, there may be risks to individuals that can be averted by breaching confidentiality. Professionals are required to report child abuse. Children are not equipped to exercise their own autonomy or to protect themselves. They are highly vulnerable and can suffer immense damage as the result of abuse. Saving a child from abuse is a significantly good consequence. Ethical dilemmas arise, though, when the professional has a *suspicion* of abuse and needs to calculate the probability of that suspicion being substantiated. If a suspicion of child abuse is reported, and there is in fact no abuse, much damage can result. Recognising this difficulty, mandatory reporting rules may require the notification of suspicion, which relieves professionals from the burden of calculating how probable it is that their suspicions are well founded. This does not entirely remove the ethical and practical difficulty of calculating probabilities, though. When does speculation about possibilities become suspicion?

Risk to others is a classic case of a clash between different ethical approaches. In principle, professionals should keep information about their clients confidential. Confidential information should not be disclosed by definition, because that is the nature of confidential information, along the lines of a categorical imperative (as discussed in chapter four on Principles). Sometimes, keeping information confidential can result in seriously harmful consequences to someone else.

How to calculate when the consequences are sufficiently serious and the calculation sufficiently certain to over ride the obligation of respecting confidentiality is extremely difficult. Ethical analysis, community attitude and legal argument conflict, as is illustrated by the famous Tarasoff case. While this case is literally a matter of life and death and hopefully most disability professionals will never find themselves in such a dilemma, the actual ethical issues it exemplifies are not uncommon.

The Tarasoff case

This dilemma of whether a professional should breach confidentiality in order to reveal a risk to another person gave rise to the famous *Tarasoff Case* in the United States [8].

In this instance, the professional was Moore, a psychologist with the student health service of the University of California. Moore's client, Poddar, confided during counselling that he intended to kill a woman who, although not named at the time, could easily be identified as Tatania Tarasoff. Tarasoff was in Brazil at the time. Moore consulted with colleagues and decided that Poddar was dangerous and should be detained in a mental hospital. He called the campus police, told them of the death threat and of his opinion that Poddar was dangerous. Although Poddar was then questioned by police, they decided he was not irrational and released him. Moore then followed up by writing to the chief of the campus police. Moore's supervisor, however, ordered that the letter and Moore's case notes be destroyed and that no further action should be taken. Tatania Tarasoff was not informed. Subsequently, after her return from Brazil, Tarasoff was killed by Poddar.

Tarasoff's parents sued, claiming that she should have been informed of the threat. They lost the case, but they appealed. They won the appeal in the California Supreme Court, which ruled that it was professionally irresponsible to fail to warn the intended victim. The key points in the ruling were:

- Therapists have a duty to warn when a client communicates to them a serious threat of physical violence against an identified victim or victims.
- The duty is discharged by the therapist making reasonable efforts to communicate the threat to the victim or victims or to a law enforcement agency.
- Therapists who make such a warning are granted immunity from any liability that may arise should the client carry out his or her threat,
- Therapists are not expected to predict violence of their clients.
- If therapists fail to warn when a threat has been made, they may be liable not only for the harm to the intended victim, but also to other victims who may be injured if the threat is carried out [9].

Prioritising principles

If a principles-based approach to ethics is applied, the case is difficult. Clearly, breaching Poddar's confidentiality would not respect his wishes, but Tarasoff did not wish to be killed. The violation of Poddar's autonomy by Moore was much smaller than the deadly violation of Tarasoff's autonomy by Poddar.

Community-based agreement

Using a community-based approach to ethics does not provide a resolution to the difficulties of this dilemma. Moore had an obligation to prioritise Poddar's needs over that of third parties, but Moore has some professional obligations to other people in the community besides his clients.

The case was very contentious and remains controversial legally, in professional ethics, within the USA and in other communities. Two courts in California disagreed, with the Supreme Court over-ruling the first court's decision. It is unknown what other courts in the United States might have decided, let alone in other countries.

Boundaries of expertise

Moore did breach Poddar's autonomy by reporting the matter to the police. The police decided that Poddar was not irrational and released him after questioning. As discussed in chapter two concerning a community-based approach to ethics, professionals have an obligation to work within their boundaries of expertise. Deciding whether Poddar was rational required the professional expertise of Moore. The police, who presumably had less professional expertise than Moore, were not convinced by his assessment and released Poddar, which led, ultimately, to tragic consequences.

Relations with employers

Moore made a professional assessment of Poddar's condition, and calculated that the risk to Tarasoff justified a breach of confidence. Moore's superior presumably disagreed. At any rate, Moore was instructed to destroy the letter he wrote and his case notes. An ethical dilemma arises when a professional's opinion is in clear conflict with an employer's instructions (as discussed in chapter six on making a decision about cleaning Julie's room). The dilemma is more difficult when, in Moore's case, both he and his employer have ethical arguments justifying their conflicting decisions.

Calculating consequences

A calculation of the immediate consequences is not difficult. Failing to warn Tarasoff resulted in her death, which is a much worse consequence than any distress Poddar might have felt because of a breach of confidence. Preventing Poddar from becoming a murderer is also in his best interests.

Applying Rule Utilitarianism may yield a different result [10]. It would be a good result if in general people who were predisposed to violence obtained professional help. There is the potential that their violent tendencies will be coped with, rather than actually carried out. But if such people do not trust that their problems will be kept in confidence, there is every likelihood they will not seek professional help. Would Poddar have told Moore he intended to kill Tarasoff if he thought that Moore would then be obliged to tell the police and Tarasoff? It seems unlikely, and he presumably would have killed Tarasoff anyway.

To make the situation even more difficult, therapists need to calculate *accurately* the consequences of warning the victim or respecting the confidence. Is this threat a real intention or a fantasy? Is it imminent or long term? Clearly a client would feel seriously and justifiably betrayed if he suddenly found himself arrested or estranged from a loved one because he revealed feelings he had no intention of acting upon. It may be extremely difficult for a professional to decide whether a threat voiced by a client actually represents a real and serious danger. Still, decisions do have consequences, and they may be difficult to predict. That difficulty is common in the consequences-based approach to ethics.

Implications of the Tarasoff case for disability professionals

The community approach is ambivalent. We want to be protected from others, but we want our own autonomy. This dilemma could be resolved if Moore had obtained Poddar's permission to reveal his threat to Tarasoff, but that was not going to happen. The principles-based approach reveals a conflict between respecting Poddar's autonomy and respecting Tarasoff's. The appeal court presumably ruled on short term consequences.

Most disability professionals will, thankfully, never face a dilemma as serious as the Tarasoff case, but it does illustrate a limit to the obligation of confidentiality. There may be an ethical obligation to breach confidentiality if that is the only way to avert a serious threat to another person. If permission from the client can be obtained, doing so resolves these ethical dilemmas. If breaching confidentiality is against the client's wishes, then to do so may be ethical if it is the only way to prevent seriously bad consequences.

Sharing confidential information may also be required by law in court cases and for the purposes of regulating funding.

Legally required disclosure

In the event of a court case or similar investigations, information may be required as evidence in the dispute [11]. Legislation generally does not formally recognize an over-riding professional-client relationship preventing disclosure of information obtained as a result of that relationship, though legal proceedings may take it into account in civil cases (rather than criminal ones). An example is a case *Campbell v Tameside Metropolitan Borough Council* where a teacher was badly beaten by a student [12]. She brought an action against the council in which she wanted access to the student's psychological records. She wanted to show that the education authority knew of the student's unstable mental condition and was therefore negligent. A court judgement recognized that the authority had a duty of confidentiality concerning the student's record, but decided that this was over-ridden by the teacher's need to pursue her case, and that it was in the public interest for people to be able to access such information for the purposes of litigation.

That case was a result of the student's own actions, but legal investigations may demand information about clients who are not actually parties in a dispute. An investigation into medical procedures demanded hospital records of patients in *Royal Women's Hospital v Medical Practitioners Board of Victoria* [13]. Again, the hospital argued it had a duty of confidentiality and would not make its records available to the investigating board, but a court ruled that it had to do so.

Clients may reasonably expect that professionals have an obligation to keep information and records confidential, but it would not be ethical for professionals to promise to do so under all circumstances. Nor is it possible to predict the circumstances in which the client or even third parties might get involved in disputes that come to court. A professional obligation of confidentiality may be over ridden by legal demands.

Insurance and welfare

There are a number of agencies and organizations that deal with welfare funding, health funding, health insurance, workers' compensation and so on, that require information about clients. Some of these organizations are government agencies and some are profit-making private organizations.

Sometimes professionals can find themselves in a situation of conflict if they are employed by such an organization, particularly if the organization has an interest in limiting funding but the client has an interest in obtaining services.

Typically, though, the provision of information about the recipient of the services to the organization supplying the services is a well-understood and essential part of the arrangement and provides no ethical dilemmas for the professionals. Recipients of welfare or disability provision understand that, in order to get services, they need to provide information about themselves and their need for the services.

This may present a dilemma for the client. People may be reluctant to admit to an impairment either because of a perceived accompanying stigma or for practical reasons. This reluctance intensifies if the impairment is going on a record which can be disseminated widely with no clear limits to unknown people, including, for example, insurance clerks.

One example of this is funding that is made available to provide services to people who are assessed with a low score on the Global Assessment of Functioning Scale [14]. The Global Assessment of Functioning Scale is a measure of functioning and competence at running one's life. A client might be rated at below 50 if they can be shown to suffer severe deficits in either social, occupational or interpersonal functioning. If they are, then they could be entitled to government-funded provision of services, such as psychotherapy [15]. To access these services, clients have to agree to labelling themselves as incompetent at running their lives, holding down a job and so on. This label goes on record. The clients cannot be certain where information might end up, nor can they control access to the records. Private Health Insurance legislation could lead to the involvement of third party funders, whose employees have no direct relationship with the client and are not even professionals. These limits to confidentiality, or rather, lack of limits to the spread of confidential information, may have poor consequences and deter clients from seeking professional services [16]. There are also impacts on the client's self-esteem and sense of identity, which are discussed in chapter nine on the ethics of identity.

However, as noted above, these are practical dilemmas for clients, rather than ethical dilemmas for professionals.

Confidentiality and its limits

There are good clear arguments why professionals have an ethical obligation to keep in confidence sensitive information about their clients.

There are ethical obligations that arise from a community-based approach. Confidentiality is a community expectation and protection of privacy is a significant contemporary concern. The use of the internet for illegitimate gathering of information is rife, and privacy legislation is still catching up. The nature of the relationship between professional and client requires that the client trusts the professional, with confidentiality an essential part of that trust. Sharing information is essential if the professional is to efficiently provide services. Clients may see information about themselves as impacting on their reputations, their standing in the community and their social identity, and so wish to determine what information should be public and what should remain private. At the same time, they are not in a position to judge which information may be necessary or relevant to the professional, so need to feel free to divulge any of it, including sensitive matters, on the understanding that it will go no further than the professional.

From a principle-based approach, clients should be recognized as autonomous and self-determining persons, so clients' wishes to control information about themselves should be respected. A practical way of respecting autonomy is to acknowledge a right to privacy and confidentiality.

If clients trust professionals, good consequences result. Services can be provided effectively and focussed on the clients' specific needs. It is difficult to imagine how a client-professional relationship could work without access to information, so keeping that information confidential is an essential condition.

Unfortunately there are a lot of practical, legal and ethical exceptions to the obligation of confidentiality.

From a community-based approach to ethics, professionals might need to divulge information to avert a risk to other people in the community. This might be a general risk, such as infectious diseases, or a specific risk to another person, such as a threat of violence. Professionals' first duty is to their clients, but they have obligations to others in the community too. There is no formula for assessing when a risk to another person becomes sufficiently large that it justifies overwhelming the professional's obligation to prioritise client confidentiality. In some cases, professionals may have contractual relationships with employers or funding agencies which require passing on information. There are also legal obligations in mandatory reporting legislation and the proceedings of court cases.

From a principles-based approach to ethics, considerations of autonomy and self-determination may not apply to clients who have significantly diminished capacity or who are children. In these circumstances, the client's substitute decision maker is entitled to information. There may be occasions, such as if a client threatens violence, when another person's rights are at risk, and they are entitled to be informed.

As is so often the case, ethical dilemmas concerning confidentiality may be a conflict between consequences and principles. Passing on confidential information may be the only way to avoid harm to others. Dilemmas can also arise when there is a conflict between calculation of short-term results and long-term consequences. If clients with violent inclinations know that information about this will be passed on, will they simply keep their intentions to themselves?

Two ethical dilemmas concerning confidentiality

Neville does not know he was adopted

Matthew is a services manager in an organization which provides supported accommodation for people with moderate intellectual disabilities. At a social event, he falls into conversation with a couple, Barbara and Ben Kams. They have recently moved into the city from interstate. He has met them a few times previously and a friendship is developing because they are pleasant people and have become members of Matthew's social circle. During this conversation, Ben asks Matthew what he does for a living and Matthew tells them what he does and the name of his employing organization.

Barbara remarks, "Well there's a coincidence, Matthew. Our son lives in that supported accommodation. You must know him".

Matthew is puzzled. "I don't think so. We don't have anybody named Kams".

Barbara explains, "Oh he's not called Kams now. He's called Linnett. Neville Linnett. We had him when we were very young, just teenagers, actually. Not even married or living together back then. Anyway, I couldn't cope, and he was adopted. Still, he's all grown up now. We know he has an intellectual disability, but he can deal with most things. Do you think it would be a good idea if we got into contact? Do the Linnetts still see him?"

Matthew replies, "Yes, the Linnetts still see him, but not often, maybe two or three times a year", but then realizes he should not be discussing a client's family affairs. "How did you know where Neville was? Did the Linnetts tell you"?

Ben and Barbara look a little embarrassed. "Well, no. Let's just say a little bird told us. The Linnetts are a bit hostile to us. You know, for being irresponsible and abandoning Neville. They know about us but don't talk to us. But that was all so long ago and Neville is an adult now. Would it be good for him to meet us?"

Matthew thinks about it. "I seem to remember that the Linnetts insisted that Neville should not be told that he was adopted. I'm not sure if I would need their permission to tell Neville about your being his biological parents, or even if he would understand".

Ben says, "Well you do whatever you think is in Neville's interests. We will leave it up to you whether you tell him or not".

When Matthew returns to work the next morning, he confirms what he had recalled. The Linnetts had insisted that Neville should not be told that he was adopted. Matthew is unsure of what to do. The Linnetts do not see Neville much now, and Neville has very little social life. He could certainly benefit from more. Barbara and Ben seem nice people. They socialize with Matthew and are bound to continue asking about Neville's welfare. They are his biological parents, after all. But Matthew cannot talk about Neville without breaching the confidentiality he owes Neville as a client.

Nor can he get Neville's permission, because to do so would mean revealing to Neville information about his adoption, information that the Linnetts insist remain confidential.

Then a thought occurs to Matthew. Who is the client to whom he owes confidentiality, Neville or his adoptive parents? If he tells Neville he is adopted, he breaches information entrusted by Mr and Mrs Linnett. But a breach of confidentiality consists of divulging information about a client to another person. Is divulging information about a client to the client himself a breach of confidentiality?

Students require information

Chloe manages a community re-entry program for people with acquired brain injury. Her program receives a lot of support from the local university. Students who are studying at the university are required to undertake practicum and Chloe takes on a lot of these students. The arrangement is good for the students' experience in disability issues and is good for the clients. The students assist in providing opportunities for the clients to redevelop life, personal and employment skills. The students also arrange social functions and accompany clients to recreational events.

The students gain considerable knowledge from their practicum placement with the community re-entry program and are keen to learn about acquired brain injury. They are frequently curious about how the brain injury was acquired by the clients they are dealing with. They want to know about brain injuries in general and they want to build a rapport with the clients with whom they are working.

This raises a concern for Chloe. In some cases, the information could be sensitive. It might even affect the rapport building process negatively. Perhaps a client who has damaged himself through drug abuse will be treated with less empathy than one who was a passenger in a road accident. On the other hand, the nature of the injury might be highly relevant. One client received the injury from an assault to the back of the head and he reacts very aggressively if approached from behind [17].

Many of the clients are not in a position to provide informed consent about discussions of their injuries. Their self-determination has been compromised by factors such as frontal lobe injury or short-term memory loss. Other clients, in contrast, can make competent decisions, but categorizing them into two groups, or deciding on a case-by-case basis, is not administratively practical.

Chloe is aware that the students discuss their work in university classes. She has talked to the relevant university lecturer about her concerns regarding confidentiality. The lecturer has assured her that students are instructed that in class discussions they are not to reveal any information that would identify clients and pseudonyms should be used. The students are taught the professional obligations concerning confidentiality. Practicum and class discussions in fact provide an excellent opportunity for that training.

Chloe is pleased that the students are enthusiastic and are receiving good training in professional obligations and conduct. They are, however, not yet qualified professionals or members of the professional association. Should she treat them as professionals and make available to them the information about their clients? Alternatively, should she decide that the information is not strictly necessary and relevant to their tasks of assisting the clients to develop skills and take part in recreational activities?

Confidentiality issues in a database

Establishing a national register or database of a disability can provide vital information about its prevalence, effective interventions and requirements for funding and service provision. A number of such registers exist in Europe, America and Australia, including registers of cerebral palsy, birth defects, vision impairment, cancer, Rett's syndrome, autism spectrum disorders and others.

Clearly, the point of these registers is to collect information about individuals and disseminate it usefully. At the heart of these registers, there are ethical considerations of confidentiality. To illustrate the issue, I will discuss the current process of establishing a National Autism Register in Australia [18].

Ethical nature of the national register

From an ethical point of view, the establishment of a National Autism Register is an exemplary project. It has the support of and expresses the wishes of the community. It aims to achieve good consequences for all involved and has no apparent bad consequences. It aims to respect the participants, facilitate their capabilities and protect confidential information about them. Despite these exemplary features, the register raises some ethical problems which need to be surmounted. Before examining the ethical issues and solutions to them, I will survey the project's positive ethical features.

A community-based project

The register has the strong support of the Autism Spectrum community, which has been promoting the need for an effective database for many years [19]. The proposal for a national register comes from the Australian Advisory Board on Autism Spectrum Disorders, which is an organization that represents people who have an ASD, their families and supporters. The national organization has member bodies in the various Australian states. The project's plan is to collect data on ASD at the state level, thus helping to situate it in local communities [20].

The establishment of the register has the support of the research community. Some researchers have made efforts to gather data about ASD but with limited success. They believe that a national database would provide reliable information, particularly about the prevalence of ASD in the community.

The Australian Government supports the establishment of the register, particularly through its Department of Families, Housing, Community Services and Indigenous Affairs which provides funding for children with ASD [21].

The register is therefore a practical example of a community-based approach to ethics through the establishment of social arrangements supported by government, and with the aim of realizing shared and negotiated goals of community members.

Intended consequences of the project

Without good data about the prevalence of ASD in Australia, it is difficult for government to make effective policy and appropriately fund services. The register aims to describe the distribution of ASD in Australia, its incidence and prevalence, and trends over time.

Research into the nature, causes and efficacy of interventions requires data. Diagnostic profiles are useful for clinicians and researchers.

An understanding of the nature and prevalence of ASD would be useful to families and individuals living with a disorder. Accurate diagnosis, effective interventions and appropriate support services would all provide tangible benefits to them.

Data on ASD in Australia has been very difficult to obtain, as it has been in other countries. Estimates of prevalence from various research studies range from 20 per 10,000 to 116 per 10,000 [22]. A study of data from the welfare agency Centrelink focussed on the number of carer allowances related to ASD. Centrelink is not a health database, but should provide a test of reliability of other data. The study estimated a prevalence of ASD across Australia of 62.5 per 10,000 of 6 to 12 year old children. Another study three years later estimated the prevalence amongst 6 to 12 year olds as 110.85 per 10,000. Either there had been a doubling of prevalence in that period, or data collection and reporting methods are unreliable [23]. ASD is associated with other disabilities, such as psychiatric, sensory/speech disorders, diabetes and cancer [24].

Clearly, the great disparities in estimates of ASD in Australia and the difference between various studies show that good data is not available. Without good data, professional services cannot be planned and provided effectively. An effective National Register is expected to have good outcomes for people affected by ASD.

Principles of respect and confidentiality

In Australia, personal information on registers is subject to national privacy legislation and state legislation. In addition, there are the requirements of the National Statement on Ethical Conduct in Human Research [25]. This legal framework respects participants' autonomy through a requirement that they consent to research and data collection. The consent obtained must follow formal legal protocols, be voluntary, be informed and be documented. Consent to be on the register is a separate process from consent to further research arising from the register data.

The ethical challenge

The challenge involves negotiating or reconciling two opposing considerations. On the one hand, the registry must respect the right of people to freely consent to participate, which obviously means their right not to participate. Whether they are on the register or not must be entirely their choice. On the other hand if people choose not to be on the register, then the effectiveness of the register is diminished, services cannot be provided effectively, research into diagnosis and intervention cannot proceed and the intended good consequences cannot be achieved.

The prevalence of ASD that is indicated by the Centrelink data is much higher than that shown by other sources. Providing information to Centrelink is not entirely voluntary, in the sense that, if you want the service, you have to provide the information. So presumably many people do not freely volunteer to provide information about ASD when it is not a condition of service provision.

Some potential register participants consider that the existence of ASD itself is sensitive information. The process of collecting information may heighten sensitivities. There is a genetic factor in ASD, so epidemiologists are interested in whether it is evidenced in other members of the family, including siblings, parents, uncles and aunts. If the National Register seeks this data then it is asking for information about people who are not participants and who have not provided informed consent. Questions about ethnicity may have a research justification, but may be considered by potential participants as irrelevant or even racist.

This reluctance to provide information about ASD might be overcome by mandatory notification, thereby placing a legal obligation on professionals and abandoning respect for the autonomy of the client. Mandatory notification is sometimes required for infectious diseases. It is not, however, appropriate in this case, since ASD is not an infectious disease and its incidence does not present a significant threat to the community.

Meeting the ethical challenge

In practice, reconciling the need to obtain consent with the need to obtain the participation of a high proportion of the ASD population requires sensitive and careful management of the interaction between the client and registry.

In order to achieve a positive, effective and ethical interaction, the National Autism Register has the following procedures.

Opt in or opt out

Typically, parents receive a diagnosis that their child has an Autism Spectrum Disorder from a professional who has the appropriate qualifications. At that point, the diagnostician informs the parents that there exists a state based organization (for example, Autism SA) which can provide information and support. The diagnostician suggests that the parents' names and address is sent to the state organization and obtains the parents' permission to do so. The parent(s) sign a consent form.

There is debate in the ethics of registers whether voluntary participation should be on the basis of the participants opting in, or whether consent should be assumed unless the potential participant opts out [26]. The Australian Commission on Safety and Quality in Health Care recommends the opt-out arrangement as a standard approach for new registers, because the participation rate may otherwise be too low to be useful. Informed consent can still be obtained and exclusion allowed for people who are actively opposed to being involved.

At the point of ASD diagnosis, the procedure of the national register is neither opt-in nor opt out, but somewhere in between. At this point, too, parents are not being asked to commit themselves to anything, nor are their details going on the national register. Contact information only is being forwarded to the state organization who will then explain the register to the parents.

If the parents do not agree to having their details forwarded, the diagnostician records that a diagnosis has been made on that date of a child of a specified age. That information only is made available to the register, so that at least the incidence and prevalence of ASD can be calculated.

The register explained

When the parents meet with the state organization, the purpose and procedures of the register are explained to them. Identifying information about them and their child will be recorded by the state organization which will send only de-identified information to the national register.

This provides an assurance of confidentiality to the parents and specified limits to the diffusion of information. Although a national register may appear to be a distant and faceless bureaucracy, the state-based organization is run by people the parents meet face-to-face. At this level, the parents have a sense of ownership and control of the process.

The state organization is also the provider of information, support and links to other services, so dealing with it results in tangible positive consequences for the family. Participants may also wish to be involved with the register for altruistic reasons or from a sense of community-based ethics. The state organization should allow for, and facilitate, these motivations.

If families, individuals and children are engaged with the process, then ethical and practical barriers dissolve.

The purposes of the register are then explained to the parent. The de-identification process is also described, making clear that the national register is not provided with any information that identifies the family or individual. If researchers wish to contact the family in order to do more research, the state organization receives the research request and contacts the family.

The consent form

The consent form that the parents are then asked to sign includes a description of how the register operates and for what purpose. From an ethical point of view, it is important that the consent form uses plain language, rather than legalese. It needs to be recognized that some people simply have a strong aversion to forms, like the person who said to health professionals "Reading paperwork is like emotional mountain climbing for me. I would rather walk 10 miles than have to read, understand and sign 2 forms. At least I know I can walk 10 miles" [27]. The ethical aim of obtaining consent to participate in the ASD National Register is to engage the clients in a fruitful relationship that respects them and furthers their interests. Sometimes organizations that are seeking agreements that have legal implications use legal jargon and stilted language to protect the organization against potential disputes, and to make the document look formal and important. The ASD Register consent form is important and has legal weight, but it also has the practical and ethical aim of obtaining genuine informed consent. Consequently, it needs to be worded in a way that will achieve both ends, as in the following example.

An exemplar of consent form for a national ASD register

I understand that the aims of the National Autism Spectrum Disorder Register are:

1. To describe ASD in Australia, how many people are affected, what they have in common and the range of their diagnoses;

2. To assist in planning services for people with ASD, and to help with policy and funding decisions;

3. To promote research into ASD, its causes and the best clinical practices;

4. To benefit people with ASD, their families and the community.

I understand that the Register

4. Respects the privacy of people on the register, and their families;

5. Collects information about people with ASD;

6. Makes information available to funders, policy makers and researchers;

7. Does not identify any individuals when it passes information on to funders, policy makers and researchers;

8. Collects information from other organizations (for example Centerlink) that already have information about people with ASD.

9. Contacts people on the Register from time to time to invite them to participate in research.

Parent section:

I, _____ (please print name) hereby give consent to the inclusion of information regarding _____ (please print name) on the National Autism Register being myself / parent / person responsible. I understand that I can withdraw this consent at any time without prejudice. I am aware that I should retain a copy of the consent form and information sheet for my records.

I consent to:

The collection, recording and permanent storage of information relating to me / my child / the person, on the National ASD Register. This may involve consulting with other records.

Yes ☐   No ☐

Transfer of de-identified information to the National ASD Register.

Yes ☐   No ☐

Receiving invitations from the National ASD Register to participate in research.

Yes ☐   No ☐

Professional(s) nominated by me / my child / the person to be contacted to assist in completing and / or verifying the details on the register.

Yes ☐   No ☐

Signature of participant.
Date.

If you have any concerns or questions regarding this form please contact:

The extent of the requested data

How much information should be sought from the clients and stored on the register? There needs to be enough so that the register can provide useful and effective data to researchers and policy makers, but a request for too much can be intrusive and burdensome. The Australian Commission on

Safety and Quality in Health Care recommends that registries should "collect only the bare minimum of easily obtained data necessary to supplement ancillary administrative data systems to accomplish their task" [29]. A User's Guide for Establishing Registers recommends,

> Elements of data to be included must have potential value in the context of the current scientific and clinical climate and be chosen by a team of experts, preferably with input from experts in biostatistics and epidemiology. Each data element should be chosen for a reason related to the purpose of the registry. Ideally, each data element should address the central questions for which the registry was designed. While a certain number of speculative fields may be desired to generate and explore hypotheses, these must be balanced against the risk of overburdening sites with capturing superfluous data [30].

In the light of these considerations, the data to be stored on the register has been refined from the original 'wish list' of consultants. A Rett disorder item was dropped because there already exists a register. A co-morbidity item, except for intellectual disability, was excluded because of issues about validity and comprehensiveness of data. Biomedical data was excluded for the same reasons. Information about relatives of the client has relevance for research, but may not be obtained without their consent. A broader, less identifying question is used instead.

The information sought can be divided into three categories. There are identifying questions that are not sent to the register, demographic questions that have varying degrees of sensitivity, and diagnostic questions. Clients may wish to abstain from answering some questions, and should be provided with the reasons for each item.

Demographic items include the following:

Year of birth

This item is necessary for data on prevalence and incidence.

Gender (M/F)

ASD is found disproportionately in males.

Place of Birth
Country of Birth - Mother
Country of Birth - Father
Primary language at home
Indigenous background

These items are useful indicators of ethnicity, though that may also be a sensitive issue. The items are useful both for research into genetic links and for provision of services.

Mother - year of birth, diagnosed ASD, diagnosed other disability
Father - year of birth, diagnosed ASD, diagnosed other disability
Marital Status - married, single, divorced, separated
Kinship - biological parent(s), foster parents, adoptive parents
Immediate or extended family member diagnosed with an ASD

These items are relevant to researchers. The marital status of the parents is important because one or both may need to be involved. If they are not together, asking one for information about the other raises ethical obstacles.

The diagnostic items include the following:
- Autistic Disorder
- Asperger Disorder
- Pervasive Developmental Disorder Not Otherwise Specified
- Atypical Autism
- Childhood Disintegrative Disorder
- Non-verbal behaviours (Y/N)
- Peer relationships (Y/N)
- Sharing enjoyment with others (Y/N)
- Social or emotional reciprocity (Y/N)
- Delay/lack spoken language (Y/N)
- Impairment in initiate/sustain conversation (Y/N)
- Repetitive use of language (Y/N)
- Lack of spontaneous/imitative play (Y/N)
- Stereotyped and restricted patterns (Y/N)
- Inflexible adherence to specific routines (Y/N)
- Repetitive motor mannerisms (Y/N)
- Preoccupation with parts of objects (Y/N)

Ending participation

Typically, parents provide information about the child to the state organization that holds the identifying information. Only de-identified data is sent to the National Register. Provision needs to be made for when the children reach adulthood. Their permission should be sought for information about them to remain with the state organization or to be deleted. Parents, too, should be able to end their participation at any time and/or have their names and contact details removed.

Conclusion

Confidentiality is an ethical imperative, whether using a community-based approach, a principles based approach or a calculation of consequences. Nonetheless, all three theories falter when people's interests conflict or their rights clash, or there is an issue of personal autonomy versus public good.

The ethical and legal obligations of professionals with regard to confidential information are challenging to manage. Some information about clients is private, some is public. Some is sensitive and some is trivial. How any particular item of information is categorised can vary greatly and unpredictably from client to client. The default position, then, is to treat all information as confidential. This includes the fact that the person is a client. In practice, treating all information as confidential may not be workable.

Information needs to be shared between professionals. The client should be aware of and consent to the furthest boundaries of information sharing. Careful de-identification of data may extend the boundaries for the purpose of research and education whilst maintaining confidentiality.

Breaches of confidentiality may be justified when there is serious risk to others. Gaining the consent of the client obviates ethical problems, but permission will not always be obtainable. Breaching confidentiality is a serious matter and should only happen with overwhelming justification.

Chapter 8
Ethics in Public Policy

In this chapter I will apply the three ethical approaches of community, consequences and principles to an issue of public policy. This is a somewhat different perspective from ethical issues that arise when professionals are dealing directly with clients. Public policy clearly impacts on the lives of people with disabilities, so it is appropriate to examine policy using ethical criteria. I will use as an example the contentious issue of the sterilisation of intellectually disabled girls [1].

Are there any circumstances in which it is justifiable for parents to arrange for the sterilisation of their daughter who has an intellectual disability such that she is unable to make such a decision for herself? There is debate about the role and responsibilities of the family in deciding whether or not to seek sterilisation, and, in contrast, the role of the state in demanding that such decisions be monitored and authorised. The issue is fundamentally ethical, but attempts to resolve it have been medical and legal. The debate has been conducted through the procedures of guardianship boards and courts, through academic articles, and in the mass media. The problem is seen by some as a private matter, by others as a medical one, by some as an example of prudence and care, and by others as an example of eugenics.

Ethical dimensions of public policy

Before examining this specific issue, it is worth looking at some more general questions about the application of ethics to policy. Why are some issues of public policy deemed by the community to be ethical issues? What features of an issue need to be apparent to have the problem seen as an ethical problem rather than solely as a technical matter, say, or a legal dispute?

An obvious first suggestion is that those policy issues that are seen to be ethical actually have a distinctive ethical feature. This does not get us very far, though. A moment's reflection reveals that all public policy issues are fundamentally ethical. Public policy arises from community concerns. It typically has some impact on people's welfare. It often involves consideration of people's rights. Any policy which impacts on people's wishes or welfare (and what policy does not?) is necessarily ethical. Furthermore, impacts on people's wishes and welfare inevitably involve the distribution of resources or power, with the potential for questions of justice to arise from that. If every public policy *is* ethical, why are some of them *seen* by the community to be ethical and others not?

Ethical questions are sometimes described as 'open' questions; that is, they are not amenable to being answered by the application of a known and agreed procedure. 'How many tables are there in this room?' is not an open question. We know how to go about answering it and will promptly reach agreement. In contrast, 'Is it ever right to kill an innocent?' is an open question. It also happens to be an ethical one. But it surely cannot be correct to *define* ethical questions as open ones. Some non-ethical questions are open. 'Is the universe infinite?' Some ethical questions are not. 'Is it ever right to torture a child for fun?' is not an open question. We would promptly agree on the answer to the last, and would have no difficulty providing reasons for our answer.

While the term 'open' does not serve, the idea of agreement is fruitful. Agreement is a significant element in a community-based approach to ethics. Perhaps the question should not be 'Why are some policies seen as ethical?' but rather 'Why are some policies seen as ethical *controversies*?'

The answer to that question is surely 'When the members of a community are not in agreement, or do not have a method for coming to an agreement'. It is worth noting that this is not a sufficient condition, but is at least a necessary one. That is, there are some controversies in community debate which are not ethical. There are also many ethical matters which are not controversial.

In his book *Ethics and Language*, Stevenson argues,

> When ethical issues become controversial, they involve disagreement that is of a *dual* nature. There is almost inevitably disagreement in belief ... but there is also disagreement in attitude [2].

By beliefs, Stevenson means opinions about the way things are and estimations of the most effective way of dealing with these matters. In this sense, there is no difference between ethical differences in beliefs and disputes in the fields of science, say, or history. But, unlike science, ethical disputes necessarily contain differences in attitude, that is, opinions about the *value* of certain ends, as well as the means of attaining them.

Stevenson's use of 'also' here might seem curious to some ethicists. Surely ethics is *about* values and attitudes [3]. Beliefs, it can be argued, are by contrast, technical, factual and testable in principle. Stevenson, though, disagrees, and insists that equal importance must be given to analysing the two factors if we are to understand ethics.

If we use Stevenson's analysis we can ask 'Why are some issues of public policy deemed by the community to be ethical issues?' We can then answer that a public policy is seen to be ethical if it is seen to be an ethical controversy. Further, it is an ethical controversy if there is a dispute involved over beliefs and attitudes.

In addition to this, I suggest, there are two more features of a disputed policy we should take into account.

One is that somebody *cares*. This is important at a number of levels. At the social level, a controversy will not gather momentum and catch the communal eye unless there are people in the community who care enough about it to raise the matter. At an ethical level, attitudes matter, as Stevenson has said. In chapter two, on a community-based approach to ethics, I referred to the ethical theorist David Hume. Hume saw passion as the very source of ethics, particularly the sentiment of sympathy. Reason, he argued, motivates no one [4]. "Reason is, and ought only to be the slave of passion ..." [5]. In modern language, the term 'emotion' is used rather than the words 'passion' and 'sentiment' that Hume used, but, nonetheless, some people need to be passionate about a policy if it is to become an ethical issue in the community.

Another important feature, as I signalled above, is that there are people involved in the issue who are in disagreement with each other and/or have no agreed method of resolving that disagreement. If such a method exists, I suggest, the issue can be resolved and either cease to be an ethical controversy, or, more likely, not be deemed to be an ethical issue in the first place.

Importantly, the method of resolution need not be ethical in nature, and indeed, may be more effective because of this. It may be medical or perhaps legal. For example, the policy that there should be welfare payments available to the unemployed could be deemed an ethical issue. There are questions here of justice, of rights, of distribution of resources, power and responsibilities. As it happens, the dole is not seen as an ethical issue because there is close to a consensus that it is necessary. There is insufficient disagreement. The question of whether a particular person is entitled to a disability pension rather than the dole is also easily resolved. Yes, if a doctor says so. The question of whether people who are obese merit special consideration is showing signs of becoming a controversy, because we do not have agreement on whether obesity is a medical condition or a matter of personal responsibility.

To summarise so far, a public policy may be seen to be of an ethical nature if it fulfils the following criteria:
- It is ethical, that is, it relates to the ethical theories discussed in this book, particularly the dominant theories that drive the communitarian approach, the consequences approach and the principles approach. An ethical policy is one which impacts on people's wishes or welfare, with consequent questions about the distribution of power or resources.
- Some significant number of people in the community cares about the issue and the outcomes of the policy.
- Some significant number disagrees with each other in beliefs or attitudes about what should be done.
- There is no obvious and agreed method of resolving these differences.

These criteria are evident in the controversy concerning the sterilisation of girls with intellectual disabilities.

The sterilisation controversy

Are there any circumstances in which it is justifiable for parents to arrange for the sterilisation of their daughter who has a severe intellectual disability, such that she is unable to make such a decision for herself? Does the parents' estimation of their daughter's welfare, and that of the rest of the family, have any stand-alone moral force, or is the daughter's inability to consent an overwhelming factor? Does she have the same rights as any other human being, or fewer rights, or perhaps more rights? [6]

This question qualifies as an example of the four conditions that define an ethical controversy in public policy. It impacts on the rights, interests, wishes and welfare of people. It is the subject of passionate debate which takes place in the community, the public service, the parliament and the courts. The sterilisation controversy has been the subject of newspaper articles, television documentaries, scholarly articles and court cases. I will provide a sample of these genres and comment on them.

A Court Case

A significant example of a court case concerning this controversy is known as the 'Marion' case, which took place in the Family Court of Australia in 1992 [7]. Some people see the case as an unjustified constraint and burden on disabled girls and their families, and some have the opposite view, seeing at as a regrettable liberalisation that provides legal excuses for unnecessary sterilisation [8].

There were two questions to be considered. The first was whether the parents had the right to make a decision regarding the sterilisation of their intellectually disabled daughter or whether they were legally required to seek authorisation from the court. Eventually it was decided that they did need to seek authorisation. The second was whether sterilisation was justified. The court ruled that in this case it was, but on some grounds and not on others.

It was put to the Court that:

1. The applicants are the parents of the child, Marion, who was born on 6 August 1977.

2. The child suffers from mental retardation, severe deafness and epilepsy, has an ataxic gait and behavioural problems.

3. The child commenced to menstruate in or about February 1990.

4. The child is incapable of caring for herself physically and/or properly understanding the nature and implications of sexuality, pregnancy and motherhood.

5. It is in the best interests of the child that she undergo hysterectomy and oviarectomy for the reasons pleaded hereunder:

Hysterectomy – to prevent pregnancy,

– to prevent menstruation and menstrual bleeding with consequent psychological and behavioural problems.

Ovarienectomy (*sic*) – to stabilise and prevent hormonal fluxes with consequential stress and behavioural problems [9].

There were submissions from paediatricians, gynaecologists, psychologists, a neurologist, a psychiatrist, the principal of the child's special school, and from the Human Rights and Equal Opportunity Commission.

Their submissions, and the judge's discussion of them, used the terms 'rights', 'interests', 'welfare', 'integrity' and 'consent', so the matter was clearly of an ethical nature, and not merely technical/legal.

The judge did not consider that avoiding pregnancy was a justification for sterilisation. Nor did he consider that sterilisation was justified by the parents' judgements, wishes or responsibilities. The impact on the family of the child's condition and the consequent burden on parents and sibling were acknowledged, but dismissed.

> The reasons advanced for the procedures have included making Marion easier to care for, and for her parents particularly the prevention of pregnancy. Without wishing to diminish the validity of these concerns on the part of the parents, it must be remembered that these are proceedings where the welfare of the child is paramount. As I said in *In re Jane* (supra) at page 77,253, the decision cannot be made to suit the convenience of caregivers, however valid their concerns may be [10].

In terms of the rights of the child, the judge quoted:

> ... children, like other persons, are entitled to be free of non-consensual invasions of their physical integrity

but balanced this with:

> I was assisted in this case by the helpful submissions from counsel for the respondent and counsel for the intervening Human Rights and Equal Opportunity Commission. The Commission made the particularly apposite observation that:

"In cases where strong medical reasons are established in support of a medical operation, refusal of that operation to an adult with an intellectual disability might constitute discrimination on the grounds of disability if the treatment could be made consensually to an adult of normal intellect" [11].

The Family Court then authorised sterilisation of 'Marion' on the grounds that in this case it was in the child's best interest. Interestingly, the judge came to the view eventually that this was primarily a medical matter, rather than an ethical controversy.

Ironically enough, this case probably falls into the category of cases where the Court's consent is unnecessary since, on the facts as I have found them, the procedure was required for medical and therapeutic reasons. It was nevertheless both prudent and correct for the applicants to have sought the consent of the Court, as this issue (whether the procedures were required for medical or therapeutic purposes) could well have been the subject of controversy [12].

Nonetheless, subsequent to and in spite of the Family Court's resolution of the particular case of 'Marion', the controversy continues to be debated by the community using the language of ethics.

One forum for the community's debate is newspapers, as exemplified by the articles summarized below. These five are cited because they come from the same jurisdiction as the Marion court case, but comparable debates can be found in other societies around the world [13].

From *The Courier Mail*:

"Human rights wronged", by Susan Booth, 5 May 2003.

This article decries legislation aimed at restricting the powers of the Human Rights and Equal Opportunity Commission. The author speaks favourably of the commission's intervention in the controversial issue of the sterilisation of women with disabilities [14].

From *The Melbourne Age*:

"Guarding the rights of the disabled", Editorial Opinion, 18 June 2003.

This editorial says it is not concerned with eugenics, but with the possibility that sterilisation puts the interests of the parents above those of the child. It maintains that the rights of the disabled person are paramount. It describes sterilisation as invasive and an abuse of bodily integrity. It refers to the 'Marion' court case but asserts that despite that case's conclusion, the law is not working [15].

Also from *The Melbourne Age*:

"Doctors illegally sterilising disabled girls – claim", by Fergus Shiel, 16 June 2003.

This reports that the Public Advocate sees a need for a review of the approval process for sterilisation of intellectually disabled girls, because the operation is irreversible, a threat to human rights, and illegal without court approval [16].

From *The Newcastle Herald*:

"Who bears the burden?" by Jeff Corbett 7 March 2005.

This article asks whether we have a right to reproduce children. It concludes we do not, but admits that sterilisation of the disabled is of concern and reminiscent of eugenics and social engineering, both of which the author is loath to defend [17].

From *Australian Associated Press:*

"Fewer disabled children being sterilised", by Peter Veness, 28 March 2008.

This article reports on a meeting of state's attorneys-general, which is pleased that doctors now have a much better understanding of their legal obligations concerning the sterilisation of intellectually disabled children. The number of sterilisations appears to have dropped significantly in recent years [18].

A Television Documentary

It is apparent that these articles represent a spread of ethical concerns and opinions. It is also apparent that the Marion case did not settle the controversy, which is further demonstrated in subsequent television documentaries, notably the 'Four Corners' program "Walk in our shoes" [19].

In that documentary, and in interviews from which it was drawn, a number of conflicting views are reported.

The view of a Family Court Judge

Chief Justice Nicholson, understandably, supports the intervention and decisions of the Family Court and the High Court. He refers to eugenics and to the rights of the disabled. He describes sterilisation of the intellectually disabled without Court approval as criminal assault and abuse.

> Historically the issue of sterilisation is [not] a very happy one. If one goes back to the 20s, there was a movement called eugenics which was sort of a brave new world attempt to produce a better society and that involved the rather horrifying concept that if someone had intellectual handicaps, they should be prevented from having children. That was practised in the US for quite a long time through the 20s. It was later adopted with some enthusiasm in Nazi Germany...
>
> I have said in the past that it's not always appreciated by those who carry out these proceedings without approval that what they are doing constitutes an assault, a serious assault and it may well be regarded as child abuse of the worst sort and it seems to me that those who perform these procedures are not fully aware that that's the consequence of failing to get approval whether it be from a court or a tribunal [20].

The view of a disability advocate

Francis Vicary, who has cerebral palsy, is an advocate for the rights of the disabled. She also is concerned about eugenics. She believes that hysterectomy is invasive, and that parents of intellectually disabled are insufficiently informed about alternatives.

> There's contraceptive options where you don't have to menstruate, and there's pills that can be put under the skin that are slow release hormones that are far less traumatic and less permanent than sterilisation and I feel really sorry for the parents because I think they're being pressured by the fact that they can't cope with what's going on in their child's maturity and becoming a woman and the medical profession is not helping them to deal with that and to change. I'd like to see them given options and information which we know are out there [21].

It is notable, though, that despite the options Vicary mentions, she decided to have herself sterilised by tubal ligation.

The view of a parent

Sue Ferris is the mother of an intellectually disabled girl and her position is strongly counter to that of Nicholson, Vicary and the Marion decision.

She has been refused permission by the Guardianship Board to have her thirteen-year-old daughter, Laura, sterilised. She sought sterilisation because of Laura's condition, which she describes as follows:

> Laura now is functioning at about the 14-month level. Basically we have to follow her around everywhere. She doesn't understand road rules, she can't toilet herself ... She needs help with cleaning her teeth and any hygiene routine, washing her hands ... I don't think she could manage menstruation at all. She needs a lot of help with it now. We have to give her pads and we help her if she just throws old pads on the floor, she doesn't know what to do with the old ones at all. She just doesn't have a clue. I don't think she even knows what blood is.
>
> ...she had a lot of problems with clothes ... She could take the clothes off and flatly refused to put them back on again, she'd just tantrum if anyone went anywhere near her clothes ... If Laura's menstruating, there's a total lack of dignity. There'd be blood everywhere, it's just an unhealthy situation for the family, it could be unhealthy for anyone if she does it down the street. There's no guarantee that she won't do it down the street, there's no guarantee that she wouldn't even suddenly decide to strip off in Woollies and throw pads all over the fresh fruit and vegetables ...
>
> ... I'm worried about pregnancy. I just feel that with Laura she's so vulnerable...
>
> ... if she got pregnant there's no way she could cope with it. I mean you can't ask a 14 month old baby to look after a child and in fact one of the doctors that we did talk to said to me that if Laura ever got pregnant, the Guardianship Board would make her have an abortion [22].

Ferris criticises the legal system for its inconsistencies and the expense it involves. Although the Marion decision approved sterilisation, it was for medical grounds only, and the Guardianship Board, she believes, is even less sympathetic. She believes that, as well as the child's rights, the child's welfare and others' rights are important factors.

> Marion's case has made it harder for children who are severely disabled to get the sterilisation. I think it's made it a lot harder for the families. I just think that it's the children who are going to suffer as a consequence, and it's all very well for the guardianship board to make these decisions, but then they go back to Hobart or wherever and they just get on with their lives. We have to pick up the pieces ... Marion's case has removed the rights of parents. I really be-

lieve that the parents just have no say. We have no rights; we have to look after the child. If we feel that something like this would make the child's life better, we're just ignored and from the hearing I think a lot of our responses were just rubbished and there was no respect for the parents, no respect for the family, no respect for the child whatsoever [22].

Ferris maintains that seeking sterilisation was a measured decision after considering numerous alternatives. She points out that she consulted seven or eight specialists, tried drugs and reviewed an IUD. She considers herself well-informed, well-intentioned and well-placed to make the best decision. The legal denial of her case is, as far as she is concerned, the wrong decision.

An academic article

Unsurprisingly, the legalities of this debate have received commentary in a number of academic articles [23]. In contrast to debating the legalities, Brady's article "Invasive & Irreversible: the sterilisation of intellectually disabled children" argues that any case that comes to court is a failure. Susan Brady is an advocate in "a rights-based statutory authority representing the interests of people with disabilities". She has strong reservations about the ethics of sterilisation and echoes Vicary's concern that parents who seek it are insufficiently informed of alternatives, citing a specific case of 'Annie' as an example. Annie's father "expressed extreme anger about what he perceived to be legal intervention in matters which in his view rightly belonged to the parents." However, after "advice and information on alternative and less invasive options to sterilisation ... The family decided not to proceed with the application for sterilisation" [24].

Brady counters the arguments that sterilisation would make menstruation more manageable and provide protection against the dangers of pregnancy.

> It is true that hysterectomy will solve the problem of menstrual management for care givers. The child will no longer bleed for five days a month. However, she will continue to urinate and defecate each day for the rest of her life. This is a greater nursing management problem....

> There is no data to suggest that pregnancy is a significant risk in this population ... the numbers of unwanted pregnancies (or pregnancies) in this population seem statistically insignificant. This ought to raise a cautionary note when thinking about authorising sterilisation on the basis of risk of pregnancy. This response is a matter of fear not fact. It may be camouflaged eugenics [25].

Brady sees this as a community issue that is wider than a matter of individual or parental responsibility:

> ... it takes little intellectual rigour to accommodate a justification for the sterilisation of children if you are predisposed to placing an overriding emphasis on parental burden which is, in reality, a consequence of scarce public resources and concomitant lack of service options. This reality reflects a socioeconomic problem, not a medical problem and not a legal problem. Invasive surgical interventions need to be called for what they are and what they are not. If the Court's responsiveness to scarce public resources is authorisation

of invasive and irreversible surgical intervention then it should be called that rather than 'best interests' and 'last resort' findings for the child at issue [26].

A policy paper

A policy paper by an association of women with disabilities (WWDA) is firmly opposed to the sterilisation of disabled girls. The WWDA:

> strongly recommends that sterilisation be prohibited in the absence of the informed consent of the individual concerned, except in those circumstances where there is a serious threat to health or life...

> asserts that forced sterilisation is an act of unnecessary and dehumanising violence which denies a woman's basic human right to bodily integrity and to bear children and which results in adverse life-long physical and mental health effects. Sterilisation of disabled women and girls is a form of social control in which a woman's right to bodily integrity is denied often at the behest of parents and medical or other professionals, who deem this bodily violation 'in her best interests'. Sterilisation, an irreversible medical procedure with lifelong physical, psychological and social consequences, if performed without consent, is a gross violation of human rights...

> is of the view that sterilisation is a question for adulthood not childhood.

The policy paper's definition of forced sterilisation is:

> The term sterilisation refers to surgical intervention resulting either directly or indirectly in the termination of an individual's capacity to reproduce. Forced sterilisation refers to the performance of a procedure which results in sterilisation in the absence of the consent of the individual who undergoes the procedure [27].

The paper argues that although courts and disability professionals may claim that sterilisation is in the best interests of the disabled girls, in reality, the motives are either eugenic or to relieve the state of the welfare burden presented by disabled people and their offspring.

Ethical analysis

In this debate, the emphasis on two concerns is striking. One is the frequent reference to eugenics. The other is the focus on rights, with a lesser regard to the other ethical considerations.

Eugenics

As Nicholson pointed out above, eugenics is associated with Nazism, which condoned the sterilisation and even extermination of intellectually disabled people on the grounds that this would improve 'racial purity' and benefit the human species [28].

This idea is ethically abhorrent on a number of grounds. It would be nice to say that it is clearly incompatible with all three of the approaches – communitarianism, consequences and principles, but sadly, only the last two apply unreservedly. There has been some community support for eugenics both historically and even in some contemporary societies. For example, a proposal for the sterilisation of the "mentally unstable" has been put to the Rwandan parliament recently. This is despite the fact that Rwanda is a signatory to the United Nations Convention on the Rights of Persons with Disabilities [29]. There is a flaw in the community-based approach to ethics, which is the potential for the idea of 'the good of the community' to be used to oppress the individual. Eugenics is a striking example of this. Of course, a community based approach can, in contrast, promote the idea that the entire point of having a community is to benefit the individuals that make it up. Which of these perspectives is dominant – the social good or the individual good - varies from culture to culture and from time to time. Nicholson, Brady and Vicary remind us of that, and work against the possibility of eugenics gaining a foothold in contemporary culture.

The consequences-based approach provides a stronger argument against eugenics. It is true that the utilitarian notion of the greatest good for the greatest number can be (and has been) used by the eugenics movement as a justification [30]. This justification fails on two grounds. Firstly the consequences-based response is that we should count the benefits for actual individual people, not abstracts such as society. Only real people have real interests. Sterilising people against their will is a damaging assault on actual persons. Secondly, there is no clear good that results from eugenics. The 'purity of the race' does not fall into the category of 'good' because it does not relate to people's experiences of pleasure over pain, or welfare, or satisfying lives. Nor is it justified by preference utilitarianism (as discussed in chapter three) because it is not the preferred outcome of the people who experience compulsory sterilisation. The argument that eugenics is justified on economic grounds has similar flaws. Economic arrangements should serve the interests of the people in the community. "Good for the economy" is not a viable claim in consequence based ethics. Admittedly, the consequences-based approach struggles with problems concerning the distribution of costs and benefits. It is true that economically unproductive people in a community represent a material cost to those members of the community who are economically productive, and it is true that occasionally an extreme view is advanced that the economically productive are justified in shrugging off these burdens by constructing a society composed entirely of themselves [31]. A consequences-based response would be that it is unlikely that such a society would be a desirable outcome. Furthermore, the benefits of social arrangements should accrue to everyone affected by them. The distribution problem can be met by starting with the least advantaged.

If the consequences approach argues strongly against eugenics, the principles-based approach is even stronger. Clearly, compulsory sterilisation does not respect persons or their rights. It does not promote their self-determination. It does not enhance their ability to exercise their capabilities.

Compulsory sterilisation to advance the ideology of eugenics is clearly unethical. Some proponents of eugenics do not favour compulsory sterilisation, recommending voluntary means of advancing their agenda [32]. These arguments need not be dealt with here, since it is the issue of sterilisation that is being examined, though it should be mentioned in passing that 'voluntary eugenics' remains abhorrent.

The family and the state

While the aversion to eugenics expressed by Judge Nicholson, legal adviser Brady, and disability advocate Vicary is ethically laudable, it is misplaced in this debate.

The issue under debate is whether the parents of intellectually disabled girls should be able to seek sterilisation for their daughters. The emphasis on eugenics is misplaced for two reasons. Firstly, none of the commentators assert that this is the motive of the actual parents who are seeking sterilisation for their intellectually disabled children. Indeed, some commentators go out of their way to acknowledge the good intentions of the parents. Nor is the accusation made against any other particular current persons, only historical organizations. Secondly, the parents are not in a position to promote eugenics. That is, they have not chosen to join a social movement because they espouse its ideology. Rather, they have found themselves, by chance, dealing with a particular dilemma confronting their own families. They are not seeking access to the wider population or promoting genetic outcomes for the human species. Their only concern, and only responsibilities, pertain to their own children. To be effective, eugenics needs to be a movement that is espoused by a significant number of adherents, with the support of the state or state institutions.

In the first section of this chapter, I described four significant features that are needed to characterise a public policy as an ethical issue.
- It is ethical, that is, it relates to the ethical theories discussed in this book, particularly the dominant theories that drive the communitarian approach, the consequences approach and the principles approach. An ethical policy is one which impacts on people's wishes or welfare, with consequent questions about the distribution of power or resources.
- Some significant number of people in the community cares about the issue and the outcomes of the policy.
- Some significant number disagrees with each other in beliefs or attitudes about what should be done.
- There is no obvious and agreed method of resolving these differences.

Eugenics is clearly not an ethically controversial public policy on these grounds. While it can be criticised within the realm of ethical theory, it is not a policy and it is not a current controversy over which significant numbers of people disagree, at least not in the community of people in the jurisdiction of the Marion case.

It is odd that Justice Nicholson suggests that eugenics in Nazi Germany provides the state with any justification for the intervention in a family's decisions [20].. After all, historically it was the state that was guilty of eugenics and the family its victims. The current debate about sterilisation is radically different. The question at issue is whether it is justifiable for parents to arrange for the sterilisation of their daughter who has an intellectual disability. Eugenics does not appear to be relevant in this debate, no argument has been advanced that the parents are motivated by it, and on the contrary, their best intentions are recognised.

The consideration of rights in the sterilisation debate

The arguments about rights in this debate are better founded, though problematic. The emphasis has been on the rights of the child involved. The assertions by the parents that they, too, have rights have been dismissed. That the rights of the child are primary is taken for granted by the Family Court judge who no doubt has legal reasons for doing so. Neither he nor other commentators and advocates, though, offer ethical justification for this primacy.

In chapter two on a community-based approach to ethics, I argued that a disability professional has relationships with, and therefore obligations to a number of people in a community but the client should be prioritised. The needs of the client come first, the needs of the client are the reason for having a profession in the first place, and the needs of the client drive the professional-client relationship.

A Family Court judge is not a disability professional, though a number of disability professionals were called to present expert opinion. They included paediatricians, gynaecologists, psychologists, a neurologist, a psychiatrist, the principal of the child's special school, and a representative of the Human Rights and Equal Opportunity Commission. In the light of their roles, they had particular obligations to the girl with intellectual disabilities whose case was being considered. In contrast, the title 'Family Court Judge' appears to indicate a responsibility to the entire family, rather than the children. Of course, children are more vulnerable than adults and so treatment of them requires special care. Still, vulnerability does not guide ethical decisions because it does not provide criteria in the same way that consequences and principles do. From a community-based approach, though, it is an important part of the Family Court's traditions, culture and precedents that the needs of the children before it come first. As quoted above, the judgement in this case included the reasoning that:

> Without wishing to diminish the validity of these concerns on the part of the parents, it must be remembered that these are proceedings where the welfare of the child is paramount. As I said in *In re Jane* (supra) at page 77,253, the decision cannot be made to suit the convenience of caregivers, however valid their concerns may be [10].

It could be argued that the rights and needs of the child should be balanced against the rights and needs of the parents, rather than insisting that the child's welfare is paramount. This argument has a fundamental problem in that it lacks a method for measuring rights that are in conflict with other rights, so I will leave it to one side and continue to consider arguments about the rights of the child.

The right of consent to medical treatment is taken for granted generally, and if the wishes of the person concerned can be ascertained, that is good grounds for settling the matter and resolving any debate. Certainly a rights-based approach rules out sterilising people against their expressed refusal. It would also rule out sterilising children who are currently too young to express informed consent or refusal, but who will be able to decide for themselves when they reach adulthood.

But in the issue under consideration, the daughter's disability precludes her from giving or refusing consent. It is important to realize that this should not be simply assumed in real cases. Judgement of the daughter's competency to grant or refuse consent must be made in the light of her competencies in other areas of her life, and over time [33]. Does she understand other choices? Are her competencies and understanding growing as she continues to develop?

If she is not and will not be competent to provide consent, how should the idea of the right of consent be applied? The Marion judge said:

> ... children, like other persons, are entitled to be free of non-consensual invasions of their physical integrity [11].

It might be argued then, that without consent, sterilisation is unjustifiable. However, this does not logically follow. We are considering a case where the wishes of the person, one way or the other, cannot be ascertained. After all, another competent individual might consider she will benefit if she seeks sterilisation for herself, and so has good reason to do so. To deny those benefits to someone on the grounds of their disability is discriminatory.

If people generally can access services, then people with disabilities should have the right to access those services and it is, *prima facie*, a denial of their rights to refuse them the services. People generally decide for themselves what services they want and need. If they cannot decide for themselves because of intellectual impairment, then someone else needs to decide for them. Whether that decision is made by the parents or the court, there should be good reasons for the decision. Arguments for and against should be considered and weighed. Refusal of services to disabled people is not justifiable by default, or by an inability to express either consent or refusal.

Still, sterilisation is a highly charged issue with significant impact on the person involved. It is hardly an issue that one can be neutral about. Discussing sterilisation, the Marion judgement refers to invasions of physical integrity. Similarly the legal commentator Brady describes sterilisation as invasive and irreversible. These terms could be seen as neutral ones, with 'invasive' being used in the medical sense of 'surgical' and irreversible as a statement of medical fact. However, Brady is not using the terms in a medical context, but in a polemical one. As with 'invasive', the term 'irreversible' tells more about the attitude of its user than it does of the medical procedure.

The position of Ferris, who is a parent, is that the contraceptive pill is more invasive than surgery, being a daily long-term chemical intervention with side effects [22]. How Ferris' view of physical integrity might differ from that of the Marion judge cannot be ascertained, because neither the judge, nor Brady, define or defend it. To an ethicist's eyes, there is a yawning fact/value gap here. That a particular set of circumstances naturally exists does not, in itself, provide reasons for or against intervening to change them. Some justification of an ethical nature is required. Although 'invasive' and 'integrity' sound like matters of principle, as offered in this debate they appear to be no more than unsubstantiated attitudes held by some persons and denied by others.

The Capabilities approach mentions bodily integrity as well.

> 3. ***Bodily Integrity***. Being able to move freely from place to place; to be secure against violent assault, including sexual assault and domestic violence; having opportunities for sexual satisfaction and for choice in matters of reproduction [34].

A key word here is 'choice'. Whether the sterilisation of an intellectually disabled girl would enhance or diminish her capabilities will depend upon the individual characteristics and circumstances of the particular girl. This requires a consideration of consequences, rather than rights.

A Consideration of Consequences

The loss of an organ and of reproductive capability is, on the face of it, a bad consequence. On the other hand, the ability to control their own reproductive processes is seen by many women as resulting in good consequences. Contraception through one means or another is common. Some women use the chemical means of the contraceptive pill and some use permanent surgical sterilisation. There does not appear to be any objective argument in favour of one means over another. Opinions and preferences vary.

In the case of girls with significant intellectual disability, it is not possible to ascertain what their preferences are (or even that they have any preferences). Consequences have to be calculated on the basis of the pain or pleasure, happiness or distress that the girls are exhibiting. If we are to take the welfare of the girls as paramount, then we need to have some notion of what we mean by welfare. A basic consequences approach defines welfare as good results, and defines good results in terms of the actual experiences of actual people. A decision on whether or not to sterilize should be made on the basis of whether the decision will result in a life that has more happiness, more pleasure and more comfort as apposed to more distress or more pain. Since these decisions must be made about real people in actual circumstances, they need to be made on a case by case basis.

Clearly, decisions to sterilize on medical grounds are using a consequence-based approach as a justification. But a blanket decision that in all cases, medical grounds are the only justification is not justified by a consequences approach to ethics. Allowing medical consequences to be calculated, but excluding all other considerations, is arbitrary. Women who can calculate consequences for themselves have a variety of preferences and make a variety of decisions. Intellectually disabled girls who cannot calculate consequences for themselves have to have the decisions made for them, but should have access to the same variety of means and be able to access the best life experiences with their substitute decision-makers taking everything into account.

Conclusion

Forcible sterilisation is severely unethical on a number of grounds. It shows a serious lack of respect for persons. It compromises their self-determination and violates their rights. It diminishes their capabilities and may result in life-long distress due to loss of fertility and damage to self-esteem. Sterilisation of children can have permanently damaging medical side effects. Because children are vulnerable (and disabled children are doubly vulnerable), professionals, courts and the community have special obligations to protect them until they are adult and able to make their own decisions.

Eugenics is an abhorrent ideology that attempts to justify sterilisation to preserve the 'purity of the race' or to relieve society of welfare burdens. In ethical terms, there is no such thing as the purity of the race and only individual people have interests, not races or societies.

These are powerful ethical arguments when 'forced sterilisation' is taken to mean sterilising people against their wishes. The ethical issues are not so clear when it cannot be ascertained what the wishes of the person concerned actually are or even if they have any wishes. The issue of parents considering sterilisation for an intellectually disabled daughter is significantly different from eugenics and state-imposed forcible sterilisation.

It is unfortunate that various commentators and policy makers have expanded the notion of 'forced sterilisation' and 'without consent'. These terms should be confined to situations where the sterilisation is against the wishes of the person concerned. They should not be applied in circumstances where the wishes of the person cannot be ascertained. Nor should they apply when the person concerned does not have the capacity to even form any preferences. Where there is the possibility that the girls concerned will develop into competent adults, the decision should be postponed. But where the person concerned has a severe intellectual disability, so that they do not and cannot have any preferences, their consent is not an issue. Other considerations should be used to decide the matter.

The commentators and policy makers cited in this chapter appear to be influenced by their attitudes towards sterilisation, which are intuitive rather than proposed, explained and argued. People do, of course, have intuitive positions with regard to fertility, gender and personhood, but intuitions are by no means uniform. They vary considerably from person to person (even in the small sample of people quoted in this chapter). Some people intuitively favour natural processes and decry intervention unless the organs and systems are diseased. Some people find that technological intervention, for example the contraceptive pill, a welcome liberation from the tyranny of natural processes and essential to their personal flourishing. Some believe surgical intervention preferable to the toxin of the pill. Because these attitudes are intuitive, they have not been justified by argument (and possibly could not be so justified). It is not ethical for people with an intuition to impose their intuition, without reflection or negotiation, on other people who have a different intuition.

On one hand, we have the position that intellectually disabled girls should not have their bodies violated by invasive surgery without their consent. To do so constitutes a denial of their rights, a disrespect for them as persons, a discrimination against them on the grounds of their disability, a promotion of abhorrent eugenics and economic expediency. On the other hand, we have the position that denying sterilisation to intellectually disabled girls is discriminating against them on the grounds of their disability, denying them access to services that are available to everyone else, condemning them and their families to unnecessary and avoidable distress and imposing on them unjustified intuitive ideology.

The legal permission for sterilisation on medical grounds but for not other reasons appears to be an arbitrary decision which does not satisfy either side of the debate.

The prime consideration should be the welfare of the girls concerned, that is, the quality of their actual lived experiences. The welfare of their families is also a valid consideration. Big-picture issues such as promoting respect for disabled people and denying eugenics are also important. The rights and welfare of disabled girls and their well-intentioned parents should not be lost in the big-picture debate.

Chapter 9
The Ethics of Identity

We are all disabled. We cannot see well at night time. In order to overcome this impairment, we rely on complicated and cumbersome artificial aids. We attach headlights to our cars. These do not work very well, for in order for them to be bright enough to illuminate our path, they dazzle others coming towards us. So we erect a complicated system of reflective markers and street lights. We also light our homes with lamps that require reliable electric power, with all the generating and transmission infrastructure necessary to supply it. If we leave the vicinity of the infrastructure, perhaps to go on a camping holiday in the wilderness, we find we simply cannot function very well at night, and most of our activities are restricted to the daylight hours. We may notice, though, that our vision impairment is not shared by other creatures such as owls and foxes.

'Disabled people' or 'people with disabilities'

Of course, we do not all think of ourselves as impaired because we cannot see well at night, or identify ourselves as disabled on these grounds. Furthermore, it would be insensitive and offensive for me to claim a rapport with some one who was congenitally blind on the grounds that I had the ordinary limitations of human vision.

If we described everybody as disabled because we all see poorly at night, we would rob the word *disabled* of any meaning. In order for terms such as disabled, disability and impairment to mean anything at all, they have to include the notion of abnormal. Abnormal has negative connotations. If we are to be ethical, we should counter connotations which are negative, disrespectful and harmful. We need to be respectful of others, but at the same time, we need to be realistic.

There are some negative associations with being short, but it would not make sense to attempt to overcome them by describing everybody as tall. Not only would it be untrue, it would work against designing things so that they were useful to people of varying heights. Somehow, we need to find a way of describing disabled persons in terms which do not label, stereotype or denigrate, which do not encourage an 'us versus them' mindset, which avoid the negative connotations of abnormal, which promote inclusion over exclusion, and yet which are sympathetic and responsive to particular needs. This is quite a challenge, and indeed may be impossible to meet.

Some terms are clearly intended to be demeaning and we should discourage their use, both because of their intention and because of their effect. But assuming we have good intentions, should we say *disabled people*, or *people with disabilities* or *people with impairment* or even *differently abled*?

Ethics is about how people should treat each other. That obviously includes how we speak to each other. This book is a discussion about how disabled people should be treated. Such a discussion is impossible without an agreed way of referring to them. It would be vacuous to say, "Everybody should treat everybody else equally and properly without regard to their circumstances or conditions". People are not identical and should therefore not be treated identically. It would not be fair, just or sensible to supply all poverty-stricken children with the same size shoes, no matter the size of their feet. People are different, and to be fair, should be treated differently [1]. Disabilities are amongst the range of differences found in a variety of people.

There is an implicit error here which we should take care to avoid. To say that this book is a discussion about how disabled people should be treated does not imply that we are discussing how *disabled* people should be dealt with by *non*-disabled people. It should not be assumed that we are already in an 'us and them' situation. Professional providers, policy makers and government advisers may themselves be people with disabilities, or they may not. They have ethical obligations and face challenging decisions either way. (As it happens, Jeremy Bentham, the philosopher who proposed the ethical theory of Utilitarianism, is believed by some analysts to have had Asperger's syndrome [2].) People who currently are not disabled may acquire disabilities in the future. People with disabilities are not merely passive recipients of other people's ethical actions. They have ethical obligations, to other disabled people and to everyone else in the community, as does everybody.

There are not two fixed classes of people, (i) disabled and (ii), not disabled. Somebody with a disability is not entirely disabled. Such a person will have normal abilities in other areas. As it happens, some disabled people have extraordinary abilities in other areas. Others are, dare it be said, mostly normal. A woman in a wheelchair might be an extremely competent mathematician. Or she may have very ordinary mathematical abilities. A man who to all appearances is ordinary and without physical disabilities may have learning difficulties such that mathematics is beyond him. Furthermore, people change over time. Any person can acquire a disability through accident or illness. Actually, it is a safe bet that everybody will acquire a disability through age if they live long enough. Again, acquired disabilities are not uniform, nor do they affect all functions. Somebody who is disabled in one respect is not in another.

Furthermore, it is worth repeating that even when considering disability issues in particular, ethics is about how people should treat each other. It is not about how 'normal' people should treat 'disabled' people. The two groups are not fixed and distinct, and even if they were, all people, their responsibilities as well as their welfare and rights, are the subject matter of ethics.

It is true that most professional providers of disability services are not themselves disabled. That is, statistically at least, likely. It could be argued that professionals would be better equipped if they did have first hand knowledge of the disabilities their clients experienced. This is, though, not a practical requirement. We can sympathize with the students of a college for the Deaf who demanded that the Board of Trustees of Gallaudet University appoint a Deaf President and we can understand how the politics of discrimination are entangled with judgement about professional expertise [3]. However, it is usually the case that professionals do not themselves require the sorts of services that they offer to their clients. The world might be a better place if doctors were frequently patients themselves and experienced being pushed around by an impersonal medical system, or if teachers remembered vividly what it was like to be a school child. Ethics does not rely solely upon sympathy, however. Deciding how people should treat each other, including people with disabilities, is everyone's responsibility and a matter for rational debate, as well as empathy and goodwill.

So to return to the question, what are the relative merits, if any, of the various terms such as *disabled* or *people with disabilities* or *people with impairments* and so on?

The medical model

Originally, people were categorized according to a medical description of their disability, and indeed, still are. The World Health Organization has an International Classification of Functioning, Disability and Health (ICF) and a similar classification of diseases in which it lists classifications that include, for example, Spina Bifida and Autism [4]. There are similarly-named community groups such as the Quadriplegic Association and the Cerebral Palsy Association. There are medical research journals that focus on diagnosis and treatment of particular disabilities, such as *Epilepsy* [5]. From an ethical point of view, there are advantages to the medical model. A diagnosis of a condition relies on objective observations, rather than making judgments, demeaning or otherwise, about the person. It is also solution-oriented, which suits a consequences-based approach. It is useful when applying the other two dominant ethical theories as well. It facilitates a communitarian recognition of a universal right to medical treatment. On the face of it, using a medical model to categorize disabilities allows us to be precise and pragmatic, to identify and respond to people's needs, and to do so in a way which, while not necessarily being sensitive and respectful, at least is not demeaning or disrespectful.

The medical model does have flaws, though. Its language is not always precise and not always respectful. The WHO International Classification includes the term 'feebleminded', for example. The medical model sometimes allows for some insensitive terms such as the "Home for Incurables" [6]. Having an institution called "The Home for Incurables" is a striking example of a pervasive flaw in the medical model. It implies that the correct response to disability is to identify what is wrong with the person and to cure that condition. By attempting to cure and thus normalize persons in this way, the community need not make any adaptions to accommodate their differences. If a cure is not available, that is regrettable, and the only remaining recourse is to remove them from the community and put them away in a home.

Understandably, this 'cure or forget' approach raises ire in the community of disabled people. Recognizing individual differences and structuring society accordingly is surely a better alternative than 'normalize or abandon'. One cannot help but applaud the Autism community's rejection of normalization when they use the term 'neurotypical' to refer to people who are not autistic.

> Neurotypical includes, among the many voices of autistics, those who take exception to the notion of being "cured" and those who offer, through their very lives, a view of what a fulfilling life might look like. Neurotypical does not attempt to diagnose, change or find a cure for autism. Instead, it looks at the culture of autism, as a valid and unique way of being [7].

The social model

An alternative to the medical model is the social model. The social model shifts attention from a medical description of the individual person to a consideration of how the environment creates obstacles for people who have disabilities. It is society's arrangements, social, physical and political, that need to be fixed, rather than the person with the disability.

> The benefits of the social model approach are that it shifts attention from individuals and their physical or mental deficits to the ways in which society includes or excludes them. The social model is social constructionist, or, as Michael Oliver (1990) prefers, social creationist, rather than reductionist or biologically determinist. Rather than essentialising disability, it signals that the experience of disabled people is dependent on social context, and differs in different cultures and at different times. Rather than disability being inescap-

able, it becomes a product of social arrangements, and can thus be reduced or possibly even eliminated [8].

The social model features a 'political commitment to improving the lives of disabled people, by promoting social inclusion and removing the barriers which oppress disabled people' [9]. The Union of Physically Impaired Against Segregation (UPIAS) has a policy statement which highlights barriers that effectively oppress their members.

> We find ourselves isolated and excluded by such things as flights of steps, inadequate public and personal transport, unsuitable housing, rigid work routines in factories and offices, and a lack of up-to-date aids and equipment....
> In our view, it is society which disables physically impaired people [10].

The Union of Physically Impaired Against Segregation strongly asserts an ethical claim with a community based approach when it states its position that society has a duty to make provision for disabled people.

> It is not individual limitations, of whatever kind, which are the causes of the problem, but society's failure to provide appropriate services and adequately ensure the needs of disabled people are fully taken into account in its social organization [11].

There are persuasive arguments for considering disability as a relationship between the environment and the characteristics of the individual.

> 1. A disability is a mismatch between the individual and the environment. This occurs both because of individual differences and because the environment is not adapted to accommodate the range of people. A deaf person is thus not disabled in a setting where everyone speaks sign language.
>
> 2. A disability is also situational. A person with a visual impairment is not disabled when using the telephone. Whether a specific individual limitation becomes disabling or not is linked to concrete situations.
>
> 3. A disability is relative, a continuum rather than a dichotomy. The cut-off point in impairment based disability definitions is to some extent arbitrary [12].

The social model has had a significant impact on how disability issues are discussed and described. Since its rise to a dominant position, much of the language used has changed. The 'Home for Incurables' mentioned above is now called 'Julia Farr Services'. The name of the *American Journal on Mental Retardation* has fallen from favour and has been changed to the *American Journal on Intellectual and Developmental Disabilities* [13].

The World Health Organization's International Classification of Functioning, Disability and Health (ICF) is influenced by the medical model, as quoted earlier, but it recently recognized the importance of social factors.

> The International Classification of Functioning, Disability and Health, known more commonly as ICF, is a classification of health and health-related domains. These domains are classified from body, individual and societal perspectives by means of two lists: a list of body functions and structure, and a list of domains of activity and participation. Since an individual's functioning and disability occurs in a context, the ICF also includes a list of environmental factors.

The ICF is WHO's framework for measuring health and disability at both individual and population levels. The ICF was officially endorsed by all 191 WHO Member States in the Fifty-fourth World Health Assembly on 22 May 2001 (resolution WHA 54.21). Unlike its predecessor, which was endorsed for field trail purposes only, the ICF was endorsed for use in Member States as the international standard to describe and measure health and disability.

The ICF puts the notions of 'health' and 'disability' in a new light. It acknowledges that every human being can experience a decrement in health and thereby experience some degree of disability. Disability is not something that only happens to a minority of humanity. The ICF thus 'mainstreams' the experience of disability and recognises it as a universal human experience. By shifting the focus from cause to impact it places all health conditions on an equal footing allowing them to be compared using a common metric – the ruler of health and disability. Furthermore ICF takes into account the social aspects of disability and does not see disability only as a 'medical' or 'biological' dysfunction. By including Contextual Factors, in which environmental factors are listed ICF allows to records the impact of the environment on the person's functioning [4].

The difficulty with this ICF statement, and with radical versions of the social model, is the same difficulty that was illustrated at the beginning of this chapter. We all experience some social and physical barriers in our lives. But we cannot, by definition, all be disabled. If the 'ICF thus 'mainstreams' the experience of disability and recognises it as a universal human experience' then it too, robs the term 'disability' of its meaning and works against a proper consideration of any particular needs a disabled person might have.

Impairment

If we are going to define disability as something that happens in the social arena, we still need a term that refers to an individual's characteristic such that they experience a disability. *Impairment* is one suggested term. To illustrate the difference between the concepts of disability and impairment, there is a fable of a village in which all the inhabitants are in wheelchairs [14].

> Everything is adapted to the villagers' needs and consequently they are not disadvantaged. In other words, they are people with impairments but not disabled people. When able bodied people visit the village, they experience physical and psychological difficulties [15].

H.G. Wells wrote a similar fable about a secluded valley where everyone is blind. A sighted person through misadventure falls into the valley. He is convinced of the adage "In the country of the blind the one-eyed man is king". He discovers, to the contrary, that he must adapt to their social arrangements and beliefs in order to survive [16].

So by this argument *impairment* is a characteristic of the individual, but a person is *disabled* by society, not by impairment. Besides the fictional illustrations quoted above, there are real and serious implications of this conceptualisation. A person with a cognitive disability is far more likely to be homeless, be unemployed or even be in prison than the general population [17].

The differentiation of impairment (the bodily experience) and disability (the social experience which ensues from having a bodily, sensory, cognitive or psychic constitution which deviates from so called 'normal') is one of the central debates exercising thinkers in contemporary disability studies... Someone may experience a severe impairment (e.g. mental illness such as schizophrenia) but not experience it as severely disabling due to a range of factors such as having the social and financial support of their family, while another person may have what might be diagnostically only a mild impairment but experience extremely disabling consequences, again due to a range of factors such as experiencing poverty and abuse. Clearly a critical intervening factor in this relationship is 'community supports' which alleviate or attenuate the impact of impairment [18].

Separating *disability* from *impairment* appears to be a neat and useful distinction. Nonetheless, the debate continues, with some thinkers pointing to difficulties in disentangling disability and impairment, and differentiating between personal limitations and environmental barriers.

Sally French is a person with visual impairment, who discusses these interactions in *Disabling Barriers, Enabling Environments*[19]. She points out that visual impairment results in a difficulty with recognising people or reading their non-verbal clues when interacting with them. It is difficult to see how, in practice, any amount of change to the social or technical environment could remove this problem.

In contrast, there is the view of Rebecca Atkinson, who describes the process of going blind as neither a disability nor an impairment.

It is a unique perspective. It is a grand experiment that most don't get to try. . . The loss is so gradual that as one sense dies others grow. Suddenly you can smell the world and sense when someone is standing out of your line of vision. Your brain grows on the inside and things on the outside start to matter less [20].

For both French and Atkinson, the loss of sight affects their lives in a way that cannot be attributed solely to socially constructed obstacles. Shakespeare points out that there are barriers in the natural environment, not just the social.

Wheelchair users are disabled by sandy beaches and rocky mountains. People with visual impairments may be unable to see a sunset, and people with hearing impairments will miss out on the sounds of birds, wind and waves. It is hard to blame the natural environment on social arrangements [21].

Shakespeare rejects the social model as inadequate, arguing that disability is both a social and an individual phenomenon.

So how should we define disability? Is it an individual's physical or mental limitation? Is it a failure of society to accommodate individual differences? Is it best understood as occurring in the individual *and* social arrangements? Is it a *relationship* between individual limitations and social arrangements? Does it occur at the *intersection* of society and the individual? Are all these conceptualisations valid and compatible with each other?

These are tricky questions, both philosophically and in practical application. Perhaps we should set them aside temporarily and consider the earlier and apparently simpler question. Should we use the term *disabled people* or *people with disabilities* or *people with impairments*?

Prioritising the person

We might be worried that saying *disabled person* prioritises the disability rather than the person. Any one person has a wide variety of characteristics. He or she might be male or female, a parent, a spouse, an artist or student, a volunteer, an executive, a professional ... the list is endless. A person's identity is made up of some combination of all the characteristics a person has. What is important is that this is a *person*.

So should we in preference say *a person with disabilities*? This does not sit well with the social model. It locates disability in the person, rather than in social arrangements. It implies that if we are going to alleviate disability, we should remove it from the person, rather than remove social barriers. If we say *disabled person* we can at least assert that the person has been disabled by society. If we say *person with disabilities* we are perhaps demanding acknowledgement and respect for the person, over and above the presence of a disability, but we are at the same time locating the disability in the person, and letting society off the hook.

There is a problem with using *disabled person* to imply *disabled-by-society person*. There are other socially constructed barriers to people's full participation in a satisfying, meaningful and comfortable life. Poverty is an obvious example of a condition that can be relieved or exacerbated by social arrangements. We do not want to include *disabled-by-poverty* in our definition of disability (even with the realisation that there are often strong causal links between poverty and disability). When we use the social model to say *disabled people* we want to mean people who confront difficulties caused by society's failure to accommodate the differences in their physical or mental capacities. In order to make any sense at all, we have to include reference to their limitations or impairments. This is the case, even if we say that the disabling impact comes not from the impairment but from society's failure to accommodate it.

So perhaps we should say *people with impairments*. Such a strategy, however, does nothing to resolve the issue. We still have the same conundrum concerning the relative merits of *disabled people* versus *people with disabilities/impairments*.

Let us return to the concern that *disabled person* draws attention to the disability rather than the person. This is not really a convincing argument. The fact is that in the English language, adjectives come before the noun. In a kitchen I might refer to a 'white plate'. In the wilderness, I might refer to a 'steep hill'. By saying 'steep hill' I do not draw attention to its gradient to the detriment of it being a hill. I do not deny that it is a hill, or that it has other characteristics. I say nothing about whether it is wooded or bare, rugged or pastoral, solitary or in a range. By saying 'white plate' I do not deny that in other lighting environments it may take on a different hue and appear, say, yellow. The grammatical construction *disabled person* does not draw attention towards *disability* and away from *person*.

While we are discussing grammatical constructions, it is worth noting that *person* with disability is clumsier than *disabled person*. It makes lucid discussion that much more difficult and demands an extra effort. In some circumstances, demanding an extra effort may be a good thing. It can challenge stereotyping and pressure people into examining their assumptions and prejudices. The danger is that otherwise well-meaning people will be alienated if they perceive language being tortured for the sake of unnecessary and belligerent political correctness.

An unsympathetic public may also blame political correctness for apparently pointless changes in the language used to describe specific disabilities. It is unfortunately true that some descriptors acquire negative connotations, especially when used by insensitive or malicious people. If shouting 'Retard!' at someone is a common juvenile insult, there are good reason to change the term *mental retardation* to *learning difficulties*. At the very least, shouting 'Retard!' is unlikely to be replaced with shouting 'You are a person with learning difficulties'. Despite this, there will always be some malicious and intolerant people who will consider any descriptor of disability an insult. Constantly changing the language in order to shake off demeaning associations would be a never-ending and ultimately futile task. Nonetheless, there are people who seem to be eternally dedicated to that project.

Positive badging

Actually, the main problem with stereotyping and labelling is not really narrow categorization, but the negative associations. The claim that *disabled person* substitutes a stereotype of disability for a recognition of individual personhood looks very dubious when compared with the term 'clever person' or 'generous person' or any other positive trait. If you refer to someone as a 'clever person', you are unlikely to be rebuked for unjustified stereotyping or depersonalised labelling. (Admittedly there is the phenomenon of the 'impostor syndrome'. Some clever people do not like to be called clever. Some do not consider themselves clever and are worried that they will be discovered to be 'ordinary' and consequently rejected [22]. The problem here though is a perceived misapplication of the label, rather than the stereotyping itself.) One counter to negative labelling is positive badging. As mentioned earlier, some people with Autism assert that they are members of a community that contains many an 'eccentric genius with remarkable abilities that defy explanation' and that non- autistic people are merely 'neurotypical' [7]. This is an example of claiming a positive badge rather than accepting a negative label.

Identifying with a community can have personal and political benefits [23]. It allows for political organization and activism that can learn from other liberation movements based on gender or race. It can help personal self-esteem and provide for cultural interactions similar to the membership of an ethnic group.

To what extent a disability community can be compared to an ethnic group is debatable. Some ethnic groups have physical characteristics that serve to identify them. Some ethnic groups are marginalized, and some develop strong bonds and shared values in response to the marginalisation. Against this, members of an ethnic group typically have a shared language, a common ancestry and a resulting set of traditions and values. Disabled people do not have this common ground. The Deaf community, though, claims a common language.

Being a member of an ethnic group or a comparable disability community can have disadvantages. Individual disabled people may wish to emphasize their identity as normal rather than giving much weight to an impairment as a significant feature of identity. They may be concerned about a tendency for an ethnic or disability community to foster a victim culture. They may be concerned that identifying as a member of a minority group may count against them being identified as a member of the majority group.

These concerns are real. They are reported in a paper aptly entitled "Well I know this is going to seem very strange to you, but I don't see myself as a disabled person: identity and disability". The title is a quotation from a disabled woman who was interviewed for the purpose of a study into disability and identity. Fourteen disabled men and fourteen disabled women were interviewed. Only three of them made disability a significant part of their self-identity. Certainly disability, and concomitant social disadvantages, were part of their daily lives, but typically, the participants of the study thought of themselves as 'normal'. Some comments from them illustrate this clearly (pseudonyms used) [24]. When asked how he thought of himself, Arnie said:

> A normal person. The only difference is that I'm in a wheelchair, and I try not to think of that as a difference.

Archie said:

> ... the only difference, really, is the physical difference, cos they can use their legs and I can't. That's the only difference, is the access, because of society, that they don't really make enough access for people in wheelchairs. But apart from that...

Mark's position is the same:

> I don't tend to think of myself as disabled, you know, I don't think, oh I'm in a wheelchair, disability's a major part of my life.

Joyce saw her identity as being in her social roles and relationships:

> Well I know this is going to seem very strange to you, but I don't see myself as a disabled person. I see me as an ordinary person, sort of being a housewife, being an Auntie, just doing ordinary things that ordinary people do.

For Keiron, his identity was a result of his own self-conscious definition and a rejection of other people's categorization of disabled people:

It's a difficult one to answer, I mean, the answer I used to give was a hundred percent I would have said disabled straightaway because that is all I've been taught. I'd say more of a person who happens to have a disability... So I think first and foremost I'm Keiron Brown the person, and I know how to concentrate on that side more than I did maybe 8 to 10 years ago when I'd just came away from a lot of negative things.

We can sympathize with, indeed admire, these people's efforts to define themselves as positive, effective people. But are they denying reality? Their identities are not solely in their own hands, but also inextricable from how others identify them. So how should others identify disabled people? And how does the answer to that conundrum affect ethical decisions?

One approach would be a 'realistic' or 'essentialist' approach. This approach would be to define or categorize a person as disabled if there is an impairment, and if external factors interact with the impairment such that restrictions result. This has the advantage, ethically speaking, of allowing a community to identify and make provision for people who have needs, and furthermore, to identify social barriers to their inclusion and opportunities for a satisfying, functioning life. It would allow for pragmatic and effective ethical decisions based on the calculation of consequences.

An alternative approach would be to say that anyone's identity is (or should be) a result of continuous negotiation between that person and their social circles. Identity would be seen as flexible and contextual. This approach appears ethical in the sense that the community is respecting the self-determination of people with disabilities. Presumably, though, the disabled do not entirely dictate the terms of their identity if it is a result of negotiating with the community.

Oliver tries to combine the three aspects of self identification, pragmatic reality and social forces:

the presence of an impairment;

the experience of externally imposed restrictions;

self-identification as a disabled person [25].

Oliver's perspective ducks the question of the relative importance of these three aspects and does not provide us with a way of choosing between the 'realistic' and 'negotiated' approaches. Nor does it provide any guidance to disabled people about which of the approaches they should favour.

This is a theoretical and practical paradox confronting disabled people. On the one hand, they should be able to demand recognition as people, with the same rights and respect due to members of a community. They should be able to call for the abolition of barriers against being included in normal social, technical and practical community life. On the other hand, they need to be able to access services that are particular to their disabilities. The paradox is made more complicated because of the contrasting theoretical approaches. How much of one's identity resides in one's characteristics, including physical make-up, and how much resides in social interactions? If it is mostly social interactions, how much does being a member of a minority group exclude one from being a member of the majority community?

A perspective from Philosophy

This paradox is not, as it happens, a disability issue especially. The identity conundrum has been wrangled over by philosophers for millennia. A classic starting point for the debate is the story of Theseus' ship [26]. Theseus was a legendary hero of ancient Greece. The story has it that his ship was tied up in harbour and preserved as a monument to his feats. Maintaining the ship required replacement of deteriorating parts from time to time – a rotting plank here, a sagging spar there. Eventually, all the parts of the ship had been replaced. The philosophical conundrum is this. Does it continue to be Theseus' ship?

There are a number of ways we could approach this question [27]. Do we start with the idea that something (or someone) has the same identity over time and in different circumstances? Or do we allow that identity depends on context and circumstances? Do we think identity resides in the physical object, or in its relationships with other objects, or in its social relationships? Perhaps something is whatever we decide it to be. The memorial to Theseus might be a ship, a monument, a modern fake or just a heap of wood. A building might be a church, a community hall or a private home, depending on how it is used.

Social meaning and physical properties

This argument contains some important truths and a fundamental flaw. It emphasizes the social attributes of the building whilst glossing over some important physical facts about the building. While it is true that a building might be a church or a home, it is not true that anything can be a home. A rock cannot be a home, though a cave might. A tree cannot be Theseus' ship, though humans might reshape a tree so that it can serve as a ship. A rock cannot be a home because it does not have the physical properties that allow it to function as a home. So the question remains. Does the identity of something lie in its physical characteristics, or is the identity of something defined by agreements and negotiations between people? Using Theseus' ship and buildings as examples confuses the issue because they are constructed by people, so there are embedded social features in their origins, designs and purposes. What happens if we consider objects that are not constructed by people? What if we consider molecules for instance? Carbon might be a good example, since it is a common substance, comes in a variety of forms, and currently presents challenges to people as an element in greenhouse gases and the climate change debate [28].

At ordinary temperatures and pressures, each carbon atom bonds to three others and it is graphite. Graphite is soft, black, and opaque. Because it is soft, black, and opaque, humans can make pencils out of it. Through geological forces some carbon gets subjected to great pressure and temperature. Under these conditions it crystallises. Each carbon atom bonds to four other atoms. In this form, carbon is diamond. Though graphite is soft, diamond is extremely hard. Where graphite is black and opaque, diamond is translucent. Human beings quite sensibly categorize diamonds as one substance and graphite as another, use them differently and relate to them differently. It is true that some uses of carbon are social, such as a diamond engagement ring, but others are entirely determined by its physical properties. It would be futile to attempt to use diamond as a pencil, but graphite is ideal. Graphite and diamonds are not different substances because people agree that they are. People agree to identify them as different substances because of their physical characteristics. So by this argument, the identity of anything is embedded in its physical form and not determined by its relationship with the environment.

This argument is not quite right, either. Diamonds and graphite are, after all, both carbon. At the atomic level, they are the same material. At a higher, more complex level, carbon atoms under the influence of the environment combine to become molecules. One combination of molecules is diamond. Another combination is graphite. At a higher, more complex level still, one form is an engagement ring and the other is a pencil. Carbon also bonds to other atoms to form different molecules, such as the greenhouse gas carbon dioxide. Carbon is essential to life and forms a significant proportion of the material that makes up the human body. We do not, of course, identify people as lumps of carbon. We identify each other as persons, friends, family, work mates, citizens and so on. On the other hand, we would not be able to function as friends or workmates without carbon, because we are a carbon based life form.

Can we now resolve the competition between the two approaches? Is the identity of anything embedded in the physical arrangement of the parts that comprise it, or is it a result of social interaction, definition and agreement? For material substances, it looks as if the physical arrangement is the compelling response. But what about social institutions, such as a bank?

With a little thought, we can recognize that a bank is more than just a building. A sophisticated idea of the nature of a bank may not include a building at all, but will be more concerned with concepts of institution and function, and will emphasize the people rather than the bricks, or even the internet banking website. But a bank is not just a collection of people either. Some collections of people are banks and some or not. A specific bunch of people could even be a bank on Friday and a sporting team on Saturday. Moreover, we could take a collection of individual people that comprises the bank and then remove the person who is the bank manager, replacing him or her with someone else. And the accountant. And the three tellers. And the investment advisers. And so on, until we have replaced everyone. We still have a bank. So if a bank is not a building and not a collection of people, what is it?

A bank, like everything else, is a particular arrangement of its component parts. If we take a group of people and arrange them in a particular fashion, and the way we arrange them allows them to perform the function of a bank, then a bank is what we have. If we take the same group of people and arrange them differently, then we can have a sporting team. Different arrangements enable the performance of different functions – thus graphite, diamonds, banks, universities, etcetera.

Persons and relationships

Now that the argument has reached the level of complexity that is groups of people making up social institutions, we can tackle a related tricky question in philosophy and sociology. Is society nothing more than the individuals who make it up? Or is any individual person nothing more than the sum of his/her social relations? [29] Clearly, a society is not just the people who make it up, but a particular set of relationships between those people, just as a bank or a diamond is a set of relations between component parts. In response to the first question of the pair – is society nothing but the people in it - we have to answer, not quite. A society is composed of the social relations between those people. The opposing question of the pair remains. Is a person's identity defined by a set of social relations? Or is it embedded in their physical components?

I have argued that a bank is a bank because it is a particular arrangement of manager, bank clerks and so on. It is also the case that a bank teller is a bank teller because of the position he occupies in that arrangement. Now if we do a sudden shift of position and look at it from his point of view, then he is a bank teller because of his relationship with other people in the bank. But he is not a *person* because of his relationship with other people in the bank. Customers might think of him just as a teller, but from his point of view, he is a person who *has* a relationship with customers, not a thing that is defined by the relationship. Kant admonished us in chapter four that we should never treat people just as a means to an end, but as ends in themselves. In practice, we ordinarily do treat bank tellers just as means to our ends. We just want bank services from them. Similarly, to a bank teller, customers are just customers. It is difficult to see how else the relationship could function. Other relationships are more significant. In disability services, the individual identity of a client is more significant for the professional than it is for a bank teller.

Things, and people, have both internally-based identity and external relations. Sometimes a thing's relationship with other things is really all we are interested in, so we describe it in those terms – for example, a goal post. We do not really care what internal structure it has – metal, wood or whatever – just as long as it can function as a goal post. It might not even be a post. Children kicking a ball against a wall might decide on the position of a goal by saying, "Look, we'll make that crack one goalpost and that odd coloured brick the other." When the game is over, the brick is still there, though it is no longer a goalpost. It still has the same colour, is still made of clay and still has a structure which will enable it to perform a number of functions such as being part of a wall or a children's game.

Similarly with a bank teller. As a customer, you may think of someone as being a teller, but that is because it is his relationship to the situation that you are interested in, rather than the person. If he retires and another person becomes your usual teller, you will deal quite happily with the new one – you might not even notice the change. If, over time, the retiring teller changes all his other relationships, divorces his wife, buries his father, changes his friends, then has the 'old' person been destroyed? Surely not. He has a continuous identity even if he is changing relationships.

Similarly, a person might be identified as a disabled client to the manager of an organization that has been set up and funded to provide services to people with disabilities. But from the client's point of view, as Joyce asserted earlier, she has a whole raft of relationships – Auntie, housewife, etcetera.

Even though the brick/goalpost above has a number of relationships too, bricks are not people. Apart from holding up the brick above it, bricks do not relate to the rest of the wall. A brick will not decide that it does not like the shape of the wall, nor can a collective of other bricks decide to change the identity of an odd-coloured brick. Importantly, a brick could not care less whether it is part of a wall or not.

People do care. It is in their nature to be a part of society. It is in their nature to develop, to build and to assume relationships, to want to flourish, and to flourish in society. Because people are both social and self-conscious, they affect society and society affects them.

The identity of any thing is not simply the physical object, but depends on what we call it and how it relates to us. Of course, the physical characteristics have some relevance or even be an essential feature. Any old pile of wood will not serve as a monument to Theseus. Not every collection of bricks would be able to function as a church, or a wall, or a goal in a children's game.

So if the identity of objects like ships and buildings arises from a complex interplay between their physical characteristics and their social relations, how much more complicated is the identity of a person.

Resolving the contradiction

The complications of personal identity are relevant to ethics. Different approaches to ethics intersect with different facets of personal identity. A community-based approach to ethics is compatible with a social relations perspective. In this approach, ethical decisions are derived from the roles and relationships between people. A principles based approach has a different perspective. An important principle is to prioritise the individual as a self determining person. A consequences-based approach has a different perspective again. It may find the medical model useful, aiming for pragmatic and measurable results.

Disabled people may need to identify themselves as disabled when their impairments collide with barriers in the physical and social world. They may need to be identified as disabled by government agencies or service providers in order to get access to services to which they are entitled. At the same time, they may not wish their personal identities as essentially disabled. They may think of themselves as normal and resist categorization and stereotyping. They therefore may see themselves as struggling with this contradiction.

The truth is, there is no contradiction. The identity of any one of us is depends on the circumstances. Personal identity, social identity and categorisation all depend on context. It is possible for one and the same person to be a parent, an offspring, an employee, an employer, a taxpayer, a service recipient, disabled, highly-functioning, introverted, out-going, generous and mean, not just over time, but all on the same day.

Summarizing the debate about terminology

Human beings observe the world around them, detect patterns and categorize. We notice similarities and differences and discriminate between classes of objects. It is the way our brains work and is unavoidable.

As persons, each of us likes to think of ourselves as unique, but we are not really. It is true that we each have unique lives and experiences, but it is also true that we have much in common with other people. 'Discrimination' has negative associations, but of course we could not survive without discriminating between food and poison, family and stranger, friend and foe. If we consider ourselves as unique individuals, it follows that we are actually *demanding* discrimination, because we are demanding that we are dealt with as individuals and do not get treated all alike. We do not like to be discriminated *against*. We do not like to have our freedoms, or our status in society compromised because of race, or gender, or disability. We do not mind positive discrimination, though. A person with a particular disability (or gender) may need services that others do not need.

The point about discrimination, then, is that it should be appropriate and focussed. A man who dismisses the opinions of all women because they are women is unethical as well as a fool. A quadriplegic who identifies himself as disabled when lobbying for wheelchair access should not be treated as impaired in other contexts.

Additionally, all people, whether disabled or not, should be treated as persons, as ends in themselves, and not merely as objects to be manipulated. That is a fundamental ethical principle discussed in chapter four.

Referring to *people with disabilities* rather than *disabled people* may have the admirable intention of promoting the fundamental principle that we should respect each other as persons. Whether it is effective is another matter. Debate continues about the relative merits of the terms. Both have validity, as well as the term *people with impairments*. No doubt new terminology will emerge as time goes by.

Exclusion through theories of human nature

What should not be at stake here is the fundamental idea that we are all human beings, that we all deserve the respect due to us as persons. Unfortunately, that idea is at risk. The United Nations Convention on the Rights of People with Disabilities reminds us that we are all members of the human family. It begins with:

> (a) *Recalling* the principles proclaimed in the Charter of the United Nations which recognize the inherent dignity and worth and the equal and inalienable rights of all members of the human family as the foundation of freedom, justice and peace in the world...

The Convention:

> marks a "paradigm shift" in attitudes and approaches to persons with disabilities. It takes to a new height the movement from viewing persons with disabilities as "objects" of charity, medical treatment and social protection towards viewing persons with disabilities as "subjects" with rights, who are capable of claiming those rights and making decisions for their lives based on their free and informed consent as well as being active members of society [30].

But why should it be necessary to remind us that people with disabilities are humans and not objects? And what has that to do with ethics?

The reason is that if we identify someone as a human person, then it follows that they should be treated ethically. The community-based approach identifies them as a member of a community, the consequences-based approach says that their interests matter and the principles-based approach says they should be treated with respect. But if we do not identify them as human persons, then they may not be granted ethical consideration [31]. The assertion that disabled people are people, and should not be excluded from our conceptions and definitions of persons, is very important. Unfortunately, theories of ethics can work against this agenda. Theories of ethics rest upon theories of human nature, and theories of human nature can lean towards excluding people with disabilities.

Nussbaum's theory of Capabilities could be read this way, even though it is in her work entitled *Frontiers of Justice: Disability, Nationality, Species Membership*. In her justification of her Capabilities approach she says

> The basic intuitive idea of my version of the capabilities approach is that we begin with a conception of the dignity of the human being, and of a life that is worthy of that dignity – a life that has available in it "truly human functioning"... [32].

The danger of this intuitive idea is that it can be taken to imply that someone who is not capable of "truly human functioning" is not truly human. The implication is strengthened further when Nussbaum goes on to say:

> First of all, the notion of human nature in my theory is explicitly and from the start *evaluative*, and in particular, *ethically evaluative:* among the many actual features of a characteristic human form of life, we select some that seem so normatively fundamental that a life without any possibility at all of exercising one of them, at any level, is not a fully human life, a life worthy of human dignity, even if the others are present.. If enough of them are impossible (as in the case of a person in a persistent vegetative state), we may judge that the life is not a human life at all, any more [33].

In quoting the above, I need to make two points immediately.

The first is that it is not Nussbaum's intention to exclude disabled people from ethical considerations, but quite the opposite. Her argument is that society should be arranged so that disabled people can, in fact, enjoy exercising the capabilities that make for a satisfactory human existence.

My second point is that the purpose of this book is not to provide a detailed or robust critique of specific theories or theorists. It is to examine the application of theories to professional ethics in disability, to note their strengths and weaknesses, their usefulness and their dangers. Nussbaum emphasises that her approach is political, rather than 'a comprehensive moral doctrine' [34]. Kant's Deontology and Bentham's Utilitarianism have been subjected to much analysis already by other scholars, and their theories were not constructed with disability issues in mind. Nonetheless, their theories can be, and are, applied to help ethical decision making in the context of disability provision.

The danger of excluding disabled persons from ethical consideration lurk in the standard ethical theories discussed in this book, because they lurk in the theories of human nature that underpin them.

In order to determine how to treat fellow humans appropriately, in order to establish social arrangements that meet their needs and capabilities, in order to justify theories of ethics, we need some common ground, some shared values, some agreed conception of human nature. Some people are optimistic about human nature and think that with the right social arrangements we can approach utopia [35]. Others are pessimistic and see the primary task as maintaining social order [36]. But for social arrangements to work, and ethical actions to be effective, they must presumably be reflective of what people are actually like. So can we identify some assumptions about human nature that are commonplace, not too controversial and compatible with assumptions which can be found in other relevant domains such as Politics, Sociology, Psychology and Law?

At first this might seem like a tall order. This, however, depends upon our methodology. If we were to look at all human beings, describe their characteristics and then attempt to find similarities, the complexity of the task would be overwhelming. But a much easier way is to look at what characteristics separate human beings from things that are not human beings, such as rocks or insects. Some characteristics, abilities and behaviours are immediately obvious. I have (somewhat arbitrarily) divided them into the five headings below.

Agents

First, people are agents, that is, they act, unlike rocks, say, which are acted upon [37].

When discussing terminology earlier in this chapter, I mentioned the Medical Model. It is relevant to this discussion that the word 'patient' is the opposite to 'agent' in that 'patient' means a person who is the recipient of someone else's action, typically a medical professional [38].

Rational

Second, people are rational. They have the capacity to acquire information and process it in logical and effective ways in order to decide what to do next.

Productive

Third, people are productive. They set out to make things they want and to alter the environment, rather than just be a part of it.

Gregarious

Fourth, people are gregarious. They can produce much more in co-operation than singly. They are language users.

Interests

Fifth, people have interests that they wish to satisfy. Their welfare matters to them and they take steps to fulfil their needs.

Expanding the concept of human nature

Already we have an indication here of the dangers that lurk in this conception of human nature. How should we accommodate people who are not co-operative, productive agents making rational decisions about what is in their own best interests?

Is this a valid theory of human nature, anyway? Perhaps it is overly optimistic, carefully selecting only the most positive characteristics of people, even to the extent of losing a grip on reality. Can we really say that people are rational when so many of them do stupid things? Can we really say that people are co-operative when so many quarrel, fight or even kill to get what they want?

I will spend a little time, then, expanding on the above five features of human nature, but it is important that this process does not obscure the point of the discussion. My aim is to examine how our assumptions about human nature and ethics, might impact upon disabled people. Exploring intricacies in fundamental philosophy would not serve this purpose. There are many scholarly books and articles on 'agency' alone. By expanding on the above five characteristics, I do not intend to defend them as a theory, but rather to flesh them out a little so that they can be recognized as commonly-accepted assumptions.

Agents

People are agents, that is, they act, unlike rocks, which are acted upon. To say that people act is to say a great deal. It certainly means more than to say that people are active while rocks are generally immobile. Rocks, after all, do sometimes roll downhill. But rocks do not roll downhill because that is where they have decided to go. 'Acting' assumes both having a desire and taking steps to satisfy it. In this respect, other species may be said to act. Humans go further, though. They act self-consciously. They know they have interests, they know they can act to satisfy those interests, and they can consciously decide what action to take.

This notion of agency underpins our beliefs about rights, about freedom and responsibility, and indeed our entire legal system. It is implicit in the United Nations Declaration of Human Rights (along with the other four characteristics).

Admittedly, determinists deny this [39]. Determinism is a theory which argues that a human's 'decisions' are part of the same cause and effect system that sets rocks rolling down hills and are equally involuntary. Accepting this theory would pre-empt and render futile all discussions about what decisions we ought to make, or what social arrangements we should construct or what responsibilities professionals have towards clients. It is also contrary to people's experience. We are conscious of making decisions and we value our freedom to do so. It is more fruitful, then, to leave determinism to one side and continue describing common conceptions of human nature.

Describing people as agents actually foreshadows most of the other features of human nature, those of rationality, productivity and having interests. (It is sometimes claimed, by the way, that these features are shared with other species, such as dolphins or chimpanzees. The extent to which this is true is not relevant to this discussion, though, which is concerned with how theories of human nature and ethics might impact upon disability issues.)

Rational

People are rational. They have the capacity to acquire information, processing it in logical and effective ways in order to decide what to do next. There are admittedly pitfalls in this process. Reasoning processes can be faulty. Sufficient information is commonly lacking. Estimation, speculation and just plain guesswork is often required, all of which can be influenced by wishful thinking. Nonetheless, people do have brains. They do learn from experience. People do deliberate and calculate. People do put two facts together, infer a third, and use the inference to manipulate the environment to their satisfaction. The fact that people have this capacity obviously has great impact on what social arrangements are appropriate.

The fact that some people do not or cannot function as rational agents poses a serious challenge to the practical issues of public and professional ethics, and to appropriate social arrangements.

Productive

People are productive. They set out to make things they want and to alter the environment rather than just be a part of it. They are productive in a different sense to a field of wheat or a cow. They are purposively productive. In order to satisfy their needs, they set out to alter their environment to produce not only the goods they need, but the devices and conditions useful to production. As well as producing things, they produce tools, and ideas, and social arrangements. The notion of passive contentment, perhaps on a tropic island paradise, or maybe sedated in a drug induced state of bliss, seems superficially attractive, but runs counter to our ideas of human nature.

Gregarious

People are gregarious. They can produce much more in co-operation than singly. As well as being productive, they like to make a contribution to a group and have that contribution recognized. Some contributions are recognized economically through work and income, but many other ways of contributing are not.

People are language users. They form relationships. They exchange ideas. They identify themselves as members of groups, by family, nationality or culture.

People then, are both gregarious and co-operative. Admittedly, they are also competitive. In a situation of scarcity, this may be a rational response. If there is only one piece of bread left, and two people, they will fight for it, and the struggle for survival has long dictated human behaviour (like other animals'). But unlike other animals, the two people, given the opportunity, will have previously co-operated to produce more bread.

It is true that some theories of human nature concentrate on the competitive aspect and see it as the driving force for all social arrangements [40]. Such a view may limit a government's task to the minimum role of regulating conflict, with no provision for people with disabilities. However, this bleak view flies in the face of the evidence. Some societies crumble into dysfunctional chaos, but given the opportunity, people will co-operate and it is obvious that people live longer and happier lives in flourishing, functioning co-operative communities.

Interests

People have interests that they wish to satisfy. They are, by nature, capable of pleasure or pain, happiness or misery, frustration or satisfaction. They may be sick or healthy, flourishing or repressed. Their welfare matters to them and they take steps to fulfil their needs. While people have similar interests, and can co-operate to fulfil them, people are fundamentally individuals. We each have our own experiences, we suffer our own pains, relish our own joys, live our own lives and make our own individual judgements about what most pleases us.

Theories of ethics and human nature

It is readily apparent how these features of human nature underpin theories of ethics.

The community-based approach relies on the notion that people are gregarious. It sees ethics as the process of people co-operating to meet shared goals and agreeing on how we should treat each other. It can plausibly be argued that, if people were not gregarious by nature, there would be no such thing as ethics. The philosopher David Hume maintained that the starting point of ethics was that people sympathised with each other [41]. Social arrangements are developed by communities as expressions of people's gregarious and sympathetic nature.

The consequences-based approach starts with the idea that people have interests. Consequentialism defines an ethical action as one that best satisfies people's interests, desires and welfare. In contrast to communitarianism, a consequences approach does not judge that an action is good simply because a community of people agree that it is good. Consequentialists would agree that as a matter of fact people satisfy their needs by co-operating with each other, but measurable outcomes for actual individual people are the stuff of ethics for Utilitarians.

The principles-based approach sees people as rational agents. Admittedly, humans have other characteristics too, but they are being ethical only when they are acting as rational agents. Autonomy and self-determination are key concepts in a principles- based approach. They underpin related approaches. A rights approach typically protects self-determination. In the Capabilities approach, almost all of the capabilities involve varying degrees of agency, self-determination, rationality and freedom.

The threshold

If being recognized as a person and being treated ethically by others is dependent upon having the characteristics that are taken to comprise being human, it is no wonder that many people with disabilities insist that they are 'normal' [42]. Admitting to a disability runs the risk of being excluded from the community of fully-functioning rational productive agents who have the same interests as each other. It runs the risk of falling below the conceptual threshold of being a person who therefore merits rights and respect.

Nussbaum assumes that someone in a persistent vegetative state is below the threshold and her position is plausible. But where should the threshold be? At what degree of impairment can we reasonably draw the line and say that ethical considerations no longer apply? Should we draw it as near to the bottom of functioning that we can manage, so that anyone who is just above a vegetative state merits ethical consideration? Or lower still, so that any body who was once human but now comatose, or who once had the potential of being human, such as a stillborn, merits ethical consideration? This may be a noble sentiment, but it cannot be effected in practice. We cannot come to agreements with a comatose person, or ask them what their preferences are, or promote their self-determination. So should we draw the threshold slightly higher? Or keep going up until we are sure we can have a practical impact on self-determination and effective production of shared goals? We should bear in mind that there are some people who set the threshold very high indeed, often thoughtlessly assuming that a physical impairment indicates a cognitive disability. It is not only the thoughtless and bigoted that disabled people have to contend with. Barriers to people with mobility impairments are endemic. The designers of buildings, roads and transport seem to be blissfully unaware of all but the fully-functioning members of the community, adding access only as a grudging afterthought and under pressure. Where then, between fully-functioning and not-functioning-at-all, should we set the threshold for the application of our theories of human nature and ethical approaches?

The answer is that we do not need to draw a line at all. Earlier in this chapter, I referred to the paradox of Theseus' ship, which is a thought experiment philosophers use to discuss notions of identity. A similar thought experiment is 'the paradox of the heap', which challenges assumptions that we have to draw lines or set thresholds [43]. Imagine a heap of sand. Imagine constructing a heap of sand by piling one grain of sand on another. At the start, a solitary grain does not constitute a heap. Nor do two grains. Nor three. Several hundred do, which can be achieved by piling them up one grain at a time. But is there a point at which the addition of a single grain transforms a number of individual grains into a heap? With the addition of this grain, we have achieved a heap. Without it there is no heap. Where is the threshold?

The point is, of course, that we do not need to specify one. It is convenient to think in categories and to group things in our minds on the grounds that they have similar properties. Oranges and tennis balls are 'round' objects. Knives and forks are not. But we know that nothing is perfectly round. We do not waste our mental resources agonizing over which 'roundish' or 'squarish' objects should go in which category. We just treat them as they are. We do not need a threshold for deciding whether a comatose person is human. Nor does there exist any perfect, fully functioning human being. We should, as the saying goes, treat people as we find them.

Conclusion

Identifying someone as a disabled person does not say very much about that person. Categorizing someone as a person with disabilities does not tell us whether the person is male or female, optimist or pessimist, parent or child. Even if people identify themselves as disabled, it does not tell us whether they also identify themselves as members of an ethnic group, or a political movement or the supporter of a football team, nor whether they have extraordinary artistic, intellectual, physical or social abilities, or conversely, are very ordinary people.

Identifying people's needs for wheelchair access, or special education, or supported accommodation, does not deny that they are people.

Each one of us has a multitude of identities, characteristics and relationships. Some of our characteristics are the cards that the fates have dealt us. So are some of our relationships. Others are the result of personal choice, or of negotiations with others.

Ethics is the study of how people should be treated. The ethics of identity requires that we identify the characteristics of people that are relevant to the way they should be treated. This in turn depends upon the circumstances they are in, the context, their relationships, their own perceptions and wishes, not to mention time, place, and change. Disability is a relevant characteristic in some contexts and not in others. Figuring out when it is relevant, deciding on when to use the medical model and when to use the social model, calculating the merits of terminology and the dangers of stereotyping, are all challenges, to be sure. But with some thought, some empathy and some analysis, and with contributions from Sociology and Philosophy, we can meet the challenges, both as members of the wider community and as disability professionals.

Chapter 10
Justice

Justice is a notion that everybody favours, but it has a variety of meanings and it is difficult to define. It has to do with fairness, equal treatment, impartiality, entitlements and rights, but what do these terms mean in practice? To say that justice means being fair to people does not seem to get us anywhere, but merely repeats the same vague idea. If we say that people should be treated equally, does that mean they should be treated the same? That does not seem right. If we advocate for justice for people with disabilities, surely we are arguing that people with disabilities should be treated differently. Treating everybody in the same way regardless of their differences would rule out paying any attention to people's different needs or circumstances. But if we are to treat people differently, how can we be fair to everybody, recognize everybody's universal human rights and be impartial?

The word *justice* is often used in the context of the legal system, law courts and the criminal justice system. Society seeks retribution by punishing criminals, and newspapers report court verdicts as justice being done [1].

In contrast to the *retributive* justice of criminal proceedings, there is the notion of *distributive* justice, which is about the fair allocation of resources. Debates about social arrangements, taxation and welfare services typically use notions of distributive justice. Opponents in these debates can use the ideas of justice and fairness to justify radically different and incompatible community policies. Some argue that it is obviously right, fair and just to tax the rich to assist people who are less well off, especially if their financial hardship is a result of circumstances beyond their control, such as a disability. In contrast, others argue that it is wrong, unjust and unfair to take money away from people who have worked hard to produce it, and to give it to others who have done nothing to earn it.

Another domain in which the idea of justice is discussed is professional ethics. Medical ethics features it as one of the four fundamental ethical principles, alongside autonomy, beneficence and non-maleficence. The Code of Ethics and Practice for Disability and Rehabilitation Professionals provided in chapter five requires disability professionals to be honest and fair in all aspects of their work.

These three domains of justice – retributive, distributive and professional – clearly deal with different issues. The professional domain has an immediate relevance for professional ethics in disability provision. The distributive domain is important for clients with disability. The retributive domain ought to be irrelevant to disability issues, but sadly it is not. The disproportionate number of people with cognitive disabilities and mental illnesses in prison is a matter of grave ethical concern.

Justice in professional ethics

If justice means that the same rules apply to everyone without favouritism, and that professionals should be fair and impartial, then the implication is that professionals should treat all their clients the same [2]. On the other hand, professions have been established to meet clients' needs. Clients do not all have the same needs. How can a professional, in order to practise justice, treat all clients the same and individual clients differently?

The solution is the understanding that all clients have needs and are that they are the same in the sense that they are clients who have needs. Professionals' treatment of clients should be determined by the clients' needs and not by other factors. The amount of professional attention and services a client receives should not be influenced, either positively or negatively, by other factors such as race, gender or the personal likes/dislikes of the professional. Discrimination on those grounds would be unjust.

There may be occasions when a professional has a number of clients and finds that their needs are competing for a limited amount of time and resources [3]. This situation raises questions of justice. Is a professional required, in the name of justice, to calculate carefully the amount of time and resources available, to divide them precisely by the number of clients and to dole out precisely measured equal amounts to each client? Would such a process be realistic and practical? Would it be ethical? What if one client's needs required a short amount of time and another a lot of time to achieve similarly positive results? How does a justice-oriented approach resolve issue like these?

The best response to the challenges of these questions may be to fall back on the dominant ethical approaches of community, consequences and principles. The notion of justice is something of a catch-all. Sometimes it is used to mean protecting people's rights, sometimes it means distributing resources to where there are most needs, and sometimes it relates to people's standing in the community. This ambiguity can be avoided by re-casting questions about what constitutes justice in professional practice, to what practices are justified according to the ethical theories exemplified in the community-based approach, in the calculation of consequences, in a commitment to principles, through dedication to increasing clients' welfare, a respect for persons and their rights, and a recognition of professional roles and responsibilities.

Social justice

As discussed in chapter two on a community-based approach to ethics, it is part of the role of disability professionals to advocate for their clients to the wider community. Taking part in community debates about distributive justice for disabled people is a responsibility of the profession as a whole. Achieving justice for people with disabilities is a challenge for the profession and for the wider community. Social justice has to do with the distribution of resources, property, power and responsibilities. As already noted, that can mean different things to different people. It may mean treating people equally, or conversely treating people according to their merits. It may mean entitlement to what a person has earned, or to what a person needs. Everyone wants justice, it seems, but there is no general agreement about what it means. The same lack of agreement applies to the related terms of fairness and equality.

In an attempt to provide an authoritative definition of justice, the philosopher Blackburn notes that:

> The problem is to lay down principles specifying the just distribution of benefits and burdens: the outcome in which everyone receives their due. A common basis is that persons should be treated equally unless reasons for inequality exist; after that, the problems include the kind of reasons that justify departing from equality, the role of the state in rectifying equality and the link between a distributive system and the maximization of well-being [4].

Taking up Blackburn's question, what should be 'the role of the state in rectifying equality and the link between a distributive system and the maximization of well-being'?

Rose, in a review of the role of government in disability services, refers to social justice principles that:
- ensure that all people, irrespective of race, sex, disability or financial status, have equal access to government programmes;
- ensure access to opportunities to assist people to live as equal citizens;
- provide services to people in a way that best meets their needs and respect their rights; provide people with the opportunity to complain if the support they receive is inadequate or unsatisfactory in some way [5].

In a community that values justice, what level of government services should be offered? Disability typically entails financial disadvantage. Should that burden be borne by the person with the disability, or by the family, or by the community through voluntary donations to charities, or by government through taxation?

Defining justice with a focus on needs

It would be reasonable for people with disabilities and for disability professionals to favour a definition of justice that is based on needs. A needs-based argument can start with the premise that people live in communities in order to satisfy their needs. People are gregarious by nature and sympathetic to each other's circumstances. Through their co-operative arrangements, they can satisfy their own needs and look after each other.

Using a community based approach, it can be argued that common needs, such as roads, sewerage, policing, education and health are best managed, supplied and financed by the community through government agencies and therefore taxation. Anyone of us may fall victim to criminals and we all need security and public order, so policing is a community need and therefore the responsibility of government. All children need an education and the community needs a well-educated citizenry, so education is the responsibility of government. Any of us may fall sick and the community as a whole is more prosperous if its members are generally healthy, so health, including hospitals, infectious diseases control and sewerage systems, are the responsibility of government. Any of us might be born with a disability, or acquire a disability through accident, illness or simply ageing, so provision for disability is the responsibility of government. It is true that there are individuals amongst us who are sufficiently well-off to pay for their own education and health needs and may prefer to do so, rather than through taxation. Even these individuals, though, expect the protection of police and do not want to build their own roads or sewerage systems. Furthermore, human nature is not entirely driven by calculations of self-interest, but is sympathetic to others' plights. We should, and do, band together to help each other out in times of need. Particularly when someone finds themselves in dire circumstances through no fault of their own or circumstances beyond their control, then we recognize their entitlement to turn to the community for assistance [6]. The practical way of doing so is to establish and fund government agencies whose responsibility is to look after people's needs, especially when those needs are acute. This argument simultaneously invokes enlightened self-interest, altruism and sympathy.

Justice, by this argument, is the entitlement that all citizens have to the support of the community in meeting individual needs in education, security, health and disability. Injustice would result if some people in need were abandoned by the community. In terms of distributive justice, this does not require that everybody be treated equally, or that wealth, resources or political power be equalized. It does require that resources to meet specified individual needs be communally funded.

I have presented this argument using a community-based approach, but versions of it are promoted by people who favour a principles approach or a consequences approach. So Rose, quoted above, uses the language of a principles-based approach by referring to 'respect' and 'rights' and a consequences approach by referring to services 'that best meets their needs'.

Whether the approach is from community, consequences or principles, there is a powerful argument / definition that *distributive justice consists of recognizing people's entitlement to government services that meet people's needs* in public infrastructure, in law, security and public order, in education, in health and disability.

Defining justice as individual liberty

An alternative definition of justice focuses on individual liberty rather than on community responsibilities. Flew's *Dictionary of Philosophy* defines it as

> to allocate to each their own... [the] individualistic ideal of securing for all their ... diverse entitlements.. to be contrasted with the collectivist ideal of imposing an equality of outcome [7].

If individual liberty and responsibility is the focus, rather than need, then people are entitled to what they have earned, produced or acquired through fair exchange [8]. Taxation as a means of assisting certain people on the grounds that they have needs is not justified. Such taxation is forcibly taking money away from people who have earned it and giving it to people who have not earned it. To do so would be unjust. Certainly people have needs in health and education. They also have needs in housing, food and personal relationships. It is up to people to figure out their own needs and to be responsible for meeting them. It is certainly not the government's responsibility. The role of government is to provide national security, law and public order; that is: to protect individual liberty. A libertarian might recognize the disadvantages facing a disabled person, but would argue that since disability is typically not anybody's fault, its concomitant disadvantages are not anybody's responsibility. The disadvantages are unfortunate, but not unfair.

As with the argument above that justice should be based on need, the argument that justice should be based on liberty can be couched in terms of a community-based approach to ethics, or a consequence-based approach, or from principles. A libertarian argument is that a community should be seen as individuals freely and productively co-operating with each other, not as a mass of people being coerced into uniformity. Libertarians can argue that the consequences for people's welfare are much better if they take responsibility for it themselves. According to Utilitarianism, and especially Preference Utilitarianism, it is the satisfaction of individuals that matters, not some perception of the common good. According to principles, people should be respected as autonomous, rational, self-determining persons. By this perception, liberty is sacrosanct.

In this argument, *justice is achieved when people can live their own lives as they see fit, and have their liberty and earned entitlements protected.*

A theory of justice

If we have two conceptions of justice, one based on needs and the other based on liberty, how can we reconcile them? Or, if we cannot reconcile them, how can we choose one over the other? Can we agree that needs are more important than liberty? Or is there a convincing argument that liberty must be prioritized and as a secondary consideration, we do what we can about needs?

It may be that no reconciliation is possible. People want to have their cake and eat it too. We all want to enjoy the fruits of being members of a community, but we each want our own individual unconstrained freedom to make our own decisions and live our lives as we choose. Perhaps that is just part of the human condition. The challenge of social life is to live with the tension and constantly manage it.

Certainly solving this conundrum is not the role of disability professionals. If we apply the rule that requires professionals to work within the boundaries of their expertise, then we must recognize that constructing a fundamental theory and definition of justice that would achieve community consensus is not the role of disability professionals. It is understandable that they would favour a needs-based definition, but reconciling that position with an opposing libertarian view is best left to political philosophers who are qualified to tackle it. Even then, as noted, the problem may be intractable.

When it comes to defining justice, a very influential political philosopher is John Rawls, who was mentioned briefly in chapter two on a community-based approach to ethics [9].

Let us look at the problem again, re-stating the main areas of difficulty, and examine Rawls' approach to it. Interestingly, Rawls comes from the libertarian tradition, but, despite that, his theory can be used fruitfully when constructing professional ethics in disability.

The problem is that we all want justice, but there are a variety of conceptions of justice, some of which appear incompatible with each other. Is there any method by which we can reach agreement on what constitutes justice, so that we can construct social arrangements accordingly?

It seems plausible to suggest that justice should mean a set of social arrangements that we would agree to because they were fair. In other words, the definition of a fair arrangement is an arrangement we would all agree to. So far, so good. The difficulty is finding a basis upon which we could agree. Some of us believe liberty is sacrosanct. Some of us believe that needs should be the driving consideration. Can we negotiate with each other given these differences? The challenge is heightened by the realization that any person's starting point in such a negotiation would presumably be influenced by their own circumstances. People doing poorly are likely to favour equality of outcomes, while people who are doing well are likely to favour individual entitlement. People in poverty may think it unfair that others are rich, while wealthy people may recommend recognition of individual responsibility, contribution and ownership.

Rawls proposes a notion of justice which aims to provide a basis for agreement on what constitutes fairness. Let us imagine a situation where a group of people are about to set up a society. Let us imagine that they know about economics, sociology and so on, so that they have the requisite expertise to design effective social arrangements. But to prevent their setting up arrangements that reflect their individual circumstances, let us imagine they know nothing about themselves personally, nor the role they will play in the society they are initiating. They do not know if they will be male or female, rich or poor, healthy or debilitated. What sort of society would they design? They would not choose equality, according to Rawls, because it is inefficient and too difficult to implement. But they certainly would not agree to arrangements whereby some people were severely exploited, because of the risk that they would find themselves in that exploited group. They would not choose, for example, to set up a society that practised slavery, because nobody would want to risk finding themselves as a slave.

Thinking about this hypothetical scenario can provide us with a definition of justice. According to Rawls, a set of social arrangements is just if they are the sort of arrangements that people would choose if they were ever in a position to do so, impartially. This hypothetical standard can then be applied to any actual society. Does the society exhibit arrangements which, on reflection and examination, are the sorts of social arrangements that they would have agreed to, leaving aside knowledge of their own circumstances?

Rawls' theory was intended to answer a theoretical question in political philosophy – how can justice be defined? Upon examination, it turns out to be very applicable to disability issues.

Let us imagine a situation in which people are setting up a new society. They know that some people in that society will have disabilities, but they do not know what their own personal circumstances will be, whether they will be one of the people with a disability or not. Would this original group agree that people with disabilities should be left to fend for themselves? Or, mindful that it could happen to anybody, would they agree that government services were justified? Surely the latter.

Rawls would agree. His definition of justice does not propose equality but nonetheless 'requires that social benefits and burdens are allocated in such a way as to make the position of the least well-off as good as it can be'[10].

When the disability services profession calls for justice for people with disabilities and for the provision of adequate and effective disability services, Rawls' argument could be a powerful tool. If it were accepted by the community at large and by policy-makers, it would be reasonable to expect a significant improvement in the lives of people with disabilities. Any community member, any policy-maker could be confronted with the scenario. Imagine you are in Rawls' hypothetical original position. Imagine you are setting up social arrangements concerning the provision of services for disabled people. Imagine that you do not know whether you will or will not be a disabled person in need of those services. What level of services would you decide upon in those circumstances?

Professionals can apply the same tool to ethical challenges in their own practice. Naturally enough, when professionals decide about what constitutes a fair way to treat their clients, they do so from the position of professionals. They may, of course, be empathetic to their clients' positions as well, or try to be. An application of Rawls' approach does not require professionals to make whatever decisions the clients would favour. Instead, it provides a starting point for negotiating an arrangement which is fair, or at least making a decision which is based on justice and impartiality.

Ethical dilemmas described in earlier chapters may serve as illustrative examples. In one of them, Latimer House is developing a restraint policy. The residents of Latimer House have intellectual disabilities and challenging behaviour, and they are sometimes restrained physically by the staff. This is dangerous for both resident and staff member, but not restraining can also be dangerous. Management is considering a policy of no restraint. If staff restrict residents' liberty by forcibly restraining them, is that unjust? Is it unjust for management to require staff to endanger themselves by restraining residents? Applying Rawls' approach requires management and staff to consider what they would agree to if they were in the original position If they did not know whether they would be staff, or management, or resident, would they favour a policy of restraint or not? It seems reasonable that a person in the original position might say, "Look, if it turns out that I have an intellectual disability and challenging behaviour that is dangerous to myself and others, I agree that I should be restrained, but only as a last resort, not just for staff convenience. But I don't want to put staff in danger either, if that can be avoided. That would not be fair." Thus Rawls' approach can be employed by managers, staff, disabled people, policy makers, government agencies and the community at large. Do organization policies comply with this notion of justice? Are the arrangements for service delivery the sort of arrangements we would agree to if we did not know whether we would be the provider or the recipient?

Criticisms of Rawls' theory of justice

As might be expected, Rawls' theory of justice has attracted a flood of criticism and commentary [11]. Rather than add yet another contribution to that debate in political philosophy, I will confine my discussion here to the application of Rawls' idea to disability issues. Two matters should be noted first. One is that Rawls did not intend his theory to be a contribution to debates about disability issues, so it may be that modification of them may be needed to make them applicable. This, though, is just as true of foundational theories discussed in the chapter on principles and the chapter on consequences. The other matter worth noting is that the amount of commentary generated by Rawls' critics is an indication of how influential his ideas are, rather than an implication that his theory should be dismissed because it is badly flawed.

As Nussbaum remarks, Rawls' theory is 'one of the most distinguished in the western tradition of political philosophy' and is worth examining for its implications for disability issues, even if it was not intended for that purpose. At the beginning of her critique *Frontiers of Justice: Disability, Nationality, Species Membership*, Nussbaum says:

> I focus on areas that Rawls himself regarded as unsolved problems, problems that challenge his theory in ways that he was not altogether certain it could meet. The focus is appropriate because he solved so many other problems so well. My ultimate purpose is to extend the core ideas of his theory to deal with these new issues. Although I believe that this extension cannot be done without serious alterations in the part of his theory that derive from the social contract tradition, I believe that the theory itself, its principles and its intuitive underpinnings, provides excellent guidance as we pursue these new and difficult questions [12].

Does Rawls' theory need serious alterations because of its roots in the social contract tradition? The philosophers Rousseau, Hobbes and Locke were the founders of the social contract tradition [13]. They were concerned with the question of how people could come together in communities, preserve their own individual liberties and yet at the same time construct social arrangements for mutual benefit and governments that preserved both order and freedom. This sounds very much like a libertarian approach to justice, which, as discussed earlier in this chapter, is at odds with a sense of justice derived from need.

Indeed, Rawls is a libertarian. He proposes that people in his hypothetical original position would agree on two principles of justice.

> First: each person is to have an equal right to the most extensive basic liberty compatible with a similar liberty for others.
>
> Second: social and economic inequalities are to be arranged so that they are both (a) reasonably expected to be to everyone's advantage, and (b) attached to positions and offices open to all ...
>
> These principles are to be arranged in serial order with the first principle prior to the second [14].

Rawls is explicit. Liberty comes first. Economic inequality is acceptable and needs do not get a mention.

There are also other foundational assumptions employed by Rawls that appear to rule out applying his theory to disability issues. In his hypothetical original position, individuals come together and negotiate arrangements with each other for mutual advantage. So it is no wonder they put liberty first. Apparently they already enjoy individual freedoms unconstrained by social obligations and they are now considering whether forming social relationships is going to be worth it in terms of their own self- interest. That is not the way human beings actually are, of course. Each of us is born into a set of social relationships. We start our lives dependant on those social relationships and indeed our very survival continues to depend on them for the rest of our lives. Whether any physical, intellectual or psychological impairments we may have effectively become disabilities is largely determined by social arrangements, infrastructure and services. There has never been a "pre-social" human being.

Just as worrying is Rawls' stipulation that the negotiations in the original position are between equals. They do not know what their positions will be in the actual society they are setting up. They are operating behind what Rawls calls a 'veil of ignorance' concerning their individual circumstances. But, he says:

> It seems reasonable to suppose that the parties in the original position are equal. That is, all have the same rights in the procedure for choosing principles; each can make proposals, submit reasons for their acceptance, and so on. Obviously the purpose of these conditions is to represent equality between human beings as moral persons, as creatures having a conception of their good and capable of a sense of justice... Together with the veil of ignorance, these conditions define the principles of justice as those which rational persons concerned to advance their interests would consent to as equals when none are known to be advantaged or disadvantaged by social and natural contingencies [16].

If none of the people in the original position is known to have any social or natural disadvantages, and all are equals negotiating to serve their self interests, how could we expect them to come up with any arrangements that accommodated disability issues? And why would we consider that the arrangements they did agree on could fairly be called 'justice' for people with disabilities?

People with disabilities *are* known to have social and natural disadvantages. They are not equal, independent, pre-social beings (though admittedly, nobody is). Some do not have equal competence in making proposals, submitting reasons for their acceptance and defining justice. As Nussbaum points out:

> When we discuss mental disability, we will see that the equation of citizen status with (prudential and moral) rationality is a hurdle that even the best contemporary theories cannot surmount, without losing their formative links to the social contract tradition [16].

The assumption of rationality is not just a hurdle for theories in the social contract tradition but also for theories of human nature, as discussed in the chapter on identity. A related assumption is that of productivity. Some people with disabilities are not able to make equally productive contributions to everybody's self interests. As Nussbaum complains:

> For the very logic of a contract for mutual advantage suggest that one would not include in the first place agents whose contribution to overall social wellbeing is likely to be dramatically lower than that of the others [17].

Nussbaum points out that in Rawls' later work, *Political Liberalism*, he agrees that his conception of justice presents difficulties when determining what is owed to people with disabilities [18].

If Rawls is proposing that a process of independent, pre-social, equal people rationally negotiating with each other to advance their self-interest would produce justice, let alone justice for people with disabilities, should we take him seriously? Is there any application of his theory to disability ethics? It seems unlikely, and yet, as I have already argued earlier in this chapter, Rawls' approach can be applied usefully to disability issues. How can this be?

Rethinking Rawls' theory

It does not really matter that Rawls constructed his theory without any regard for the special issues pertaining to disability. That is true of all of the ethical theories canvassed in this book. Community-based ethics, Utilitarianism and Deontology all struggle with disability issues. Actually, Rawls' proposals are more amenable than Kant's. Neither would it be a good idea to start from scratch in the development of an ethical theory that was specific to disability issues. Such a theory would lack credibility in society and would of necessity isolate disabled people, which would be an unacceptable result. What has to be done is work on existing foundational theories so that they become applicable to disability issues. That work is the purpose of this book.

Although Rawls did not have disabled people in mind, he did not rule them out. His idea was to construct a hypothetical situation in which people did not know what their abilities or disabilities would be in an actual society. He says:

> Now in order to do this I assume that the parties are situated behind a veil of ignorance. They do not know how the various alternatives will affect their own particular case and they are obliged to evaluate principles on the basis of general considerations.
>
> It is assumed, then, that the parties do not know certain kinds of particular facts. First of all, no one knows his place in society, his class position or social status; nor does he know his fortune in the distribution of natural assets and abilities, his intelligence, his strength and the like [19].

Rawls is quite clear here. The people in the original position are not constructing a society meant for a populace that is uniformly independent, rational and equal. Quite the opposite. The people in the original position understand that they must come up with social arrangements which are fair to citizens who have a range of abilities and disabilities, of status, power and assets. Using Rawls' scenario, we can easily hypothesize an original position member saying, "Look, we know that some of us in this group are going to have disabilities in this society we are setting up. We just don't know which of us that is going to be. So we had better set up some social arrangements that are fair to such people." Even Rawls' prioritizing of liberty needs to be seen within these constraints. Everyone should enjoy the most liberty compatible with the maximum liberty for all. 'Everyone' clearly includes people with disabilities. He says that:

> The denial of equal liberty can be accepted only if it is necessary to enhance the quality of civilization so that in due course the equal freedoms can be enjoyed by all [20].

Rawls insists he does not favour 'a callous meritocratic society'. He does think it is asking too much to expect society to try to even out handicaps as if all were expected to compete on a fair basis in the same race, but nonetheless he does believe that fairness requires an allocation of resources to people disadvantaged by disability. He chooses education as an example, which should be resourced:

> so as to improve the long term expectations of the least advantaged.... And in making this decision, the value of education should not be assessed only in terms of economic efficiency and social welfare. Equally, if not more important is the role of education in enabling a person to enjoy the culture of his society and to take part in its affairs, and in this way to provide for each individual a secure sense of his own worth [21].

It is easy to misread Rawls by misunderstanding the hypothetical nature of the original position. Rawls is not proposing that justice should be determined by some sort of super-class of people who are independent, rational, equal and self-interested. He recognizes that in a real society, some people are advantaged and some are disadvantaged. He proposes that social arrangements favouring the advantaged at the expense of the disadvantaged are unfair and unjust. He recommends that real people in actual society should adopt a conception of justice which could find agreement amongst everyone. We are asked to abandon the question "Do I favour our actual, current social arrangements because they are to my advantage (or not)?" and consider instead the question "Are our current, actual social arrangements fair? Are they just? That is, are they the sort of arrangements I would have chosen before I knew whether I would be powerful or marginalized, disabled or fully functioning, wealthy or poor?" If actual people in contemporary society really did ask this question, it is likely that social arrangements for disabled people would significantly improve.

Retributive justice

Ideally, the state's use of the prison system for retribution and deterrence would be confined to citizens who choose to commit crimes. The justification of retribution and deterrence assumes choice, responsibility, control over one's behaviour, an understanding of one's actions and their consequences. It also assumes a fair hearing, with no discrimination on the grounds of race, gender, poverty or class, and that all people are equal before the law. Criminal justice, then, should have no significance in a discussion of disability ethics.

Unfortunately, this ideal is not realized, as illustrated by the case of 'Boz', a disabled man in prison. Boz acquired a brain injury when he was the victim of an assault. As a result, his personality changed from his being a reasonably calm person to one who loses his temper at the slightest provocation. By his own account:

The big problem is once the rage kicks in, there's no way I can turn it off, doesn't matter whether the other guy is bigger than me, or there are cops around [22].

Because of his uncontrollable rages, Boz was convicted for assault and continues to get into trouble inside the prison, which has lengthened his stay and prevented him from getting parole. Boz is not an isolated example. One recent Australian study of 200 male prisoners found that in 82% of them, there was evidence of a traumatic brain injury (TBI) [23]. An American study reports that while 8.5% of non-incarcerated citizens have suffered a traumatic brain injury, the proportion of prisoners, male and female, with a history of TBI is up to 10 times that of the general population [24].

The issue is not confined to acquired brain injury. People with mental health disorders and cognitive disabilities are over-represented in the criminal justice system compared to the general population [25]. Learning difficulties and poor educational attainments are significant factors. A study of a sample of court defendants found that 9% had not continued schooling past year seven, 30% past year ten and 21% had difficulties reading and writing [26]. These people are clearly candidates for an allocation of resources towards the education that Rawls had in mind when he said that, in a just society:

> Equally, if not more important is the role of education in enabling a person to enjoy the culture of his society and to take part in its affairs, and in this way to provide for each individual a secure sense of his own worth [21].

These studies have established a worrying correlation between a cluster of factors comprising mental illness, cognitive disability and acquired brain injury on the one hand, and incarceration on the other hand. Researchers are still working on the causative mechanisms of the correlation. It is possible that in some cases criminal lifestyles bring about acquired brain injuries, rather than the other way around. Drugs and alcohol can exacerbate mental illness. It is not plausible, though, that this is the explanation for the correlation in the majority of cases. Research indicates that the presence of a cognitive disability is a significant causal factor for imprisonment – a classic example of the social model of disability. As a recent study argues:

> ... it is necessary to bring together an analysis of the synergistic interactions of impairment and its disabling consequences, the systemic and institutional contexts of crime and criminalisation... to create a hybrid framework for conceptualising the individual, institutional, systemic, social and political factors that appear to propel increasing numbers of people with mental health disorders and cognitive disabilities into, through and back to the criminal justice system [25].

That people are being imprisoned because of their disabilities is a serious injustice and of grave ethical concern.

A principles-based approach to ethics requires us to treat people as self-determining. Courts of justice assume that people accused of crimes are, in fact, self-determining. Concepts of guilt, responsibility and retribution make no sense otherwise. Indeed, imprisonment is a sanction against self-determination. It removes people's freedom because they have chosen to abuse it in criminal ways. It is not an ethical response to use prison as a sanction for anti-social behaviour which is *not* freely chosen because the behaviour was influenced by a cognitive disability or similar disorder.

Imprisonment is intended to be a punishment and to cause distress to convicted criminals. From the perspective of a consequences-based approach, imprisonment is a bad outcome, justified only because it is intended to prevent worse outcomes. That is, it is predicted to be a deterrent, both to the offender and to others contemplating crime. Again, the assumption here is that the targets are people who are contemplating various choices of behaviour, calculating consequences, and reflecting upon their decisions. If their ability to do so is compromised by disabilities, then imprisonment is not justified by a consequences-based approach.

Imagine people in Rawls' hypothetical original position debating imprisonment for crime. They discuss a scenario in which one of their number – they do not know which one, becomes the victim of an assault. The assault causes a brain injury, which results in the victim's changed personality and an inability to control sudden bouts of inexplicable anger. This is turn results in the person being imprisoned. Would the negotiators in Rawls' original position permit that scenario, knowing it could happen to any one of them? Or would they think that justice requires them to put in place proper safeguards to prevent it happening? One such safeguard would be requiring a response from the health system, rather than the criminal justice system. They would also, surely, require similar safeguards to deal with the effects of other disabilities and mental illness.

For retributive justice to actually be justice for people with disabilities, a society needs to understand the interactions between impairments, the demands of society and the criminal justice system and it needs ways to deal with these interactions so that people with disabilities are not unjustly imprisoned.

Conclusion

There are three domains in which the notion of justice is relevant to disability issues. One is the domain of professional ethics and practice. Another is the domain of social and distributive justice. A third is the domain of retributive justice and the criminal justice system. In each of these domains the idea that justice should mean equality and impartiality struggles with the idea that justice should mean appropriate treatment of individuals.

In the domain of professional ethics, there is an apparent contradiction that practitioners should treat their clients equally and impartially, but at the same time respond to them as individuals. The contradiction can be resolved through the realization that all clients have needs. The definition of a client is someone in need of professional services. To treat clients equally and impartially, professionals should treat clients according to their needs and not discriminate on other grounds such as gender, race, class or personal preference. When the needs of one client conflict with another's, the conflict should be resolved through the application of the standard strategies, that is, a community-based approach to ethics, a calculation of consequences and an adherence to principles.

In the domain of social and distributive justice, there is a struggle between a needs-based conception of justice and a libertarian conception of justice. A libertarian approach favours social arrangements which promote the maximum freedom for all, which implies minimum government interventions and constraints. In contrast, a conception of justice based on needs favours social arrangements that promote maximum welfare, especially for the most disadvantaged. This implies that the community, through government, has the responsibility for considerable intervention in supplying services, in taxation and in regulation, such as building codes and anti-discrimination legislation. Disability practitioners are likely to favour a needs-based conception of justice, but libertarian ideals are also very influential in contemporary communities, and there is no sign that the tensions between the two positions will be resolved any time soon.

In the domain of retributive justice, it is a serious ethical issue that the criminal justice system deals with a disproportionate number of people with cognitive disabilities, acquired brain injuries and mental illness. A community-based approach to ethics can argue that imprisoning criminals is justified on a number of grounds. In principle, it is a just response to criminals who choose to compromise other people's freedoms and self-determination. It is also expected to result in deterring people from committing crimes. These justifications are very suspect if applied to people with cognitive disabilities and mental illness.

The philosopher John Rawls has proposed a conception of justice. It comes from the libertarian tradition but it can be applied to disability issues. He proposes that social arrangements are just if they would have been agreed to by people in an original position who are negotiating agreements. Importantly, these hypothetical people would not know what their own personal circumstances would be in the society they were setting up. Rawls argues that they would not choose to set up a slave society because of the risk they would find themselves to be slaves rather than masters. This argument can be adapted for disability issues. Presumably, people in the original position would not set up social arrangements in which disabled people were abandoned to their fate by the community, because of the risk that any of the negotiating people might find themselves disabled. Rawls' proposal can be used fruitfully by professionals reflecting on their practices, by managers of organizations, and by government policy advisers in both the welfare system and the criminal justice system.

Chapter 11
An Ethical Society

I began this book by noting that our social arrangements suit most people most of the time. Government provides security and public infrastructure. Professions supply expert advice when needed. The assumption, though, is that for most of the time, most people are independent agents. That is, they are expected to look after themselves and make their own decisions. This assumption holds in the theories of ethics that underpin our social arrangements. The model of autonomous individuals recognizing each other's rights whilst trading with each other for mutual benefit is a common ideal. Admittedly it is not accepted by everybody or by every community. Of course, none of us is truly independent. None of us is fully self-sufficient, rational, productive and co-operative all of the time. But this ideal is very influential in contemporary societies that feature professions and in the traditional ethics that inform professional practices.

What happens, or rather, what *should* happen, when this idea is challenged? What social arrangements and what professional practices should be in place for people made vulnerable by disability? If you are a professional, how should treat people who are dependent on your services? How should you go about making decisions for clients if they are not well placed to make decisions for themselves? Can there be procedures in professional ethics that can deal with this situation? Are there ethical guidelines that can be applied by managers of service organizations, or by policy writers, or by government officials? Can our assumptions and underlying ethical theories be reworked, modified and effectively applied?

Yes, they can. They need work in three areas. That work has been the project of this book. One necessary modification is to focus on the client. Another is to cope with compromised self-determination. A third task is that theory needs to be applied to actual circumstances and real issues in disability.

Typically, the scope of ethical theories is very broad, and so it should be. If an ethical theory recommends that we should promote people's welfare, it should not propose that we should advance some people's well-being by making some other people miserable. We should calculate the consequences for all the people affected. If an ethical theory recommends that we should respect each other's rights, that must mean respecting everybody's rights, all of the time. The practice of professional ethics should not deny these universal concerns, but professionals also have specific obligations. Professions exist because clients have needs. Disability professions exist because their clients' well-being has been significantly affected or their autonomy significantly compromised by disability. Rather than worry about all people, professionals need to focus on their clients.

A lot of ethical debate revolves around autonomy. Typically, it is assumed that people are self-determining, and that they should be treated as such. This assumption underpins many arguments about rights and much legislation. But disabilities can, by their very nature, make it difficult for people to be self-determining in practice. This presents a challenge for professional ethics. In some circumstances, professionals can give too much weight to the assumption that people's autonomy should be respected. In other circumstances, they can give too little.

Having too little respect for autonomy is perhaps the more obvious danger. Professionals have more power than clients. It is only too easy for confident, knowledgeable professionals to make decisions without making sufficient effort to involve the client in the decision-making process. A number of factors can make this situation worse for clients with disabilities. They may be dependent on the professional services. They may not be able to discard a particular professional and choose another. People with physical disabilities can find themselves being treated as if they had cognitive disabilities. Institutions and organisations tend to develop inflexible routines and systems.

Conversely, professionals can have too much respect for autonomy and become stymied when it does not exist. Clients who are unable to either provide or refuse consent should not be denied services that other people can access. Substitute decision- makers, such as parents, should be respected.

Finally, professional ethics needs to be practical. As I mentioned above, ethical theories tend to be broad, abstract and universal. Applying them to actual cases can require careful and methodical thought. What exactly will be the consequences of a decision? How much practical determination does a particular client have? What is the extent of a particular professional's obligations, or contract, or expertise?

Let us assume for a moment that the work has been done to make ethical theories applicable to disability issues. Let us imagine an ethical society. It is a society that recognises its obligations to people with disabilities. In this ethical society, services to disabled people are provided by professionals, practitioners and policy makers who are skilled in professional ethics. What would life in such a society be like? There is a tendency to discuss professional ethics from the point of view of the professional, so let us counter that by looking at it from the client's point of view. If you have a disability, what are your experiences and expectations in this ethical society?

You are a member of that society. You are acknowledged as an individual, as part of the community and as a citizen. The community recognises that its reason for existence is to meet the needs of all of its members. You have access to adequate services provided by government and by professionals.

Your community knows that its members are varied. It also knows how easy it is to be thoughtless or careless when it designs infrastructure and social arrangements that only suits mainstream needs, so it makes an effort not to throw up social barriers. It has building codes and anti-discrimination legislation. Its politicians and bureaucrats listen to you. Your society has just signed the United Nations Convention on the Rights of Persons with Disabilities. You particularly like article 4f, which requires your community to develop universally-designed goods and services that require the minimum possible adaptation to meet your specific needs.

You can identify yourself as a person with these specific needs when you want to access services, but the rest of the time you are not labelled or stereotyped. Your needs relating to your disability do not overshadow your identities of a citizen, a family member, in the work place or in recreation.

When you do access the services of professionals, you find that they are competent. They discuss with you the levels and limits of their expertise and what services they can provide. They negotiate their relationship with you. They are familiar with the relevant professional codes of ethics. They respect you and your rights. They set out to maximise your capabilities and your opportunities for self-determination.

They are primarily concerned with your welfare. They provide expert advice which they calculate will result in the best consequences for you. They recognise that you have to live with the consequences and that you are an expert on your own preferences, desires, ambitions and experiences. They see you and them as making up a team with the same goal of maximising your well-being.

Your disability might reach a level that prevents you from being able to make decisions for yourself. Other people have to make them for you. These people will not shirk that task, but will have the courage to make decisions that promote your welfare. Your family, your substitute decision makers and your professional providers may have differences of opinion from time to time, but they will negotiate them on the basis of the shared goal of providing you with the best actual life experiences.

Otherwise, if you are capable of making your own decisions, your right to do so will be respected. You recognize, though, that in order to make informed decisions you will have to rely on the advice of experts. This may be complicated, and the best course of action, either technically or ethically, will not always be clear.

You know that from time to time, ethical dilemmas will arise. Some dilemmas will come about because it is not always possible to get the best consequences for everybody involved. Good results for some people entail that other people miss out. Other dilemmas are a result of a conflict between respecting people's rights and producing the best consequences.

You know that there will always be problems in trying to get the best consequences for everybody and distributing them fairly. That is a fact of life. In every society, resources are limited. You wish that the philosophers working on the consequences theory of ethics could solve the problem, but it looks as if that hope is unrealistic. In the meantime, you have two expectations. One is that the ethical society you live in will pay special attention to its worst-off members when it is allocating resources and constructing policy. The other is that professionals will pay special attention to the needs of their clients. In their professional practice, they will prioritise clients, and in society they will advocate for clients.

You also know that tensions will arise between ethical principles and consequences. You know there are some ethicists who regard outcomes as the only important consideration and you know there are other ethicists who think we should conform to principles regardless of the outcomes. Neither of these extremes is convincing, and you know that, in practice, some compromise position is necessary. You certainly want your autonomy to be respected, and at the same time you want to be the one who decides what constitutes the best outcomes for yourself.

That compromise will not resolve all the tensions, though. You know that justice requires fairness, consistency and the impartial application of known rules. But it cannot be fair to completely disregard individual circumstances. You know that respect for people's autonomy and their self-determination is vitally important, but it is not black and white. There are degrees of autonomy. It is not something you either have or do not have.

So even in an ethical society, where policy is framed by experts and decisions are made by knowledgeable professionals, you do not expect that things will be perfect. Dilemmas will arise, negotiations will be required and social arrangements will need constant discussion and refinement.

Those discussions should not be confined to ethical theory. You expect contributions from other thinkers, scholars, researchers and practitioners. You look forward to advice from feminism, from the philosophy of care, from legal experts, from psychology, politics and sociology.

After all, you might ask these experts, is there any better challenge, is there any application of their expertise that is more worthy than the resolution of disability issues and the improvement of disabled people's lives?

References and Notes

Full Publication details can be found in the bibliography.

Chapter 1. The Ethical Challenge

1. See, for example, Cohen, S. *The Nature of Moral Reasoning* p. 12 or Singer, P. *Practical Ethics* p.1

2. Kuhse, H. *Caring: Nurses, Women and Ethics*

3. Aristotle ([c330 BC] *The Ethics of Aristotle: The Nicomachean Ethics* Book one 1102b28-1103a10 p. 90. Or more currently, Blackburn, S. *Oxford Dictionary of Philosophy* p. 126

4. Hume, D. *A Treatise of Human Nature*
Kant, I. *Grounding for the Metaphysics of Morals*
Nussbaum, M. *Frontiers of Justice – Disability, Nationality, Species Membership*
Dworkin, R. M. *Taking rights seriously*

5. Kant, I. *Grounding for the Metaphysics of Morals*

6. Hume, D. *A Treatise of Human Nature*

7. Bentham, J. *An Introduction to the Principles of Morals and Legislation*

8. Gauthier, D. *Morals by Agreement*

9. Stevenson C. L. *Ethics and Language*

10. Baker, S. What is a Profession? *Professional Ethics* p. 73–99

11. Bayles, M. *Professional Ethics*

12. Laver, P. *Professional Education and Credentialism* p. 77

13. High Court of Justice Family Division Case No: FD04C01788 UK 2004

14. Jewell, P.D. Policy as Ethics: Sterilisation of Girls with Intellectual Disability in *Policy and Society*

15. Key thinkers who discuss communitarianism are
Hobbes, T. *Leviathan*
Locke, J. *Two Treatises of Government*
Hume, D. *A Treatise of Human Nature* and
Rawls, J. *A Theory of Justice*
A modern critique of these ideas is by Martha Nussbaum *Frontiers of Justice – Disability, Nationality, Species Membership*

16. Kant, I. *Grounding for the Metaphysics of Morals*

17. United Nations Convention on the Rights of Persons with Disabilities 2007 http://www.un.org/disabilities/
United Nations Universal Declaration of Human Rights 2009 http://www.un.org/en/documents/udhr/ accessed 27.8.9

18. Bentham, J. An Introduction to the Principles of Morals and Legislation, in *Sections from Classical and Contemporary Writers*, Johnson, O. p. 202–215.
Also Mill, J. *Utilitarianism, on Liberty and Considerations on Representative Government*

19. Aristotle *The Ethics of Aristotle: The Nicomachean Ethics.* Book Two 1107b 18-20 p. 104.

20. Russell, B. *A History of Western Philosophy* p.300

21. Blackburn, S. *Oxford Dictionary of Philosophy* p.118

22. A contemporary argument for intuition is Margaret Somerville's *The Ethical Canary.*
Difficulties with intuition are pointed out in
Ayer, A.J. *Language, Truth and Logic* p.141 and
Rosen, B. *Ethical Theory – Strategies and Concepts* p. 5

23. Rosen p.180
Ladd, J. *Ethical Relativism*

Chapter 2. A Community Based Approach to Professional Ethics

1. For example, Marcuse, H. *One Dimensional Man*

2. Mill, J. *Utilitarianism, on Liberty and Considerations on Representative Government.* This idea is also in the United Nations *Universal Declaration of Human Rights* http://www.un.org/Overview/rights.html

3. Rousseau, J. *The Social Contract* and *Discourses*

4. Hobbes, T. *Leviathan*

5. Locke, J. *Two Treatises of Government*.

6. Jewell, P.D. Competing Roles of Dogma and Humour in the Construction and Critique of Social Arrangements. *New Zealand Sociology*

7. Thoreau, H. D. *Walden and Civil Disobedience*.

8. Hume, D. *A Treatise of Human Nature*.

9. Norman, R. *The Moral Philosophers*

10. Bayles, M. *Professional Ethics*

11. Jewell, P.D. Distributing Responsibility for Decision Making in Medical Ethics. *Australian Review of Public Affairs* October 2008 http://www.australianreview.net/

12. Davis, L. Rights Replacing Needs: A New Resolution of the Distributive Dilemma for People with Disabilites in Australia? In Hauritz, M., Sampford, C. and Blencowe, S. *Justice for People with Disabilities: Legal and Insitutional Issues* p.17

13. Blackburn, S (1994). *Oxford Dictionary of Philosophy* p. 279

14. Brown, R. in *A Comprehensive Guide to Intellectual and Developmental Disabilities*

15. Arranging an alternative to avoid a clash with personal beliefs is explicit in a Psychiatrists Code of Ethics. Royal Australian and New Zealand College of Psychiatrists (RANZCP) *Code of Ethics* http://www.ranzcp.org/

16. Jean-Jacques Rousseau asked this question in 1792 in *The Social Contract* . See also Trigg, R. *Ideas of Human Nature: An Historical Introduction*

17. Todd, S. and Jones, S. 'Mum's the Word!': Maternal Accounts of Dealings with the Professional World. *Journal of Applied Research in Intellectual Disabilities* 16, 229-244, 2003

18. Swain, J. and Walker, C. Parent-Professional Power Relations: parent and professional perspectives. *Disability and Society* Vol 15, No 5

19. The United Nations' Convention on the Rights of Persons with Disabilities 2007 http://www.un.org/disabilities/

20, United Nations' Universal Declaration of Human Rights http://www.un.org/Overview/rights.html
Convention on the Rights of the Child http://www.unhchr.ch/html/menu3/b/k2crc.htm

21. Deloughery, G. History of the Nursing Profession. *Issues and Trends in Nursing* p. 23

22. Rawls, J. *A Theory of Justice*

23. Clause 4.1 (a) in the DARPA Code of Ethics in the next chapter.

24. Jewell, P.D. Policy as Ethics: Sterilisation of Girls with Intellectual Disability. *Policy and Society* 2007 Vol 26, No. 3

Chapter 3. A Consequences Approach to Professional Ethics

1. Cohen, S. *The Nature of Moral Reasoning: the framework and activities of ethical deliberation, argument and decision making* p. 36

2. Bentham, J. An Introduction to the Principles of Morals and Legislation, in *Ethics: Selections from Classical and Contemporary Writer*
Mill, J. S. *Utilitarianism, on Liberty and Considerations on Representative Government*

3. Bayles, M. and Hurley, K. *Right Conduct: Theories and Applications* p. 95

4. Rachels, J. *The Elements of Moral Philosophy* p. 107-121

5. Johnson, O., *Ethics: Selections from Classical and Contemporary Writers* p. 202

6. Rawls, J. Classical Utilitarianism. In Scheffler, S, (ed) *Consequentialism and its Critics*

7. Rawls, J. *A Theory of Justice.* Or for a summary, see Blackburn, S. *Oxford Dictionary of Philosophy* p. 235

8. Rosen, B. *Ethical Theory – Strategies and Concepts* p. 105

9. Mill, J. S. *Utilitarianism, on Liberty and Considerations on Representative Government.* p. 7

10. Bentham famously said that pushpin (a trivial card game) is as good as poetry. Johnson, O., *Ethics: Selections from Classical and Contemporary Writers* p. 203

11. Hare, R. *Moral Thinking Its Levels, Method and Point.*

12. Jewell, P.D. Regulating Medical Procedures. *The Voices and Silences of Bioethics* p. 159

13. Sen, A. & Williams, B. *Utilitarianism and Beyond* p. 9

14. Warnock, M. *Ethics Since 1900* p. 42

15. This debate will be taken up in the next chapter.
Kant, I. *On a Supposed Right to Tell Lies from Benevolent Motives* An appendix to *Grounding for the Metaphysics of Morals*

16. Beauchamp, T. *Philosophical Ethics* p. 117

17. Brandt, R. Some Merits of One Form of Rule Utilitarianism in Beauchamp, T. *Philosophical Ethics*

18. This hypothetical case is discussed by J. Rachels in *The Elements of Moral Philosophy* p. 109, but there is also a real life parallel. The life and career of the renowned cellist Jacqueline du Pres was tragically cut short by multiple sclerosis. Recordings of her work can be heard on the EMI CD set *Impressions: Jacqueline de Pres* CMS 7 69707 2.

19. Scanlon, T. M. Rights, Goals and Fairness in Scheffler, S, (ed) *Consequentialism and its Critics.*

Chapter 4. A Principles Approach to Professional Ethics

1. Rosen, B. *Ethical Theory – Strategies and Concepts.* p.14

2. Kant, I. [1797] *Grounding for the Metaphysics of Morals.* p.31, section 422 and p. 35, section 428 and p. 39 section 431

3. United Nations *Universal Declaration of Human Rights* http://www.un.org/Overview/rights.html

4. Bidmeade, I. *National Standards for Disability Services and the Law*

5. Article 3 of the United Nations *Convention on the Rights of Persons with Disabilities* 2007 http://www.un.org/disabilities/

6. Paraphrase of Articles 4 to 30 of the United Nations *Convention on the Rights of Persons with Disabilities*

7. Nussbaum, M. *Frontiers of Justice* p. 77-78

8. Kant, I. *On a Supposed Right to Tell Lies from Benevolent Motives* An appendix to *Grounding for the Metaphysics of Morals*

9. Havemann, P. No rights without responsibilities? Third way and global human rights perspectives on citizenship. *Waikato Law Review* 2001 WkoLRev 4.

10. Beauchamp, T and Childress, J *Principles of Biomedical Ethics*
Kerridge, I., Lowe, M. and Stewart, C. *Ethics and Law for the Health Professions*

11. Australian Electoral Commission

Chapter 5. A Code of Ethics and Practice for Disability and Rehabilitation Professionals

1. Disability and Rehabilitation Professionals' Association (dArpa)
Acknowledgements: This document is heavily based on the earlier "Code of Ethics and Practice for Developmental Educators" (1999). The work of Eddie Bullitis and many others on DEA committees over the years has provided a sound base for the current document and the current dArpa Committee thanks them for their work and acknowledges their major contribution to the current document.

2. The bibliography of the Code of Ethics and Practice for Disability and Rehabilitation Professionals is as follows.
American Psychological Association. (1992). 'Ethical principles of psychologists 2nd edition code of conduct'. American Psychologist , 47, (12), 1597-1611.
Australian Association of Social Workers Ltd. (1996). Code of ethics. By - Laws on ethics.
Bidmeade, I. (1994). Justice for all. Adelaide: Intellectual Disability Services Council, State Information Service.
Connelly, J., Rosser, K., White, M., & Wilson, H. (1992). A question of

rights. Chippendale, NSW: Redfern Legal Centre Publishing.
Developmental Educators' Association. (undated). Ethics & practice. Adelaide: Flinders University.

3. DEA is the acronym for Developmental Educators Association.

4. Brian Matthews, B. On behalf of the dArpa Committee March, 2002.

Chapter 6. Making Ethical Decisions

1. Rest, J. R., Narvaez, D., Thoma, S. J., & Bebeau, M. J. A Neo-Kohlbergian approach to morality research. *Journal of Moral Education*
Also Foot, P. *Moral dilemmas and other topics in moral philosophy*

2. High Court of Justice Family Division Case No: FD04C01788 UK 2004

3. Solomon, R.C. *Ethics, a Short Introduction,* p. 82
Moore, G. *Principia Ethica.* p. 9

4. Originally the term 'stakeholder' referred to a neutral person who held the stakes of other people who were betting against each other. The meaning of the word has changed over time and now usually means the people who have something to gain or lose, depending on the outcome. http://www.businessdictionary.com/definition/stakeholder.html

5. Rawls, J. *A Theory of Justice*

6. Brown, R.I. Roles, Education, Training, and Professional Values of Disability Personnel

7. United Nations *Universal Declaration of Human Rights* http://www.un.org/Overview/rights.html

8. United Nations *Convention on the Rights of Persons with Disabilities* 2007 http://www.un.org/disabilities/

Chapter 7. Confidentiality

1. Kerridge et al *Ethics and Law for the Health Professions* p.220

2. Draper, H. and Rogers, W. Re-evaluating confidentiality: using patient information in teaching and publications

3. Macquarie Dictionary

4. Rowan, J. and Zinaich, S. *Ethics for the Professions.* p 146

5. Welfel, E.R. *Ethics in Counselling and Psychotherapy* p.144

6. Hawley, G. and Lansdown, G. *Eastern Philosophical Traditions* p.133

7. Kerridge et al *Ethics and Law for the Health Professions* p.230

8. Corey, G., Corey, M.S., Callanan, P. *Issues and Ethics in the Helping Professions.* p.225

9. Corey, G., Corey, M.S., Callanan, P. *Issues and Ethics in the Helping Professions.* p.226

10. See chapter three, A Consequences Approach to Professional Ethics

11. Kerridge et al *Ethics and Law for the Health Professions* p 237

12. *Campbell v Tameside Metropolitan Borough Council* [1982] QB 1065 cited in Kerridge et al *Ethics and Law for the Health Professions* p.238

13. *Royal Women's Hospital v Medical Practitioners Board of Victoria* cited in Kerridge et al *Ethics and Law for the Health Professions* p.237

14. Le Feuvre C. Managed Care and Medicare. Item 319: GAF or Gaffe? *Australasian Psychiatry*

15. Commonwealth Department of Health and Aged Care. *Medicare Benefits Schedule.* November 2001, page 157. Also at http://www.health.gov.au/internet/wcms/publishing.nsf/Content/Medicare+Benefits+Schedule-2

16. Jewell, P.D. & Anaf, G. Medicare Item 319, 1996-2006: a ten-year follow up with concerns and potential side effects. *Australasian Psychiatry* Vol 15, number 5 2007, 372-375

17. There are implications here for justice issues too, as discussed in chapter ten.

18. Martin, J. and Ridley, G. *Proposal for a National Autism Spectrum Disorders Register*

19. Australian Associated Press. *National autism register to be established.* 20 August 2009

20. This is a somewhat different approach to the national autism register in the United States of America. That register was spearheaded by individuals, Doctors Paul and Kiely Law, who are physicians, researchers and the parents of a son with autism. Autism Speaks. *Kennedy Krieger Institute Launches First National Online Autism Registry* http://www.autismspeaks.org/press/ian_launch.php

21. Australian Government Department of Families, Housing, Community Services and Indigenous Affairs (FaHCSIA) *Helping Children with Autism* http://www.fahcsia.gov.au/search/Results.aspx?k=autism&s=All%20Sites

22. Williams, K. MacDermott, S. Ridley, G, Glasson, E and Wray, J. 2008 The prevalence of autism in Australia. Can it be established form existing data? Journal of Pediatrics and Child Health, 44, 504-510
Baird, G., Siminoff, E. Pickles, A., Chandler, S. Loucas, T. Medrum, D. and Charman, T. Prevalence of disorders of the autism spectrum in a population cohort of children in South Thames: The Special Needs and Autism project (SANP) *Lancet* 2008 368: 201-215
Both cited in Martin, J. and Ridley, G. *Proposal for a National Autism Spectrum Disorders Register*

23. MacDermott et al. *The Prevalence of Autism in Australia. Can it be established from existing data?*

24. Australian Institute of Health and Welfare. *Disability in Australia: multiple disabilities and need for assistance.* Disability series. Cat. no. DIS 55. Canberra: AIHW 2009
Cited in Martin, J. and Ridley, G. *Proposal for a National Autism Spectrum Disorders Register*

25. National Health and Medical Research Council. *The National Statement on Ethical Conduct in Human Research*

26. Australian Commission on Safety and Quality in Health Care. *Operating Principles and Technical Standards for Australian Clinical Quality Registries*

27. McGreevey, M. *Patients as Partners: How to involve patients and families in their own care.* p. 69

29. Australian Commission on Safety and Quality in Health Care. *Operating Principles and Technical Standards for Australian Clinical Quality Registries* p.19

30. Gliklich R. and Dreyer N. (eds) *Registries for Evaluating Patient Outcomes: A User's Guide.* p.24

Chapter 8. Ethics in Public Policy

1. Jewell, P.D. Policy as Ethics: Sterilisation of Girls with Intellectual Disability. *Policy and Society* 2007

2. Stevenson C. L.. *Ethics and Language* . p.11

3, Solomon, R.C. *Ethics, a Short Introduction*

4. Mackie, J. L. *Hume's Moral Theory*

5. Hume, D. *A Treatise of Human Nature.* p. 415

6. Bunney, L. The Capacity of Competent Minors to Consent to and Refuse Medical Treatment. *Journal of Law and Medicine* 1997, 5: 52-80
Sandor, D. Sterilisation and Special medical Procedures on Children and Young People: Blunt Instrument? Bad Medicine? *Controversies in Health Law*

7. Family Court of Australia . *Re Marion*

8. Dowse, L. Sterilising by stealth? Safeguarding the human rights of girls with disabilities in Australia. *The Australian Health Consumer* 3, 2004
Four Corners *Walk In Our Shoes.* Australian Broadcasting Corporation 2003

9. Re Marion 1992:80,655

10. Re Marion 1992:80,665

11. Re Marion 1992:80,664

12. Re Marion 1992:80,668

13. For example NewsRx. Equip for Equality; Passage of Illinois House Bill 2290 Adds Crucial Due Process Protection Governing Sterilisation of Adults With Disabilities *Health & Medicine Week*

14. Booth, S. Human rights wronged. *The Courier-Mail.* Queensland. 5 May 2003

15. Editorial. Guarding the rights of the disabled. *The Age.* 18 June 2003

16. Shiel, F. Doctors illegally sterilising disabled girls - claim. *The Age.* 16 June 2003

17. Corbett, J. Who bears the burden. *The Newcastle Herald.* 7 March 2005

18. Veness, P *Fewer disabled children being sterilised.* Australian Associated Press, 28 March 2008

19. Four Corners *Walk In Our Shoes.* Australian Broadcasting Corporation 2003

20. Nicholson, A.. Four Corners: Interview with Chief Justice Nicholson

21. Vicary, F. (2003). Four Corners: Interview with Francis Vicary

22. Ferris, S. Four Corners: Interview with Sue Ferris 2003

23. Rhoades, H. Intellectual Disability and Sterilisation - An Inevitable Connection? *Australian Journal of Family Law* 1995 (9): 234-251
Ford, J. The Sterilisation of Young Women with an Intellectual Disability: A Comparison between the Family Court of Australia and The Guardianship Board of New South Wales. *Australian Journal of Family Law* 1996 10(3): 236-262. Nicholson, A., Harrison, M., & Sandor, D. The Role of the Family Court in Medical Procedure Cases. *Australian Journal of Human Rights* 1996 **2**(2): 242-261. O'Neill, N. Sterilisation of Children with Intellectual Disabilities. *Australian Journal of Human Rights* 1996 **2**(2): 262-277

24. Brady, S. Invasive & Irreversible: the sterilisation of intellectually disabled children. *Alternative Law Journal* 1996 21(4). p.160

25. Brady p. 162

26. Brady p. 164

27. Frohmader, C. *Policy & Position Paper: The Development of Legislation to Authorise Procedures for the Sterilisation of Children with Intellectual Disabilities*

28. Bullock, A. and Stallybrass, O. (eds) *The Fontana Dictionary of Modern Thought* Fontana Collins 1977

29. BBC Monitoring Africa. *Rwandan parliament considers sterilizing "mentally unstable" persons.* The British Broadcasting Corporation. 2 July 2009

30. Allen, G. E. *Social Origins of Eugenics,* p 4

31. Rand, A. *Atlas shrugged*

32. Van Court, M. The Case for Eugenics in a Nutshell

33. Jewell, P.D. Regulating Medical Procedures

34. Nussbaum, M. *Frontiers of Justice* p. 77-78

Chapter 9. The Ethics of Identity

1. Jewell, P.D. Autonomy and Liberalism in a multicultural society. *International Education Journal* 2005 6(4), 494-500

2. Lucas, P. and Sheeran, A. Asperger's Syndrome and the Eccentricity and Genius of Jeremey Bentham. Journal of Bentham Studies 8 2006

3. Shakespeare, T. *Disability Rights and Wrongs* p.69

4. World Health Organisation. *International Classification of Functioning, Disability and Health (ICF)*

5. *Epilepsy* http://www3.interscience.wiley.com/journal/117957420/home

6. Home for Incurables http://history.dircsa.org.au/1800-1899/home-for-incurables/

7. Larsen, A. *Neurotypical* 2007 http://www.neuro-typical.com/

8. Shakespeare, T. *Disability Rights and Wrongs* p.29

9. Shakespeare, p.9

10. Shakespeare, p.11-12

11. Oliver, C. *Understanding Disability: from theory to practice* p. 32, cited in Shakespeare p. 38

12. Tossebro, J. Understanding Disability *Scandinavian Journal of Disability Research* 2003, 6, 1, 3-7, cited in Shakespeare p 25

13. AJIDD formerly AJMR www.aamr.org

14. Finkelstein, C. To deny or not to deny disability

15. Shakespeare, p.43

16. Wells, H.G. The Country of the Blind

17. Dowse, L., Baldry, E. and Snoyman, P. Disabling criminology: conceptualising the intersections of critical disability studies and critical criminology for people with mental health and cognitive disabilities in the criminal justice system. *Australian Journal of Human Rights* 2009 Vol 15(1)

18. Baldry, E., Dowse, L., Snoyman, P., Clarence, M and Webster, I. A critical perspective on Mental Health Disorders and Cognitive Bisability in the Criminal Justice System in Cunneen, C. and Salter, M. *Proceedings of the 2nd Australian & New Zealand Critical Criminology Conference* 19 – 20 June 2008 Sydney, Australia p. 40

19. French, S. Disability, impairment or something in between, in Swain, J., French, S., Barnes, C. and Thomas, C (eds) *Disabling Barriers, Enabling Environments* cited in Shakespeare p. 39

20. Atkinson, R. 'Do I want my sight back? 'The Guardian 17 July 2007 quoted in p. 4 Barnes, E. Disability, Minority, and Difference. *Journal of Applied Philosophy* 26, 4, 337-355

21. Shakespeare, p.45

22. Gravois, J. You're Not Fooling Anyone *The Chronicle of Higher Education* Nov9 2007

23. Shakespeare, p.68

24. Watson N. Well I know this is going to sound very strange to you, but I don't see myself as a disabled person: identity and disability. *Disability & Society* 2002; 17(5): 509-29

25. Oliver, M. *Understanding Disability: from theory to practice* p5, cited in Watson p. 513

26. Chisolm, R.M. *Person and Object*

27. Quinton, A. *The Nature of Things*

28. Askeland, D.R & Phule, P.P. *The Science and Engineering of Materials*

29. Marx, K. *A Contribution to the Critique of Political Economy*.
and
Hook, S. Marx against Der Einzege in Krimemrman, L.I. and Perry, L (eds) *Patterns of Anarchy*

30. United Nations Convention on the Rights of Persons with Disabilities

31. There are some arguments that objects that are not human, such as other species or the environment as a whole, should be treated ethically, but those arguments have not achieved a community consensus by any means. One significant proponent of the claim that non-humans should also be treated ethically is the philosopher Peter Singer. See Singer, P. *Animal Liberation: A New Ethics for our Treatment of Animals*.
Singer has been strongly criticised by disability advocates *because* he does not champion human rights for example by DeMarco, D. "Peter Singer: Architect of the Culture of Death." *Social Justice Review* 94 no. 9-10 September/October 2003:154-157

32. Nussbaum, M. *Frontiers of Justice – Disability, Nationality, Species Membership*. p. 74

33. Nussbaum p. 181

34. Nussbaum p. 155

35. Plato. *The Republic*

36. Hobbes, T. *Leviathan*

37. Blackburn, S. *Oxford Dictionary of Philosophy* p.9

38. Macquarie Dictionary p.490

39. Blackburn, S. *Oxford Dictionary of Philosophy* p.102

40. Hobbes, T. *Leviathan*

41. Hume, D. *A Treatise of Human Nature*

42. Watson N. Well I know this is going to sound very strange to you, but I don't see myself as a disabled person: identity and disability. *Disability & Society* 2002; 17(5)

43. Known technically as Sorites paradox. Blackburn S. *Oxford Dictionary of Philosophy* p. 357

Chapter 10. Justice

1. A guilty verdict is seen as justice. Failure to achieve a guilty verdict is seen as a failure of justice. For example, 'No justice for Diane Brimble' The Advertiser p 1. October 21, 2009. Newscorp

2. Fremgen, B.N. *Medical Law and Ethics.* p.12

3. Veatch R. M. and Fry, S.T. *Case Studies in Nursing Ethics* p. 84 Lippincott, USA 1987

4. Blackburn, S. *Oxford Dictionary of Philosophy* p. 203

5. Rose, A.D. *Australian Law Reform Commission Review of the Disability Services Act 1986* (CTH) p. 97

6. Daniels, Norman, 1990, "Equality of what: Welfare, resources, or capabilities?" *Philosophy and Phenomenological Research*, 50 273-296

7. Flew, A. *A Dictionary of Philosophy.* p. 188

8. Nozick, R. *Anarchy, State and Utopia*

9. Rawls, J. *A Theory of Justice*

10. Blackburn, S. *Oxford Dictionary of Philosophy* p. 105

11. Perhaps the best way to gain a comprehensive grasp of the theory, its strengths and weaknesses, is to read Rawls, J. *A Theory of Justice*
and then
Wolff, R.P. *Understanding Rawls: A Reconstruction and Critique of A Theory of Justice.*

12. Nussbaum, M. *Frontiers of Justice – Disability, Nationality, Species Membership* p. ix

13. Rousseau, J. *The Social Contract* and *Discourses*
Hobbes, T. *Leviathan*
Locke, J. *Two Treatises of Government.*

14. Rawls, J. *A Theory of Justice* p. 60-61

15. Rawls, J. *A Theory of Justice* p. 19

16. Nussbaum, M. *Frontiers of Justice – Disability, Nationality, Species Membership* p. 54

17. Nussbaum, M. *Frontiers of Justice – Disability, Nationality, Species Membership* p. 20

18. Nussbaum, M. *Frontiers of Justice – Disability, Nationality, Species Membership* p. 23
Rawls, J. *Political Liberalism*

19. Rawls, J. *A Theory of Justice* p. 137

20. Rawls, J. *A Theory of Justice* p. 542

21. Rawls, J. *A Theory of Justice* p. 101

22. Boz. Problems on the Inside – acquired brain injury and the prison system. *Synapse – the Official Journal of the Brain Injury Associations of Australia*, Summer 2005 p.23

23. Schofield, P.W., Butler, T.G., Hollis, S.J., Smith, N.E., Lee, S.J., Kelso, W.M. Traumatic brain injury among Australian prisoners: rates, recurrence and sequelae. *Brain Injury* 2006 May;20(5):499-506

24. Wald, M. A., Helgeson, S., Langlois, J.A. Traumatic brain injury among prisoners. *Brain Injury Professional* (publication of the North American Brain Injury Association). Vol 5, Issue 1, 2008

25. Dowse, L., Baldry, E. and Snoyman, P. Disabling criminology: conceptualising the intersections of critical disability studies and critical criminology for people with mental health and cognitive disabilities in the criminal justice system. *Australian Journal of Human Rights* 2009 Vol 15(1)

26. Baldry, E., Dowse, L., Snoyman, P., Clarence, M. and Webster, I. A critical perspective on Mental Health Disorders and Cognitive Disability in the Criminal Justice System in Cunneen, C. & Salter, M. (eds) *Proceedings of the 2nd Australian & New Zealand Critical Criminology Conference* Sydney 19-20 June 2008

Bibliography

Allen, G. E. *Social Origins of Eugenics*, Cold Spring Harbor Laboratory USA http://www.eugenicsarchive.org accessed 2 October 2009

Aristotle [c330 BC] *The Ethics of Aristotle: The Nicomachean Ethics.* Translated by J.A.K Thomson. Penguin Books, UK 1976

Askeland, D.R & Phule, P.P. *The Science and Engineering of Materials.* Thomson USA 2005

Atkinson, R. 'Do I want my sight back?' The Guardian 17 July 2007 in Barnes, E. Disability, Minority, and Difference. *Journal of Applied Philosophy* 26, 4, 337-355

Australian Associated Press. *National autism register to be established.* 20 August 2009 http://a4.org.au/a4/node/144 accessed 14 Oct 2009

Australian Commission on Safety and Quality in Health Care. *Operating Principles and Technical Standards for Australian Clinical Quality Registries.* Australia 2008

Australian Electoral Commission http://www.aec.gov.au/Enrolling_to_vote/Eligibility.htm Accessed 20 April 2009

Australian Government Department of Families, Housing, Community Services and Indigenous Affairs (FaHCSIA) *Helping Children with Autism* http://www.fahcsia.gov.au/search/Results.aspx?k=autism&s=All%20Sites accessed 2 November 2009

Australian Institute of Health and Welfare. *Disability in Australia: multiple disabilities and need for assistance.* Disability series. Cat. no. DIS 55. Canberra: AIHW 2009

Autism Speaks. *Kennedy Krieger Institute Launches First National Online Autism Registry* http://www.autismspeaks.org/press/ian_launch.php accessed 14 October 2009

Ayer, A.J. *Language, Truth and Logic.* Penguin, UK 1986

Baird, G., Siminoff, E. Pickles, A., Chandler, S. Loucas, T. Medrum, D. and Charman, T. Prevalence of disorders of the autism spectrum in a population cohort of children in South Thames: The Special Needs and Autism project (SANP) *Lancet* 2008, 368: 201-215

Baker, S. What is a Profession? *Professional Ethics* 1992, 1 (1&2): 73–99

Baldry, E., Dowse, L., Snoyman, P., Clarence, M and Webster, I. A critical perspective on Mental Health Disorders and Cognitive Disability in the Criminal Justice System in Cunneen, C. and Salter, M. *Proceedings of the 2nd Australian & New Zealand Critical Criminology Conference* Sydney, Australia 19 – 20 June 2008

Bayles, M. *Professional Ethics.* Wadsworth, USA 1989

Bayles, M. and Hurley, K. *Right Conduct: Theories and Applications* Random House USA 1983

BBC Monitoring Africa. *Rwandan parliament considers sterilizing "mentally unstable" persons.* The British Broadcasting Corporation, 2 July 2009

Beauchamp, T. *Philosophical Ethics* McGraw Hill USA 2001

Beauchamp, T and Childress, J *Principles of Biomedical Ethics* Oxford University Press, New York 2009

Bentham, J. [1873] An Introduction to the Principles of Morals and Legislation, in *Ethics: Selection from Classical and Contemporary Writers,* Johnson, O.,, Holt, Rinehart and Winston USA 1965

Bidmeade, I. *National Standards for Disability Services and the Law.* ANGOSA, Australia 2004

Blackburn, S. *Oxford Dictionary of Philosophy.* Oxford University Press, UK 1994

Booth, S. Human rights wronged. *The Courier-Mail.* Queensland. 5 May 2003

Boz. Problems on the Inside – acquired brain injury and the prison system. *Synapse – the Official Journal of the Brain Injury Associations of Australia,* Summer 2005

Brady, S. Invasive & Irreversible: the sterilisation of intellectually disabled children. *Alternative Law Journal* 1996 21(4)

Brandt, R. Some Merits of One Form of Rule Utilitarianism in Beauchamp, T. *Philosophical Ethics* McGraw Hill USA 2001

Brown, R. Roles, Education, Training, and Professional Values of Disability Personnel in Brown, I & Percy, M (eds) *A Comprehensive Guide to Intellectual and Developmental Disabilities* Brookes, USA 2007

Bullock, A. and Stallybrass, O. (eds) The Fontana Dictionary of Modern Thought Fontana Collins, 1977
Bunney, L. The Capacity of Competent Minors to Consent to and Refuse Medical Treatment. *Journal of Law and Medicine* 1997, 5: 52-80
Chisolm, R.M. *Person and Object: a metaphysical study.* Routledge, London 2002
Cohen, S. *The Nature of Moral Reasoning: the framework and activities of ethical deliberation, argument and decision making.* Oxford University Press, Australia 2004
Commonwealth Department of Health and Aged Care. *Medicare Benefits Schedule.* 2001
Corbett, J. Who bears the burden. *The Newcastle Herald.* 7 March 2005
Corey, G., Corey, M.S., Callanan, P. *Issues and Ethics in the Helping Professions.* Thomson USA 2007
Daniels, Norman, 1990, "Equality of what: Welfare, resources, or capabilities?" *Philosophy and Phenomenological Research*, 50 273-296
Davis, L. Rights Replacing Needs: A New Resolution of the Distributive Dilemma for People with Disabilities in Australia? In Hauritz, M., Sampford, C. and Blencowe, S. *Justice for People with Disabilities: Legal and Institutional Issues.* The Federation Press, Australia 1998
DeMarco, D. "Peter Singer: Architect of the Culture of Death." *Social Justice Review* 94 no. 9-10 September/October 2003:154-157
Disability and Rehabilitation Professionals' Association. *A Code of Ethics and Practice for Disability and Rehabilitation Professionals* dArpa PO Box 1088, Unley Business Centre, South Australia 5061, 2002
Deloughery, G. History of the Nursing Profession. *Issues and Trends in Nursing.* C. V. Mosby USA, 1995
Dowse, L., Baldry, E. and Snoyman, P. Disabling criminology: conceptualising the intersections of critical disability studies and critical criminology for people with mental health and cognitive disabilities in the criminal justice system. *Australian Journal of Human Rights* 2009 Vol 15(1)
Dowse, L. Sterilising by stealth? Safeguarding the human rights of girls with disabilities in Australia. *The Australian Health Consumer* 3, 2004
Dowse, L., Baldry, E. and Snoyman, P. Disabling criminology: conceptualising the intersections of critical disability studies and critical criminology for people with mental health and cognitive disabilities in the criminal justice system. *Australian Journal of Human Rights* 2009 Vol 15(1)
Draper, H. and Rogers, W. Re-evaluating confidentiality: using patient information in teaching and publications *Advances in Psychiatric Treatment* 2005 11: 115-124
Dworkin, R. M. *Taking rights seriously.* Harvard University Press, Cambridge 1977
Editorial. Guarding the rights of the disabled. *The Age.* 18 June 2003

Family Court of Australia . *Re Marion.* Darwin, CCH: 80652 - 80668. 1992
Ferris, S. Four Corners: Interview with Sue Ferris. 2003 http://www.abc.net.au/4corners/content/2003/20030616_sterilisation/default.htm accessed 11 November 2009
Finkelstein, C. To deny or not to deny disability, in Brechin, A., Liddiard, P and Swain, J. (eds) *Handicap in a Social World* Sevenoaks Hodder & Stoughton 1971
Flew, A. *A Dictionary of Philosophy.* MacMillan UK 1979
Foot, P. *Moral dilemmas and other topics in moral philosophy.* Oxford University Press. 2002
Ford, J. The Sterilisation of Young Women with an Intellectual Disability: A Comparison between the Family Court of Australia and The Guardianship Board of New South Wales. *Australian Journal of Family Law* 1996 10(3): 236-262
Four Corners *Walk In Our Shoes.* Australian Broadcasting Corporation 2003
Fremgen, B.N. *Medical Law and Ethics.* Pearson, USA 2009
French, S. Disability, impairment or something in between, in Swain, J., French, S., Barnes, C. and Thomas, C (eds) *Disabling Barriers, Enabling Environments* London, SAGE 1993
Frohmader, C. *Policy & Position Paper: The Development of Legislation to Authorise Procedures for the Sterilisation of Children with Intellectual Disabilities* Women With Disabilities Australia (WWDA). 2007 http://www.wwda.org.au/polpapster07.htm accessed 11 November 2009
Gauthier, D. *Morals by Agreement..* Oxford University Press, UK 1986
Gliklich R. and Dreyer N. (eds) *Registries for Evaluating Patient Outcomes: A User's Guide.* AHRQ, USA 2007
Gravois, J. You're Not Fooling Anyone *The Chronicle of Higher Education* Nov9 2007 http://chronicle.com/article/You-re-Not-Fooling-Anyone/28069 accessed 6 August 2009
Hare, R (1981). *Moral Thinking Its Levels, Method and Point.* USA, Oxford University Press
Havemann, P. No rights without responsibilities? Third way and global human rights perspectives on citizenship. *Waikato Law Review* 2001 WkoLRev 4
Hawley, G. and Lansdown, G. Eastern Philosophical Traditions in Hawley, G. (ed) *Ethics in Clinical Practice* Pearson, UK 2007
High Court of Justice Family Division Case No: FD04C01788 UK 2004
Hobbes, T. [1651] *Leviathan.* Collins, UK 1962.
Hook, S. Marx against Der Einzege in Krimemrman, L.I. and Perry, L (eds) *Patterns of Anarchy* Andhor USA 1966
Hume, D.[1888] *A Treatise of Human Nature.* Oxford University Press, USA 1978
Jewell, P.D. Regulating Medical Procedures. *The Voices and Silences of Bioethics* Australian Bioethics Association 2000
Jewell, P.D. Autonomy and Liberalism in a multicultural society. *International Education Journal* 2005 6(4), 494-500

Jewell, P.D. Policy as Ethics: Sterilisation of Girls with Intellectual Disability. *Policy and Society* 2007 Vol 26, No. 3

Jewell, P.D. Competing Roles of Dogma and Humour in the Construction and Critique of Social Arrangements. *New Zealand Sociology* Volume 22, Number 1 2007

Jewell, P.D. Distributing Responsibility for Decision Making in Medical Ethics. *Australian Review of Public Affairs* October 2008 http://www.australianreview.net/

Jewell, P.D. & Anaf, G. Medicare Item 319, 1996-2006: a ten-year follow up with concerns and potential side effects. *Australasian Psychiatry* Vol 15, number 5 2007, 372-375

Johnson, O., *Ethics: Selections from Classical and Contemporary Writers*, USA, Holt, Rinehart and Winston 1965

Kalaitzidis, E. & Harris, H. Moral Agents and the Nurse-patient relationship: A Critique of the Philosophy of Care as a Professional Ethic. *Australian Journal of Professional and Applied Ethics* Vol 6, no 2 Sep 2004

Kant, I. [1797] *Grounding for the Metaphysics of Morals.* Translated by J Ellington., Hackett Publishing Company USA 1981

Kerridge, I., Lowe, M. and Stewart, C. *Ethics and Law for the Health Professions* Federation Press, Australia 2009

Kuhse, H. *Caring: Nurses, Women and Ethics.* Blackwell, UK 1997

Ladd, J. *Ethical Relativism* Wadsworth USA 1973

Larsen, A. *Neurotypical* 2007 http://www.neuro-typical.com/ accessed 6.8.9

Laver, P. *Professional Education and Credentialism.* Australian Government Publishing Services 1996

Le Feuvre C. Managed Care and Medicare. Item 319: GAF or Gaffe? *Australasian Psychiatry* 1998; **6:** 123-125

Locke, J. [1689] *Two Treatises of Government.* Cambridge University Press UK 1962

Lucas, P. and Sheeran, A. Asperger's Syndrome and the Eccentricity and Genius of Jeremey Bentham. Journal of Bentham Studies 8 2006 http://www.ucl.ac.uk/Bentham-Project/journal/aspergers.pdf accessed 6.8.9

MacDermott S, Williams K, Ridley G, Glasson E and Wray J. *The Prevalence of Autism in Australia. Can it be established from existing data?* Australian Advisory Board on Autism Spectrum Disorders, 2006

Mackie, J. L. (1980). *Hume's Moral Theory.* London, Routledge & Kegan Paul

Macquarie Dictionary. Macquarie Library, Australia 1982

McGreevey, M. (ed) *Patients as Partners: How to involve patients and families in their own care.* Joint Commission Resources USA 2006

Marcuse, H. *One Dimensional Man: Studies in the Ideology of Advanced Industrial Society.* Routledge & Kegan Paul, UK, 1986

Martin, J. and Ridley, G. *Proposal for a National Autism Spectrum Disorders Register.* Australian Advisory Board on Autism Spectrum Disorders 2009

Marx, K. *A Contribution to the Critique of Political Economy.* Lawrence and Wishart, London 1971

Mill, J. [1861] *Utilitarianism, on Liberty and Considerations on Representative Government.* Edited by H Acton, J M Dent & Sons, UK 1984

Moore, G ([1903] 1971). *Principia Ethica.* Great Britain, Cambridge University Press

National Health and Medical Research Council. *The National Statement on Ethical Conduct in Human Research.* Commonwealth of Australia, Canberra. 2007

NewsRx. Equip for Equality; Passage of Illinois House Bill 2290 Adds Crucial Due Process Protection Governing Sterilisation of Adults With Disabilities *Health & Medicine Week via NewsRx.com* 1 June 2009

Nicholson, A.. Four Corners: Interview with Chief Justice Nicholson. http://www.abc.net.au/4corners/content/2003/20030616_sterilisation/default.htm ABC Online. 2003 accessed 11 November 2009

Nicholson, A., Harrison, M., & Sandor, D. The Role of the Family Court in Medical Procedure Cases. *Australian Journal of Human Rights* 1996 **2**(2): 242-261

Norman, R. *The Moral Philosophers* Oxford: The Clarendon Press 1983

Nozick, R. *Anarchy, State and Utopia.* New York: Basic Books, 1974

Nussbaum, M. *Frontiers of Justice – Disability, Nationality, Species Membership.* The Belknap Press of Harvard Univeristy Press. USA 2006

Oliver, M. *Understanding Disability: from theory to practice* Basingstoke. Macmillan. 1996

O'Neill, N. Sterilisation of Children with Intellectual Disabilities. *Australian Journal of Human Rights* 1996 **2**(2): 262-277

Plato. *The Republic.* Penguin UK 1955

Quinton, A. *The Nature of Things* Routldege & Kegan Paul, UK 1973

Rachels, J. *The Elements of Moral Philosophy* McGraw-Hill USA 1999

Rand, A. *Atlas shrugged.* N.Y. : New American Library, 1959

Rawls, J. Classical Utilitarianism. In Scheffler, S, (ed) *Consequentialism and its Critics.* Oxford University Press UK 1988

Rawls, J. *A Theory of Justice.* Harvard University Press, USA 1971

Rawls, J. *Political Liberalism.* New York: Columbia University Press 1993

Rest, J. R., Narvaez, D., Thoma, S. J., & Bebeau, M. J. A Neo-Kohlbergian approach to morality research. *Journal of Moral Education,* 2000 *29*(4), 381-395

Rhoades, H. Intellectual Disability and Sterilisation - An Inevitable Connection? *Australian Journal of Family Law* 1995 (9): 234-251

Rose, A.D. Australian Law Reform Commission Review of the Disability Services Act 1986 (CTH) in Hauritz, M., Sampford, C. and Blen-

cowe, S. *Justice for People with Disabilities: Legal and Institutional Issues*. Australia: The Federation Press 1998
Rosen, B. *Ethical Theory – Strategies and Concepts*. Mayfield, USA 1993
Rousseau, J. *The Social Contract* and *Discourses* Dent, London 1983
Rowan, J. and Zinaich, S. Ethics for the Professions. Wadsworth, USA 2003
Royal Australian and New Zealand College of Psychiatrists (RANZCP) *Code of Ethics*. http://www.ranzcp.org/publicarea/ethics.asp Accessed 1.9.9
Russell, B. *A History of Western Philosophy* Unwin, UK 1984
Sandor, D. Sterilisation and Special medical Procedures on Children and Young People: Blunt Instrument? Bad Medicine? *Controversies in Health Law*. I. Freckleton. Sydney, Federal Press. 1999
Scanlon, T. M. Rights, Goals and Fairness in Scheffler, S, (ed) *Consequentialism and its Critics*. Oxford University Press UK 1988
Schofield, P.W., Butler, T.G., Hollis .SJ., Smith, N.E., Lee, S.J., Kelso, W.M. Traumatic brain injury among Australian prisoners: rates, recurrence and sequelae. *Brain Injury* 2006 May;20(5):499-506
Sen, A. & Williams, B. *Utilitarianism and Beyond* Cambridge University Press UK 1982
Shakespeare, T. *Disability Rights and Wrongs*. Routledge UK 2006
Shiel, F. Doctors illegally sterilising disabled girls - claim. *The Age*. 16 June 2003
Singer, P. *Animal Liberation: A New Ethics for our Treatment of Animals*, New York Review/Random House, New York, 1975
Singer, P. *Practical Ethics*. Cambridge University Press, UK 1979
Solomon, R.C. *Ethics, a Short Introduction*. Brown and Benchmark USA 1993
Somerville, M. *The Ethical Canary*: Science, Society and the Human Spirit. Viking/Penguin, Canada 2000
Stevenson C. L.. *Ethics and Language* .Yale University Press, USA 1944
Swain, J. and Walker, C. Parent-Professional Power Relations: parent and professional perspectives. *Disability and Society* Vol 15, No 5. pp. 547-560, 2003
The Advertiser, *No justice for Diane Brimble* October 21, 2009. Newscorp
Thoreau, H. D. *Walden and Civil Disobedience*. Signet, USA 1960
Todd, S. and Jones, S. 'Mum's the Word!': Maternal Accounts of Dealings with the Professional World. *Journal of Applied Research in Intellectual Disabilities* 16, 229-244, 2003
Tossebro, J. Understanding Disability *Scandinavian Journal of Disability Research* 2003 6, 1, 3-7
Trigg, R. *Ideas of Human Nature: An Historical Introduction*. Basil Blackwell Oxford 1988
United Nations Convention on the Rights of Persons with Disabilities 2007 http://www.un.org/disabilities/ accessed 19.1.9

United Nations Universal Declaration of Human Rights 2009 http://www.un.org/en/documents/udhr/ accessed 27.8.9

Van Court, M. The Case for Eugenics in a Nutshell. *The Occidental Quarterly* Winter 2004 http://www.eugenics.net accessed 2.10.9

Veatch R. M. and Fry, S.T. *Case Studies in Nursing Ethics.* Lippincott, USA 1987

Veness, P *Fewer disabled children being sterilised.* Australian Associated Press, 28 March 2008

Vicary, F. (2003). Four Corners: Interview with Francis Vicary, http://www.abc.net.au/4corners/content/2003/20030616_sterilisation/default.htm ABC Online accessed 11 November 2009

Wald, M. A., Helgeson, S., Langlois, J.A. Traumatic brain injury among prisoners. *Brain Injury Professional* (publication of the North American Brain Injury Association). Vol 5, Issue 1, 2008

Warnock, M. *Ethics Since 1900.* Oxford University Press, UK 1978

Watson N. Well I know this is going to sound very strange to you, but I don't see myself as a disabled person: identity and disability. *Disability & Society* 2002; 17(5): 509-29

Welfel, E.R. *Ethics in Counselling and Psychotherapy.* Brooks/Cole USA 2010

Wells, H.G. The Country of the Blind *Strand Magazine* 1904 http://www.horrormasters.com/Text/a0159.pdf accessed 16.3.2010

Williams, K. MacDermott, S. Ridley, G, Glasson, E and Wray, J. 2008 The prevalence of autism in Australia. Can it be established form existing data? *Journal of Pediatrics and Child Health*, 44, 504-510

Wolff, R.P. *Understanding Rawls: A Reconstruction and Critique of A Theory of Justice.* Princeton University Press, USA, 1977

World Health Organisation. *International Classification of Functioning, Disability and Health (ICF)* http://www.who.int/classifications/icf/en/index.html accessed 6 August 2009

www.ingramcontent.com/pod-product-compliance
Lightning Source LLC
Chambersburg PA
CBHW070828300426
44111CB00014B/2491